Brazil

WORLD BIBLIOGRAPHICAL SERIES

General Editors:
Robert G. Neville (Executive Editor)
John J. Horton

Robert A. Myers   Hans H. Wellisch
Ian Wallace   Ralph Lee Woodward, Jr.

John J. Horton is Deputy Librarian of the University of Bradford and was formerly Chairman of its Academic Board of Studies in Social Sciences. He has maintained a longstanding interest in the discipline of area studies and its associated bibliographical problems, with special reference to European Studies. In particular he has published in the field of Icelandic and of Yugoslav studies, including the two relevant volumes in the World Bibliographical Series.

Robert A. Myers is Associate Professor of Anthropology in the Division of Social Sciences and Director of Study Abroad Programs at Alfred University, Alfred, New York. He has studied post-colonial island nations of the Caribbean and has spent two years in Nigeria on a Fulbright Lectureship. His interests include international public health, historical anthropology and developing societies. In addition to *Amerindians of the Lesser Antilles: a bibliography* (1981), *A Resource Guide to Dominica, 1493-1986* (1987) and numerous articles, he has compiled the World Bibliographical Series volumes on *Dominica* (1987), *Nigeria* (1989) and *Ghana* (1991).

Ian Wallace is Professor of German at the University of Bath. A graduate of Oxford in French and German, he also studied in Tübingen, Heidelberg and Lausanne before taking teaching posts at universities in the USA, Scotland and England. He specializes in contemporary German affairs, especially literature and culture, on which he has published numerous articles and books. In 1979 he founded the journal *GDR Monitor*, which he continues to edit under its new title *German Monitor*.

Hans H. Wellisch is Professor emeritus at the College of Library and Information Services, University of Maryland. He was President of the American Society of Indexers and was a member of the International Federation for Documentation. He is the author of numerous articles and several books on indexing and abstracting, and has published *The Conversion of Scripts and Indexing and Abstracting: an International Bibliography*, and *Indexing from A to Z*. He also contributes frequently to *Journal of the American Society for Information Science*, *The Indexer* and other professional journals.

Ralph Lee Woodward, Jr. is Professor of History at Tulane University, New Orleans. He is the author of *Central America, a Nation Divided*, 2nd ed. (1985), as well as several monographs and more than seventy scholarly articles on modern Latin America. He has also compiled volumes in the World Bibliographical Series on *Belize* (1980), *El Salvador* (1988), *Guatemala* (Rev. Ed.) (1992) and *Nicaragua* (Rev. Ed.) (1994). Dr. Woodward edited the Central American section of the *Research Guide to Central America and the Caribbean* (1985) and is currently associate editor of Scribner's *Encyclopedia of Latin American History*.

VOLUME 57

Brazil

Revised Edition

John Dickenson

Compiler

CLIO PRESS

OXFORD, ENGLAND · SANTA BARBARA, CALIFORNIA
DENVER, COLORADO

British Library Cataloguing in Publication Data

Dickenson, John P.
Brazil, Rev. Ed. – (World bibliographical series; v. 57)
1. Brazil – Bibliography
I. Title
016.9′81

ISBN 1–85109–259–5

ABC-CLIO Ltd.,
Old Clarendon Ironworks,
35A Great Clarendon Street,
Oxford OX2 6AT, England.

⎯⎯⎯⎯⎯

ABC-CLIO Inc.,
130 Cremona Drive,
Santa Barbara,
CA 93117, USA.

Designed by Bernard Crossland.
Typeset by Columns Design Ltd., Reading, England.
Printed and bound in Great Britain by Bookcraft (Bath) Ltd., Midsomer Norton.

THE WORLD BIBLIOGRAPHICAL SERIES

This series, which is principally designed for the English speaker, will eventually cover every country (and some of the world's principal regions and cities), each in a separate volume comprising annotated entries on works dealing with its history, geography, economy and politics; and with its people, their culture, customs, religion and social organization. Attention will also be paid to current living conditions – housing, education, newspapers, clothing, etc. – that are all too often ignored in standard bibliographies; and to those particular aspects relevant to individual countries. Each volume seeks to achieve, by use of careful selectivity and critical assessment of the literature, an expression of the country and an appreciation of its nature and national aspirations, to guide the reader towards an understanding of its importance. The keynote of the series is to provide, in a uniform format, an interpretation of each country that will express its culture, its place in the world, and the qualities and background that make it unique. The views expressed in individual volumes, however, are not necessarily those of the publisher.

VOLUMES IN THE SERIES

In memory of
Nilo Bernardes (1922-1991)
Lysia Bernardes (1924-1991)
Geographers and friends

Contents

Contents

Contents

Contents

Preface

In common with the other volumes in this series, this book seeks to provide an annotated survey of the recent literature on Brazil. Its aims are to provide an introduction to Brazil for the general reader, and to assist those with some previous knowledge of the country to explore particular fields. The literature cited is primarily in English, but some non-English sources are given. To exclude these, particularly works in Portuguese, would be to ignore important scholarly and popular work, and would require the omission of important sources for researchers already familiar with Brazil. Some material from academic journals is also included, particularly relating to topical issues or recent research. This is drawn from major Latin-Americanist, Brazilianist, or disciplinary journals. The Introduction provides a brief overview of Brazil in terms of its geography, history, economy, society, and culture, as a frame for the more detailed annotations. There is also a substantial listing of bibliographical sources, to enable both the expert and the beginner to explore beyond what is of necessity a selective listing.

A substantial majority of the material included here has been published since Solena Bryant's first edition of this book, in 1984, and the reader is referred to that volume for work from the 1970s and early 1980s. Where older material is cited, it represents 'classic' work on Brazil, items which have not been superseded by more recent work, or it offers a contemporary portrait of the time or circumstances in which it was published.

The structure of the book follows the standard format of the series, with a few minor adjustments. There are some shifts in emphasis compared to the first edition. For example, considerably less weight is given to agriculture, as a reflection of the greater importance of manufacturing and the tertiary sector in the Brazilian economy and employment structure. The sections on history, ethnicity and gender, the city, and the arts are considerably enlarged. Given recent interest in the consequences of Brazil's advance into Amazonia, there is a specific section on the 'frontier' and a subsection on environmental issues.

Preface

Some sections of the bibliography are clearly self-contained, but others incorporate works which another compiler might have classified differently. For example, the dynamic political circumstances of Brazil since 1960 are such that the division between politics and recent history is blurred. In some cases sections end with brief lists of cross-referenced material, but it is hoped that the subject index will provide appropriate guidance for the reader searching a particular topic. All works which are exclusively bibliographical are included in the bibliography section, even where they deal with a specific field identified in the body of the book.

Within each section, works are ordered alphabetically by the surname of the author. It is the compiler's experience that, after the broad 'subject' sweep, most users of increasingly computer-based library systems search by author. This system does pose certain problems with regard to Portuguese names, as they may be complex and there is no consistent practice, particularly in Brazil. Thus Christian names may be complex (Maria de Jesus), and surnames can include both maternal and paternal elements (Cabral de Oliveira). There may also be some elements of kinship, for example Filho (son) or Sobrinho (nephew). It is hoped that within the text the alphabetical logic is clear, though the otherwise laudable practice followed by the series, of including the fullest possible name entries, may lead to some problems for the unwary in separating Christian and surnames, as in Maria de Jesus Cabral de Oliveira. The reader should also note that libraries may vary in their cataloguing practice, so that this (fictional) example might be sought under both 'Cabral' and 'Oliveira'. Place names and proper nouns are cited consistently in the annotations, but are left in their original form in all titles of books and articles.

In producing this book, I am grateful to Dr. Robert Neville for his tolerance of some slippage in the date of submission, but which allowed exploration of some of the byways of Braziliana, and the inclusion of some material from 1996. I am also most grateful to Anna Fabrizio for her editorial skills in picking up errors and inconsistencies, and for acquiescing to my stylistic foibles. In the Department of Geography, University of Liverpool, I am grateful to Sandra Mather, who drew the map; to Steve Reddy, who introduced me to computer library searches; and to Mansell Prothero for an introduction to the literature of tropical medicine.

Much of the research for this volume was undertaken in the libraries of the University of Liverpool, and I am grateful for its resources, and especially the unsung 'shelvers' of the Sydney Jones Library, who put away the innumerable caches of books and journals left by my searches. The libraries of the Liverpool School of Tropical Medicine, and Canning House, London, were invaluable for particular fields. Over a longer period, work on a number of research topics has illumined my knowledge of the Brazilian literature. In this, the following libraries have been invaluable: those of the Royal Geographical Society and the Royal Botanic Gardens, London; the Hunter Library of Carnegie Mellon University, Pittsburgh, and the Hillman Library, University of Pittsburgh; the Biblioteca Municipal of Oporto and the Arquivo Ultramarino, Lisbon; and the Instituto de Geociencias, Federal University of Minas Gerais, Belo Horizonte. In Brazil also, the personal libraries of Nilo Bernardes and Oswaldo Bueno Amorim Filho provided cool places to browse and to discuss the literature of Brazil.

As ever, a great debt is owed to my family – to Bonnie for forbearance of further disappearances to Brazil, the study and the library; to Stephanie, for her challenging company on a 'Brazilian adventure'; and to Maria Gabriela, who cast critical and first-class eyes over a draft of the text.

John Dickenson
Liverpool
15th November, 1996
(*Proclamação da República, 1889*)

Introduction

Brazil is a country frequently portrayed in superlatives – as 'the country of the future', 'the land of tomorrow', a 'sleeping giant', and 'the infinite country'. The name conjures up images of dense tropical forest, exotic native peoples, riotous *carnaval*, startling architecture, and magical soccer or, more prosaically, urban poverty, international debt, and burning forest. In more pragmatic terms Brazil is the world's fifth largest country. Its population of over 159 million people ranks it behind China, India, and the United States. Perhaps more surprisingly it ranks as the world's tenth largest economy, as measured by Gross Domestic Product.

With an area of 8.5 million square kilometres, it is the largest country in South America, and has borders with all but two of the other countries. It extends from north of the Equator to south of the Tropic of Capricorn, and its north-south and west-east axes are both some 4,300 kilometres long. The country's highest point is the Pico da Neblina (3,014 metres), on the border with Venezuela. Almost two-thirds of the country lies between 200-1,200 metres above sea level, and the major physiographic feature is an upland which is tilted to the south and east from the Amazon lowland. Much of this upland is a plateau. Its eastern edge, the Serra do Mar, parallels the coast from Santa Catarina to Espírito Santo, and contains some of the highest areas. There are also two significant mountain ranges in Minas Gerais and Bahia, the Serra da Mantiqueira and the Serra do Espinhaço. North of the Amazon, along Brazil's northern borders, is a smaller upland area, the Guiana Highlands.

Parts of the Serra do Mar drop sharply to the sea. This created a barrier to early penetration of the interior, and still poses an obstacle to transport. There are short rivers from this edge, but much of Brazil's drainage is circuitous, rising close to the coast, but flowing west and south, to join the Plate estuary, or northwards into the Amazon.

The principal lowland is that of the Amazon basin. The river, which is the world's largest in terms of flow of water, drains almost sixty per cent of the country, though not all of this is lowland. The Amazon lowland proper, however, consists of gently undulating terrain. There are other significant lowlands in the seasonally flooded Pantanal, in the Centre-West region; in Rio Grande do Sul, where the pampaen lowlands extend northwards from the River Plate; and a generally narrow coastal strip extends from French Guiana to Uruguay.

Over a large part of northern Brazil a tropical climate, of high rainfall, temperature, and humidity, prevails. Seasonal variations in temperature and rainfall are limited, with annual temperatures in Amazonia averaging 24-27°C. Over the interior highlands the semi-humid tropical climate has greater seasonal variation in rainfall and temperature. The latter averages 20-28°C but may be modified by altitude or latitude. In the southern states the climate is subtropical, with rainfall distributed throughout the year, and a more marked seasonality of temperature, which may include frost. Part of the interior of the Northeast has a tropical semi-arid climate, with average temperatures of 24-27°C, and a low and very seasonal rainfall, which occasionally fails altogether.

The best-known element in the vegetation cover is the tropical rainforest of Amazonia, which in fact has a degree of internal diversity. It contains possibly one-tenth of the planet's plant and animal species. Brazil's advance into this area since the 1970s has provoked considerable controversy abroad, because of its perceived impact on the flora, fauna, and surviving tribal Indian groups, and possible wider implications for the global environment. Against that, Brazil has begun to create substantial forest parks and reserves.

When the Europeans arrived, the coastal regions also had a substantial forest cover, but much of that has been cleared by five centuries of agricultural development. In the south a distinct subtropical forest is associated with the araucaria pine. Over much of the interior uplands a savanna vegetation is dominant. This varies from an almost continuous tree cover (the *cerradão*), to a mixed tree and grassland (the *campo sujo*, or 'dirty' grassland), and the more open *campos* grassland. There are smaller areas of distinct vegetation in the semi-arid Northeast (the *caatinga* scrub), the grassland/woodland of the Pantanal, and mangroves, palms, and dune vegetation along the coast. Despite the apparent luxuriance of the tropical rainforest, many of Brazil's soils are of limited fertility and modest agricultural potential. Brazilian soil scientists suggest that at least one-third of the soils are unsuited to agriculture because of steep slopes, low fertility, or salinity. Exceptions are the fertile *massapé* soils of the Northeast, and the *terra roxa* soils of São Paulo. If soils are generally poor, Brazil has a rich endowment of mineral resources, especially iron, manganese, bauxite, gold and gemstones. Fossil fuels are limited, though offshore oil deposits have become significant in recent years. In compensation the rivers offer very considerable hydro-electric potential, estimated at 255,000 megawatts, of which only about one-quarter has been tapped to date.

Brazilian geographers divide the country into five macro-regions. The North is the area of the Amazon, the least developed and least populous part of the country, but which accounts for forty per cent of the national territory. The Northeast region, about one-fifth of the country, was the first to be settled, but it has suffered relative decline and is an area of marked poverty. This derives from intermittent drought, uneven land distribution, and population pressure. It is traditionally divided into three subregions. The formerly wooded coastal strip of the *zona da mata* was the area of the colonial sugar economy; the interior *sertão* is the area affected by low rainfall and drought, and has been associated with extensive pastoralism. Between these two lies the narrow *agreste* zone.

The Southeast contains only one-tenth of the country, and consists of a narrow coastal plain and extensive interior plateaux. However, it is Brazil's economic, demographic, and political heartland, focusing around the metropolises of São Paulo and Rio de Janeiro. It contains forty per cent of the population and two-thirds of the industrial production. The South is the smallest region, about seven per cent of the national area, and comprises the three southern states of Paraná, Santa Catarina and Rio Grande do Sul. It is an area associated with substantial European immigration in the late 19th century. The Centre-West is the second largest region, but is relatively sparsely populated. However, the construction of Brasília, and the advance of an agricultural frontier from the Southeast, have made it an area of rising prosperity. Politically the country is divided into twenty-six states and the federal district of Brasília, and a lower tier of *municipios*, equivalent to an American county.

There was no native population in Brazil, the earliest inhabitants being part of the prehistoric settlement of the Americas from Asia. A very controversial site in northeast Brazil would put human occupation of the territory at more than 30,000 years Before Present. This, however, does not accord with the conventional wisdom, and would contradict the usual interpretation of the migration pattern, and the evidence of settlement from other parts of the American continents. The earliest generally accepted date of settlement in what is now Brazil is that of Lagoa Santa man, in Minas Gerais. The earliest human fossils there date to circa 10,000 years BP.

However, the level of development achieved by the Indian population appears to have been modest. There is no evidence of advanced civilizations resembling those of the Andes or Central America, and few substantial artefacts have been discovered. At the time of the arrival of the Europeans five centuries ago, the Indian population consisted of hundreds of small tribal groups who were mainly hunter-gatherers, or simple farmers. They may, however, be categorized into four main language groups – Tupi, Gê, Carib, and Aruak. The Tupi occupied the coastlands at the time of European contact, the Gê the interior plateaux, and the Carib and Aruak the more northerly areas. Evidence to date suggests that the most sophisticated pre-conquest groups had evolved on Marajó island, at the mouth of the Amazon, and along that river's central lowland. Calculating the Indian population in 1500 is extremely difficult, given the lack of records and the dearth of artefacts. One careful estimate suggests 2.4 million inhabitants, but some estimates put the figure as high as 5 million.

Europeans arrived in Brazil when Pedro Alvares Cabral made an unanticipated landfall on the coast of Bahia in 1500, on what was the second Portuguese voyage to India. Under the 1494 Treaty of Tordesillas, which divided the world then in process of being 'discovered' by Europeans between Spain and Portugal, the eastern part of what was to become Brazil became Portuguese territory.

Initially the Portuguese showed little interest in it, being more attracted by the greater evident wealth of the Orient. Its coastal forests were exploited for the dyewood, *pau brasil*, from which the country derives its name. It was not until 1530 that a modest attempt at organized colonization was attempted, and only in 1549, when a governor-general was appointed, with Salvador as the capital, did significant development begin. This took the form of a plantation sugar economy, on the fertile coastlands of the Northeast. The Portuguese failed to attract or enslave the Indians into labouring on the plantations, and from the 1540s to 1889 slaves of African origin or descent were the major component in the labour force.

Sugar was the first of a series of economic cycles which have dominated Brazil's economy and shaped its geography. The principal commodities have been sugar in the Northeast (1550-1700), gold and diamonds in Minas Gerais (1690-1800), and coffee in Rio de Janeiro and São Paulo (1840-1930). There were lesser cycles of spices and rubber in Amazonia, cotton in the Northeast, and cocoa in Bahia. Each 'cycle' was associated with rapid exploitation of the resource, an influx of population, considerable prosperity, and a subsequent decline, which might be absolute if the resource was worked out, or relative, if another commodity became more important. Together, however, these cycles accounted for the occupation and settlement of much of the national territory.

The Portuguese ruled Brazil for just over three centuries, initially with Salvador as capital, and after 1763 from Rio de Janeiro. Sugar, gold and diamonds were the keys to the colonial economy, together with cattle in the far South and the interior Northeast, and gathering of spices along the Amazon. Between 1630 and 1654 the Dutch, attracted by sugar prosperity, occupied the Northeast coastal strip. The territory was expanded beyond the original Tordesillas divide, particularly by the roving explorer groups (the *bandeirantes*), mainly from São Paulo, who pushed into the interior in search of Indians to enslave, and precious metals.

In 1808 the Portuguese court fled to Brazil to escape the Napoleonic invasion of Iberia, and between 1808 and 1821 the Portuguese empire was ruled from Rio de Janeiro, which underwent considerable improvement. After the court returned to Lisbon, European liberal ideas prompted a desire for independence, and in September 1822 the Prince Regent, who had remained in Brazil, declared independence and became emperor. The economy continued to be dominated by export commodities, but from the middle of the century elements of modernization, such as the railway and telegraph, began to arrive from Europe, along with foreign investment in utilities and the productive sector.

European views also began to influence the issue of slavery, which remained a key element in economic activity. Under external pressure, the slave trade was abolished in 1850, and other measures diminished the scale of slavery. Recognition that the institution was doomed led to considerable debate in Brazil between abolitionists and their opponents. The fiercest opposition came from São Paulo coffee planters, but recognizing the survival of slavery was untenable, they began to search for alternative labour sources, in the form of European immigrants. The emperor favoured abolition, but a pro-republican alliance of liberals, the military, and landowners resulted in his dethronement in 1889, a year after slavery was abolished by the 'Golden Law'.

Brazil then became a republic, initially with considerable military influence. Coffee became a dominant element in the economy (and indirectly in politics). In Amazonia rubber stimulated a brief and notorious boom. There was some political unrest during the early 20th century, with Messianic movements and banditry in the Northeast, some separatist movements, and an emerging urban working class. The world depression of the late 1920s had an adverse effect on the export economy, with the value of the country's foreign trade falling by two-thirds between 1929 and 1931.

A disputed presidential election in 1930 led to a revolt in the states of Minas Gerais, Rio Grande do Sul and Paraíba. This marked the end of the Old Republic, and the coming to power of Getúlio Vargas, who governed as a dictator from 1937-45. His *Estado Novo* (New State) saw a centralization of government control and an effort to diversify the economy away from dependence on a few primary products. There was a strong element of economic nationalism in Vargas' policies, with the State becoming involved in the economy, in organized labour, and in social welfare. In 1942 Brazil joined the Allies in the Second World War, and a Brazilian Expeditionary Force served in the Italian campaign.

Vargas was deposed by the military in 1945, but democratically re-elected president in 1950, again with a strong nationalistic element to his policies. Between 1945 and 1964 Brazil was a democracy, though on occasion a somewhat fragile one. The election of Juscelino Kubitschek to the presidency in 1956 saw a period of considerable economic progress. Kubitschek's electoral slogan was 'Fifty years progress in five'. There were high rates of economic growth and considerable industrialization, especially of steel, other heavy industries, and automobile production. President Kubitschek was a key figure in the transfer of the capital to the interior. Brasília was inaugurated in 1960, and in addition to the symbolism of its architecture, the city was the focus for the opening up of the interior, with the construction of the first roads along the margins of Amazonia.

A period of political and economic uncertainty followed the end of Kubitschek's term of office in 1961, and in 1964 the military, deeply suspicious of the left-wing tendencies of President Goulart, staged a coup. Military presidents ruled Brazil for the next twenty-one years. The period of the late 1960s was one of considerable repression, with leftist guerrilla opposition to the régime. Segments of the Roman Catholic Church, traditionally close to the State, also formed part of the resistance to the military, influenced by the emergence of 'liberation theology' in Latin America. The military period was, however, also one of considerable economic prosperity. During the government of President Medici (1969-74) economic growth rates were around ten per cent a year. This was in part the product of an alliance of the State, domestic capital and multinational concerns. The military perspective was also significant in the moves to develop Amazonia, where a strategic wish to fully occupy the national territory, secure its borders, and exploit its resources, was articulated by military geopoliticians.

However, changing economic circumstances and growing antipathy to the régime saw gradual moves towards *abertura* (opening up) in the early 1980s. Direct elections for state governorships were permitted in 1982, and in 1985, under an electoral college system, the opposition candidate, Tancredo Neves, defeated the government candidate for the presidency, but died before he could take office. A full return to democracy came with the direct presidential election of 1989, which elected Fernando Collor. His attempts to deal with Brazil's problems of chronic inflation and debt failed, and he was impeached on charges of corruption in 1992. The country's return to democracy has therefore been complicated by the death of Neves and the impeachment of Collor, who were both succeeded by somewhat ineffective vice-presidents. In addition, there has been a need to recreate democratic institutions and political parties, which had atrophied or been disbanded by the military. A new constitution had to be drawn up, the country's third since 1945. Political difficulties were compounded by external and domestic economic circumstances.

In 1994 Fernando Henrique Cardoso was elected to the presidency, and there has been some progress towards economic stability. In addition, and in response to the influence of the free-market ideas of the World Bank, there have been moves to privatize sectors of the economy and major companies in which the State has been influential since the Vargas era. The external economic circumstances of the global economy remain significant for Brazil's economic development, having encouraged the 'boom' periods of the late 1950s and early 1970s, but also being partly responsible for the economic crises of the early 1990s. In addition, long-standing (and long-avoided) issues of poverty, social inequality and lack of social provision, land reform, and unemployment remain to be tackled.

In spite of these difficulties, over the past half-century Brazil has succeeded in becoming a major economic power. It is now categorized by the World Bank as an Upper Middle Income economy, a category which includes Greece, Portugal, Hungary, Venezuela and Saudi Arabia. Gross National Product per capita was $2,970 in 1994, and if the economic growth rate could not match that of the 'economic miracles' of the 1950s and 1970s, it still grew at over two per cent a year over the period 1980-92.

A major element in the economic pattern has been the shift from the colonial and 19th-century dependence on primary product exports. From President Vargas onwards, there have been strong efforts to diversify the export economy, and create a broader economic structure, in which improved infrastructure and industrialization have been key features. This has involved formal state planning, and the pursuit of foreign investment. Early industrial strategies followed a line of import-substitution, but more recently there has been a strong element of export-oriented industrial activity. By 1994 agriculture contributed only thirteen per cent of Gross Domestic Product, with thirty-nine per cent coming from industry and the remainder from the tertiary sector.

Introduction

Only about thirteen per cent of the workforce is now employed in agriculture. As recently as 1970 primary products accounted for over eighty per cent of Brazil's exports. By 1994 this had fallen to forty per cent, with manufactured goods providing sixty per cent of exports.

This economic growth and diversification has not been fully matched by an expansion of jobs to absorb population growth, so that there is unemployment or under-employment in the rapidly modernizing agricultural sector, and in the cities, where there is a significant 'informal sector'. Lack of employment opportunity is a factor in migration from country to city, and also to the agricultural frontiers of Amazonia.

The GNP per capita of $2,970 is only about one-sixth that of the United Kingdom, and one-tenth that of the United States. Moreover, income distribution in Brazil is profoundly skewed. World Bank figures suggest that the richest one-fifth of households control over two-thirds of household expenditure, while the poorest fifth disburse only two per cent.

The population of Brazil is estimated at 159 million. At the time of the first census, in 1872, it was 9.9 million; by 1900 the figure was 17.4 million; in 1950 it had reached 51.9 million; and in the last census of 1991, the figure was determined at 146.8 million. Throughout the 20th century there has been a high rate of population growth, reaching 2.9 per cent in the 1950s, but slowing down to 1.93 per cent in the 1980s. Even so, one-third of the population is below fifteen years of age, which has implications for the growth rate and the need to create employment. Despite this growth of population, the overall density is still below twenty persons per square kilometre, and in Amazonia and the Centre-West it remains below five per square kilometre.

Since 1945 the population has become increasingly urbanized. By the 1960s a majority of the population lived in urban areas, and since the 1970s there has been an absolute, as well as a relative, decline in the rural population. Growth has been particularly marked in the major cities. Half of the urban population, and more than one-third of the total population, lives in cities of over one million inhabitants. São Paulo, with more than 9.5 million inhabitants, and Rio de Janeiro, with 5.5 million, are the principal cities, but there are a further nine metropolitan areas with over 1 million inhabitants. This growth is the product of both natural increase and also rural-urban migration. The rapidity of urban expansion has been such that the provision of jobs and urban services has lagged behind demand, giving rise to significant areas of urban deprivation, the *favelas*. Associated with this has been a marked social segregation in the cities, between areas of great affluence and those of extreme poverty.

As a legacy of the diverse pattern of immigration, the Brazilian population is derived from the Indian, Portuguese and African elements of the pre-colonial and colonial periods, and significant migration from eastern and southern Europe in the late-19th century. There has also been considerable intermingling between these groups, particularly in the emergence of the mulatto, of mixed African and European origin. In 1990 fifty-five per cent of the population was categorized as white, five per cent as black, and thirty-nine per cent as brown (mulatto). These figures are debatable but give some indication of the racial mix. The percentage of whites tends to be slightly higher in the urban areas (fifty-eight per cent), and higher for brown in the rural areas (forty-eight per cent). There are also regional variations, with the North, Northeast, and Centre-West having higher percentages of black and brown inhabitants, whereas two-thirds of the inhabitants of the Southeast are defined as white, and over eighty per cent in the South, which was the main recipient of 19th-century European immigration. There was also a small migration of Japanese to São Paulo and Paraná between 1904 and 1935.

Brazil has a reputation as a racial democracy, partly as a response to its 'melting-pot' of racial mixing, but this has been questioned. In the late 19th century the search for European migrants was partly to replace black slave labour after the end of the slave trade and slavery, but there was also discussion of the desirability of 'whitening' the population. Today there is little evident racial friction, and no institutional discrimination. Certainly the general impression is of a freely mixing society. However, there is a distinct social stratification in Brazil, between rich and poor, and there is a *tendency* for this to have a colour dimension, in which the black and brown groups *tend* to form the bulk of the poorer population, and live in the poorer areas, and for whites to be more affluent. As a consequence, social differentiation may have a racial dimension, which is perpetuated by deficiencies in education, health, and employment for the poor brown and black population.

The position of the surviving Amerindians is also difficult. Their numbers have been much reduced since the colonial period by European diseases, warfare, and enslavement, and surviving tribal groups have been pushed into the interior. The Indian Protection Service (SPI), established in 1910, was initially seen as a model for guarding the interests of the Indians, but it and its successor, the National Indian Foundation (FUNAI, which replaced SPI in 1967), have been subject to criticism. There has also been a conflict of interest in the State's role in developing the Amazon frontier, and protecting its native inhabitants. There has been considerable friction between the Indians and squatter farmers and mineral prospectors (*garimpeiros*) in Amazonia.

Introduction

If the notion of the racial melting-pot is being called into question, there is little doubt as to the diversity created in Brazilian culture by its racial mix. There are significant Indian and African components in the Portuguese language used in Brazil, as well as contributions to diet, and the use of hammocks and canoes, etc. The African contribution to religion is also important. Although over ninety per cent of the population is nominally Roman Catholic, Afro-Brazilian cults are significant. These are *candomblé*, a cult brought from West Africa and with African deities (*orixas*), and *umbanda*, which is a mixture of *candomblé* and spiritism, and where the gods involve figures from Africa, Catholicism, and Brazilian society.

The African contribution to Brazilian music is also of major importance, in its rhythms and instruments. In the 20th century varieties of Brazilian music have had international impact. They include samba, choros, lambada, and bossa nova. There are, in addition, ethnic and regional components of popular and folk music, as well as a classic component which, in the music of Brazil's best-known composer, Heitor Villa-Lobos, blends European classical and African and Indian traditions.

Brazil has a strong literary heritage, although the lack of translations from Portuguese means it is not all well known. A particularly important event in Brazil's cultural formation was the Week of Modern Art, held in São Paulo in 1922, which had a profound impact on literature, painting and architecture. It rejected previous models and led to experimentation in all of these art forms. One of its results was to give Brazilian writers, musicians and artists an international reputation. A particularly innovative element in Brazil's culture has been in the field of architecture, most obviously in the capital city of Brasília.

If Brazil is a country of superlatives, it is also a country of diversity. This is evident in the natural environment, the ethnic mix, and the economic contrasts. It is also expressed in regional identities, in which different historical and cultural experiences find expression. There is thus a rivalry, usually good-humoured, between Paulistas (from São Paulo), Cariocas (Rio de Janeiro), Mineiros (Minas Gerais), Gauchos (Rio Grande do Sul), and Nordestinos (the Northeast).

The Country and Its People

General

1 Fighting for the soul of Brazil.
Edited by Kevin Danaher, Michael Schellenberger. New York: Monthly
Review Press, 1995. 274p.

Despite its popular style, this disparate collection of contributions from journalists,
academics, missionaries and others provides a useful introduction to contemporary
Brazil. The volume explores problems facing the country in the 1990s, and sets the
International Monetary Fund's vision of the benefits of a market economy against the
people-centred activities of trades unions, women's organizations and environmental
groups. Its major themes are the nature and economic impact of IMF policies, the
elections of 1994, Amazon issues, street children, and the position of minority groups.

2 The Brazilian world.
Robert Ames Hayes. St. Louis, Missouri: Forum Press, 1982. 88p.

A brief survey, which provides a very basic introduction to Brazilian history up to
1980. It covers the principal economic, social, political and cultural issues for the
main periods of the country's history.

3 Brazil, world frontier.
Benjamin H. Hunnicutt. New York: Greenwood Press, 1969. 388p.

This is a reprint of a book that was originally published in 1949 (New York: Van
Nostrand), and it is thus very dated. However, it provides a fascinating contemporary
picture of the land, peoples, agriculture, industry and culture of the country half a
century ago.

1

4   **Growth and development in Brazil: Cardoso's *Real* challenge.**
     Edited by Maria D'Alva Kinzo, Victor Bulmer-Thomas.   London:
     Institute of Latin American Studies, University of London, 1995. 190p.

Offers a very useful, up-to-date view of Brazil's attempts to create new economic and
political structures after two decades of authoritarian government. The main focus of
this academic study is on the period since 1990 and, for the social scientist and
business person, the volume represents a good introduction to topical issues. It
explores Brazil's position in the global and regional economies, provides detailed
consideration of the social issues of land, the law, and education, and includes a
commentary on the national election of 1994.

5   **Brazil: a mask called progress.**
     Neil MacDonald.   Oxford: Oxfam, 1991. 122p. map. bibliog.

Presents an Oxfam perspective on the impact of economic development in Brazil,
exploring the problems of the Indians, the landless, and the urban poor. Adopting a
critical view of the negative consequences of Brazil's development strategies, the
work is well illustrated and makes effective use of topical 'boxes' on particular issues.
This small volume will be of most interest to readers concerned with poverty issues
and the work of NGOs. It includes a brief listing of other agencies, of suggestions for
campaigns, and of Oxfam publications, videos and other resources.

6   **Brazil: the land and the people.**
     Rollie E. Poppino.   New York; Oxford: Oxford University Press, 1973.
     2nd ed. 386p. maps. bibliog.

Despite its age, this work remains one of the most readable accounts of Brazil's social,
economic and cultural development, couched in terms of the major phases of
economic activity. Thus, it deals with the land, the arrival of the Portuguese, and the
economic boom products, such as sugar, gold, coffee and rubber, which have
dominated different phases of the country's economic history and shaped its
geography. There is a good discussion of immigration from Europe at the end of the
19th century, of the process of economic development in the 20th century, and of the
societal changes these have prompted. The volume also contains a useful historical
chronology, and helpful annotated bibliography.

7   **Brazil: the giant of Latin America.**
     Alan Robinson.   London: Euromoney Publications, 1993. 198p.

This useful basic guide for business people provides an introduction to history and
geography, but its main importance is in substantial detailed material on the economy,
finance, labour conditions, the law and taxation. It affords a valuable commercial
introduction to the country.

8   **Brazil. Culture and politics in a new industrial powerhouse.**
     Ronald M. Schneider.   Boulder, Colorado; Oxford: Westview Press,
     1996. 256p. maps.

Although it is an academic work, this volume is also a worthwhile study for the
serious general reader, as it represents an excellent all-round introduction to
contemporary Brazil. Opening with a geographical introduction to each of the
country's five major regions, identified as the Heartland (the Southeast), the South,

Centre-West, Northeast, and North (Amazonia), the volume goes on to deal with Brazil's historical experience from the colonial period to the present day, devoting particular attention to the military period (1964-85) and the return to democracy (up to 1994). It also discusses recent economic development, social issues, foreign relations, and the diversity of the cultural scene. No bibliography is included, but the chapter notes are an excellent introduction to recent work on the various topics.

9 **Democratizing Brazil: problems of transition and consolidation.**
Edited by Alfred C. Stepan.   New York; London: Oxford University Press, 1989. 404p.

A useful introduction to contemporary Brazil, this work explores the early post-military years of the process of democratization. This process is presented in this volume as being incomplete and uncertain, a reflection of the initial difficulties faced by the country in re-establishing political parties, writing a new constitution, and restoring democratic institutions after two decades of authoritarian rule. The essays it contains discuss the political background, the development process, the debt problem, gender, and the activities of the Church, trades unions, and popular movements.

10 **Brazilian mosaic: portraits of a diverse people and culture.**
G. Harvey Summ.   Wilmington, Delaware: Scholarly Resources, Inc., 1995. 212p. bibliog.

Compiled from the writings of thirty-five foreign, and nine Brazilian, writers, the sequence of this 'mosaic' is historical, but it covers a wide range of themes, including people, history, race, gambling and soccer. It is a fascinating pot-pourri, which conveys an excellent sense of the variety of Brazil to the general reader. The extracts are from the work of past and contemporary observers, for example: the 19th-century travellers, Auguste de Sainte-Hilaire and A. R. Wallace; the American poet, Elizabeth Bishop, who lived for many years in Brazil; and the sociologist, Gilberto Freyre, a major commentator on the theme of race in Brazil.

For children

11 **Let's go to Brazil.**
Keith Lye.   London; New York: Franklin Watts, 1983. 32p.

Covering basic topics of place, people and lifestyle, this is a very simple introduction, for young readers, which contains good photographs.

12 **People and places in Brazil.**
Marion Morrison.   London: Macmillan, 1988. 46p. maps.

Aimed at early secondary-school pupils, this authoritative book deals with geography, history, the economy, and how people live, devoting particular attention to topical issues such as urbanization and deforestation.

Geography and Geology

General

13 **Brazil: a new regional power in the world economy. A regional economy.**
Bertha K. Becker, Claudio A. G. Egler.   Cambridge, United Kingdom: Cambridge University Press, 1992. 206p. maps. bibliog.
Despite its subtitle this work is essentially an economic geography which sets Brazil in the context of the world economy, and seeks to explain the process and pattern of the country's economic development as a function of the world capitalist market. The volume's scope is wide-ranging, offering a historical perspective, an interpretation of the regional development and urbanization of Brazil, and an assessment of the country's place in the global and continental economies. Although intended primarily for geography students, this work would be of interest to other social scientists.

14 **Brazil.**
John Dickenson.   London; New York: Longman, 1982. 220p. maps. bibliog.
Provides an account of the evolution of the cultural landscape of Brazil. Beginning with a discussion of the physical environment, the work goes on to examine the role of the Amerindians, the colonial period, the 19th century, and modern development strategies in the shaping of the cultural landscapes of contemporary Brazil. Particular attention is given to the diversity of townscapes and to the frontier, and to more esoteric landscapes created by tourism or as portrayed in literature and the media.

15 **Brazil.**
    J. H. Galloway. In: *Latin America: geographical perspectives*.
    Edited by Harold Blakemore, Clifford T. Smith. London; New York:
    Methuen, 1983, 2nd ed., p. 325-82. maps. bibliog.
This substantial chapter comes from a book intended for the university student. It offers a highly useful introduction to the geography of Brazil, containing an excellent review of the 'economic cycles', such as sugar, gold and coffee, which have affected the country's development, and a sectorial analysis of the modern economy. The volume also provides a good survey of trends in agriculture and industrialization.

16 **Portuguese South America.**
    Preston E. James, Clarence W. Minkel. In: *Latin America*. New
    York; Chichester, United Kingdom: John Wiley, 1986. 5th ed.,
    p. 463-533. maps.
'Preston James' has been a classic American college text on Latin America for over fifty years. In the earlier editions, by James alone, the Brazilian section was more extensive. However, this traditional regional geography offers a useful portrait of Brazil. It provides an outline of the environment and economic history of the country, and then discusses each of six macro-regions, with some emphasis on their varying characteristics.

17 **Brazil.**
    C. Gary Lobb. In: *Latin America and the Caribbean. A systematic and
    regional survey*. Edited by Brian W. Blouett, Olwyn M. Blouett.
    New York; Chichester, United Kingdom: John Wiley, 1997, 3rd ed.,
    p. 353-84. maps. bibliog.
Offering a brief introduction to the historical and contemporary human geography of Brazil, this essay is aimed mainly at the American college market. Excellent summaries of the modern economy, social problems, and the Amazon frontier are accompanied by useful maps.

18 **Brasil. Uma visão geográfica nos anos 80.** (Brazil: a geographical
    view of the 1980s.)
    Edited by Solange Tietzmann Silva. Rio de Janeiro, Brazil: Instituto
    Brasileiro de Geografia e Estatística (IBGE), 1995. 354p. maps.
The IBGE (Instituto Brasileiro de Geografia e Estatística – Brazilian Institute of Geography and Statistics) is a governmental agency and this volume represents a statement of the human geography of Brazil in the 1980s, as interpreted by its leading geographers. An up-to-date and definitive source of reference on the country, the volume deals with agriculture, industry, infrastructure, health, population and environment, and includes numerous maps relating to these topics.

Regional studies

19 The land and the people of Northeast Brazil.
Manuel Correia de Andrade, translated by Dennis V. Johnson.
Albuquerque, New Mexico: University of New Mexico Press, 1980.
250p. map. bibliog.

Provides a detailed examination of northeastern Brazil and its agricultural traditions. The volume presents a thorough survey of land ownership and land use in the three environmental zones of the Northeast – the formerly wooded coastal strip of the *zona da mata*, the dry interior (*sertão*), and the intermediate *agreste* zone between them. Although the study has been updated since it was originally published in Portuguese as *A terra e o homen no Nordeste* (São Paulo, Brazil: Editôra Brasiliense, 1963. 266p.), it retains a discussion of the prospects for a radical transformation of landholding which was never realized.

20 Le nordeste Bresilien. (The Brazilian northeast.)
Manuel Correia de Andrade. *Les Cahiers d'Outre-Mer*, no. 193 (1996), p. 3-30.

Represents a reliable introduction to this region beset by problems, describing its environment, population, economic activities, and subregions.

21 Out of the Amazon.
Sue Cunningham, Ghillean T. Prance. London: HMSO, 1992. 122p. map.

A richly illustrated study of the Amazon region, with excellent colour photographs of the forest, its peoples, and the impact of development. The photographs would be of particular use in the classroom, but the text is of broader interest, dealing with the river and rainfall, wildlife, and the Indians and their decorative arts and use of plants for medicinal purposes.

22 Amazonia: past, present and future.
Alain Gheerbrant. London: Thames and Hudson, 1992. 192p. maps. bibliog.

Outlining the historical development of the Amazon region, this pocket book is heavily illustrated and also contains a series of 'documents' – short pieces by the author, or past and present commentators, on a range of topics. These include the idea of the 'noble savage', Indian myths, wildlife, and the Amazon in literature.

23 A socioeconomic regionalization of Brazil.
Archibald O. Haller. *Geographical Review*, vol. 72 (1982), p. 450-64.

This article is a technical exercise which makes uses of a range of social and economic data to identify macro-regions in Brazil. It identifies a core 'South' which consists of São Paulo, Rio de Janeiro, the three southern states (Rio Grande do Sul, Santa Catarina and Paraná) and parts of Minas Gerais, and a surrounding 'periphery'. The remainder of the country is defined as the 'unevenly developed Northeast', the 'developing Amazon frontier', and the 'underdeveloped interior Northeast'.

24 **Maracá: rain forest island.**
John Hemming, James Ratter.   London: Macmillan, 1993. 134p. map.
bibliog.
A popular account of the Royal Geographical Society/SEMA (Brazilian Environmental Secretariat) expedition to Maracá Island, Roraima. Describing the land and
water environments in particular, the volume is rich in photographs of flora and fauna.
It represents a good introduction to this remote part of Amazonia, and an interesting
and readable account of field research into the natural environment and the impact of
human activity.

25 **The logic of poverty. The case of northeast Brazil.**
Edited by Simon Mitchell.   London; Boston, Massachusetts: Routledge
& Kegan Paul, 1981. 190p.
Although dated, this is a useful collection of essays on the Northeast, which focuses
on the area's social and economic difficulties. Discussing hunger, subsistence and cash
agriculture, fishing, and regional planning, the book provides a critical review of the
experiences of this deprived region.

26 **Vanishing Amazon.**
Mirella Ricciardi.   London: Weidenfeld and Nicholson, 1991. 240p.
map. bibliog.
Essentially a coffee-table book comprising fine photographs of native people, together
with some commentary. The volume covers the Kampa, Marubo and Yanomami
tribes.

27 **Amazonia.**
Eneas Salati et al.   In: *The earth as transformed by human action:*
global and regional changes in the biosphere over the past 300 years.
Edited by B. L. Turner II, W. C. Clark, R. W. Kates, J. F. Richards,
J. T. Mathews, W. B. Meyer.   New York; Cambridge, United
Kingdom: Cambridge University Press, 1990, p. 479-93.
A useful overview of the physical environment of the Amazon region, covering
geomorphology, climate, hydrology and vegetation. The processes of human activity
in the region since 1500 are discussed, along with their impact on the wildlife.

28 **L'Amazonie à la fin du XXème siècle.** (Amazonia at the end of the
20th century.)
Orlando Valverde.   *Les Cahiers d'Outre-Mer*, no. 193 (1996),
p. 53-94.
The author is one of Brazil's most distinguished geographers, and a pre-eminent
student of Amazonia. This wide-ranging and thoughtful survey of the region explores
the 'notion' of Amazonia, and describes its characteristics, ecological subregions and
human occupation. The article concludes with a commentary on the region's
biodiversity and future, with an appraisal of winners and losers from various possible
utilization strategies.

Geology

29 **The Brazilian marginal basins.**
H. E. Asmus, F. C. Ponte. In: *The ocean basins and margins: 1. The South Atlantic*. Edited by Alan E. M. Nairn, Francis G. Stehli. New York: Plenum, 1973, p. 25-86.

This is an essay for the specialist, describing ten small geological basins along the coast of Brazil from the Northeast to the far South. These consist of rocks of mainly Jurassic to Recent date. A useful introduction and bibliography is included, but the reader should note that knowledge about several of these basins has much increased over the past twenty years due to the discovery of petroleum deposits.

30 **Geology of the Amazon and Parnaíba basins.**
J. J. Bigarella. In: *The ocean basins and margins: 1. The South Atlantic*. Edited by Alan E. M. Nairn, Francis G. Stehli. New York: Plenum, 1973, p. 87-133.

Despite the title of the book, this chapter covers the geology of the entire Amazon and Parnaíba basins, outlining their structural history and geological succession. An extensive, though now dated, bibliography is included.

31 **Geological sciences in Latin America: scientific relations and exchanges.**
Edited by Silvia F. M. de Figueirôa, M. Margaret Lopes. Campinas, Brazil: Universidade Estadual de Campinas, 1994. 402p.

A collection of conference papers on the history of geology, including a number on Brazil. These include the exploration of Brazil's geology in the 19th century, particularly the role of American and English geologists, the development of the discipline and the display of geological collections.

32 **Caves: the fascination of underground Brazil/Cavernas: o fascinante Brasil subterrâneo.**
Clayton Lino. Rio de Janeiro, Brazil: Editora Rio, 1989. 280p. maps. bibliog.

Handsomely illustrated, this bilingual introduction to Brazil's spectacular limestone caves examines the nature of karst limestone, and the morphology of the caves and their wildlife, attempting to conserve them against extractive industry and touristic 'improvement'.

33 **Cretaceous echinoids from northeast Brazil. Fossils and Strata 31.**
Andrew B. Smith, Peter Bengtson. Oslo: Universitetsforlaget, 1991. 88p. maps. bibliog.

This detailed report is part of a long-term research project on the Cretaceous rocks of the eastern South Atlantic. Though intended for the fossil-specialist, it provides a useful introduction to the geology of the northeast coast.

Climate and soils

34   On the 1983 drought in North-East Brazil.
V. Brahmananda Rao, P. Satyamurty, José Ivaldo de Brito.   *Journal of Climatology*, vol. 5 (1986), p. 43-51.
1983 was a year of extensive drought in the interior of the Northeast, with wet-season rainfall falling forty per cent below normal levels. This is attributed to the combined effect of several physical processes, most notably shifts in the El Niño current and the Southern Oscillation in atmospheric pressure in the Pacific Ocean.

35   On the severe drought of 1993 in North-East Brazil.
V. Brahmananda Rao, Kioshi Hada, Dirceu L. Herdies.   *International Journal of Climatology*, vol. 15 (1995), p. 699-704.
The Northeast experienced a dry spell from 1990-93, culminating in a drought in 1993 which was comparable in severity to those of 1915, 1919, 1932 and 1958. In this article the cause is suggested as being a combination of an unusual El Niño condition and the creation of climatic anomalies, referred to as ENSO (El Niño-Southern Oscillation) events.

36   Management of the cerrado soils of Brazil.
W. J. Goedart.   *Journal of Soil Science*, vol. 34 (1983), p. 405-28.
An assessment of the potential utility of Brazil's savanna soils for agriculture, this study notes that they are mainly acidic and of low fertility. However, experiments in the use of lime and fertilizer suggest that these savanna soils may have considerable potential.

37   Late Quaternary environmental and climatic changes in central Brazil.
Marie-Pierre Ledru.   *Quaternary Research*, vol. 39 (1993), p. 90-98.
This is a research study of palaeo-environmental changes using pollen data. The advance and retreat of *Araucária* pine forest is seen as particular evidence of such fluctuations, and the research suggests a number of phases of alternate dry and cool, moist climatic periods.

38   Physical environments of Latin America.
Tom L. Martinson.   In: *Latin America and the Caribbean: a systematic and regional geography*.   Edited by Brian W. Blouett, Olwyn M. Blouett.   New York; Chichester, United Kingdom: John Wiley, 1997, 3rd ed., p. 11-44. maps.
A sound general introduction to the environment, covering climate, soils, vegetation, hydrology and landforms of the continent, and providing a broad introduction to these phenomena in Brazil. Its discussion of landforms is rather brief, but the material on the climates of the continent, and on the hydrologic cycle, is valuable.

39 **The climate of Brazil.**
L. R. Ratisbona. In: *Climates of Central and South America. World Surveys of Climate. vol. 12.* Edited by Werner Schwerdtfeger. Amsterdam; Oxford; New York: Elsevier Scientific Publishing Company, 1976, p. 219-93. maps. bibliog.

Provides a basic account of the factors which influence Brazil's climate, and the main climatic elements of temperature and rainfall, etc. The chapter discusses the types of climate of the various regions, and the 'problem' climates of the dry Northeast and variable rainfall patterns of the east coast and the interior. It also contains tables of climate data for the main cities.

40 **Amazon soils: a reconnaissance of the soils of the Brazilian Amazon region.**
W. G. Sombroek. Wageningen, Netherlands: Centre for Agricultural Publications and Documentation, 1966. 292p. map. bibliog.

Though this study predates Brazil's advance into Amazonia, its use of previously inaccessible Portuguese material makes it a useful source not only on soils, but on the general physical environment. Its coverage encompasses climate, geomorphology and vegetation. The types, distribution, and chemical and physical properties of soils are discussed, as well as their relationships with vegetation cover, and with agricultural land use and land capability.

Maps and atlases

41 **As peças raras da Mapoteca do Ministério das Relações Exteriores.**
(Rare items in the map room of the Ministry of Foreign Affairs.)
Isa Adonais. Rio de Janeiro, Brazil: Museu Histórico e Diplomático do Itamaraty, 1956. 68p.

Provides detailed descriptions of forty rare maps of Brazil held in Brazil's Foreign Office, spanning the period 1512-1940. The volume includes some facsimile reproductions of these maps.

42 **Mapas e planos manuscritos relativos ao Brasil colonial, 1550-1822.**
(Maps and manuscript plans relating to colonial Brazil, 1550-1822.)
Isa Adonais. Rio de Janeiro, Brazil: Ministério das Relações Exteriores, 1960. 692p.

A detailed and annotated commentary on over 800 antique maps of Brazil. This publication is an important cartographic reference source, which provides a listing of maps of the whole country, and of the regions and the various provinces.

43   **A cartografia da região Amazônica. Catalogo descritivo (1500-1961).**
(The cartography of the Amazon region. Descriptive catalogue,
1500-1961.)
Isa Adonais.   Rio de Janeiro, Brazil: Conselho Nacional de Pesquisas,
1963. 2 vols.

The coverage provided by this book is more extensive than its title implies, as it includes smaller-scale maps which encompass Amazonia, as well as more specific maps of the region and its provinces and states. The annotations are very detailed.

44   **Atlas nacional do Brasil.** (National atlas of Brazil.)
IBGE.   Rio de Janeiro, Brazil: Instituto Brasileiro de Geografia e
Estatística, 1992. 2nd ed. 198p.

This is the official national atlas of Brazil, produced by the country's Geographical Institute. It is organized on a thematic basis, and covers physical, economic and social phenomena. Containing over 250 maps, mainly at a scale of 1:10 million, this atlas is an extremely useful source of thematic maps of the country.

45   **Brazil.**
Palmyra V. M. Monteiro.   In: *A catalogue of Latin American flat maps
1926-1964. Volume 2: South America, Falkland (Malvinas) Islands &
the Guianas.*   Austin, Texas: Institute of Latin American Studies,
University of Texas, 1969, p. 89-168.

Provides a systematic listing of maps of Brazil, categorized as topographic, economic, demographic, political, etc. Although the catalogue is almost thirty years old, it remains probably the best comprehensive listing of Brazilian maps available in English. It supplies details of the dates, scales, and publishers of the maps listed.

Travel Guides

46   AA Baedeker: Brazil.
Baedeker.   London: Macmillan, 1995. 476p. maps.
An English version based on the standard format of Baedeker guides, this volume provides an alphabetical listing of places. It includes introductory essays on facts and figures, history, people, and art, and some special features on topics such as carnival, the Amazon, and 'green' issues.

47   Brazil. The Rough Guide.
David Cleary, Dilwyn Jenkins, Oliver Marshall, Jim Hine.   London: Rough Guides, 1994. 678p. maps.
An extensive guide which provides comprehensive information on travel, health matters, accommodation and communications, etc. Tourist information is presented on a regional basis, including material on the major cities regarding access, accommodation, sightseeing, restaurants and bars. A 'Contexts' section provides interesting essays on topics such as environmental issues in Amazonia, race, and popular music. The book also contains a helpful guide to literature on a range of Brazilian themes, and a very brief listing of useful Portuguese phrases.

48   Rio de Janeiro: a Lonely Planet city guide.
Andrew Draffen.   Oakland, California; London, Paris: Lonely Planet Publications, 1995. 264p. maps.
A conveniently-sized guide, providing information for visitors, such as travel advice, things to see and do, excursions, accommodation and eating places.

49   **Brazil: a travel survival kit.**
      Andrew Draffen, Robert Strauss, Deanna Swaney.   Hawthorn,
      Australia; Berkeley, California; London: Lonely Planet Publications,
      1996. 3rd ed. 704p. maps.

Probably aimed at the younger and less-affluent tourist, this is a compact and helpful guide. An informative introduction to the 'do's and don't's' of travelling in Brazil is followed by detailed coverage of each state, including the major cities and tourist attractions, places to stay and eat and local travel. It is a good pocket book for the traveller, which contains useful street plans of the major towns, showing hotels, restaurants, utilities and sights.

50   **Brazil.**
      Fodor.   New York; London: Fodor Travel Publications, 1991. 214p.
      maps.

Follows the standard Fodor pattern, providing general information, regional coverage, and guidance for travellers.

51   **Rio de Janeiro: cidade e estado.** (Rio de Janeiro: city and state.)
      Rio de Janeiro, Brazil: CBP Michelin, 1990. 312p. maps.

A standard Michelin guide, in the format familiar in Europe and North America, but in Portuguese. The volume contains a substantial introduction to the State of Rio, which covers physical geography, history, the arts, popular customs, and gastronomy. Coverage of the tourist attractions of the city of Rio and other parts of the state is excellent.

52   **Guia Brasil: Quatro Rodas.** (Brazil Guide: Four Wheels.)
      São Paulo, Brazil: Editora Abril. annual. maps and street plans.

This motorists' handbook claims 'it is impossible to travel without it'. Written in Portuguese, but with brief English summaries, it is a standard guidebook for the motorist, with an alphabetical listing of cities and towns. It uses symbols to indicate accommodation and restaurant standards, along with principal tourist sights and the location of garages and banks, etc. Covering over 800 towns, this publication is more detailed than the standard European and American guides, which makes it particularly useful to independent tourists using a car or Brazil's good inter-urban bus system to travel away from the major cities. Maps of routes between major cities are contained. Quatro Rodas guides are also available for some states, and can usually be purchased from news-stands.

53   **Insight guides: Brazil.**
      Edited by Edwin Taylor, revised and updated by Deirdre Ball.
      Singapore: APA Publications Ltd., 1992. 2nd ed. 412p. maps. bibliog.

Illustrated with excellent photographs, this book would serve both the armchair traveller and the tourist, although it is perhaps a little heavy for the rucksack. Consisting of a series of substantial essays on Brazilian history, race and society, and a more eclectic collection on topics such as Rio, Minas Gerais, Bahia, food and wine, the book also contains features on music, art and architecture, soccer, and Amazonia. In addition, the guide includes a basic guide for visitors on matters of travel, accommodation, services and shopping. Although intended primarily for the tourist, it is a useful general introduction to the country.

Travellers' Accounts

54   A journey in Brazil.
Lóuis Agassiz, Elizabeth Agassiz.   New York; London: Praeger, 1969.
540p.

Agassiz was a Swiss-born naturalist who became an American citizen. This is the narrative of his scientific expedition to Amazonia, the Northeast and Rio de Janeiro in 1865-66. Largely written by his wife, Elizabeth, the book was originally published in 1868.

55   The naturalist on the River Amazons.
Henry Walter Bates.   London: John Murray, 1876. 4th ed. Reprinted,
New York: Dover Publications Inc., 1975. 394p.

First published by John Murray (London) in 1863, Bates' account of eleven years spent in Amazonia as an insect collector is partly a detailed diary and partly a travel narrative. Also containing portraits of the forest, wildlife and native peoples, with some quite detailed commentaries on specific animals and insects, and Indian activities, the book remains a classic account of the rainforest.

56   Pioneering in south Brazil.
Thomas P. Bigg-Wither.   New York: Greenwood Press, 1968. 2 vols.
map.

Originally published by John Murray (London) in 1878, this is the account of a railway engineer surveying routes in Paraná. It includes some detailed and elegant descriptions of the landscape and is evocative of adventures along the frontier, in its accounts of native peoples and of hunting expeditions.

57   Assault on the Amazon.
Richard Bourne.   London: Victor Gollancz Ltd., 1978. 320p. bibliog.

One of the first accounts of the development of the Transamazonica highway, begun in 1970, to open up Amazonia and to facilitate agricultural colonization by migrants from the impoverished Northeast. Although essentially a journalistic report, it conveys a lively and immediate sense of the dynamism of the project and the people involved in it. The volume deals with the major themes of the building of the road, colonization schemes, mining and ranching, and the impacts on the environment and native peoples.

58 **Exploration of the highlands of Brazil.**
Richard F. Burton. New York: Greenwood Press, 1969. 2 vols.
An account of Sir Richard Burton's travels from Rio, across Minas Gerais and down the River São Francisco, first published in 1869 (London: Tinsley. 2 vols.). The volume contains comments on people, places, scenery and economic activities. It is a very detailed report, in which Burton's preferences and prejudices are evident, and it can be read either as a very informative description of southeast Brazil or as a rather tedious compendium of facts.

59 **The voyage of Pedro Alvares Cabral to Brazil and India, from contemporary documents and narratives.**
Translated by William B. Greenlee. London: Hakluyt Society, second series LXXXI, 1938. 228p. map. bibliog.
Brings together a collection of documents from 1500-01, relating to Cabral's discovery of Brazil, together with a brief biography of Cabral and an account of his voyage. Cabral (1467-1520?) was leading the second Portuguese voyage to India in 1500, when he made landfall on the east coast of Brazil and claimed it for Portugal.

60 **Brazilian sketches.**
Rudyard Kipling. Bromley, United Kingdom: P. E. Walter and Associates, 1989. 64p.
Kipling visited Brazil while recuperating from illness in 1927. This is a collection of newspaper articles he wrote in that year, which provide sketches of Rio de Janeiro, coffee plantations, the Butantã snake farm and the Santos-São Paulo railway.

61 **History of a voyage to the land of Brazil, otherwise called America.**
Jean de Léry, translated by Janet Whatley. Berkeley, California; London: University of California Press, 1990. 276p. bibliog.
De Léry formed part of an early Protestant mission to the New World, which was sent to the short-lived French colony at Rio de Janeiro in 1557-58. He provides a very early portrait of Brazil, especially of Guanabara Bay and of the Tupinambá Indians. The book covers his voyage, wildlife, foodstuffs, and the people and their behaviour. First published in 1578, this volume is a translation of the second edition of 1580.

62 **Travels in the interior of Brazil, particularly in the gold and diamond districts of that country, by authority of the Prince Regent of Portugal.**
John Mawe. London: Longman, Hirst, Rees, Orme and Brown, 1812. 368p. map.
Mawe was one of the first non-Portuguese permitted to visit Brazil, in 1809-10. He was interested in mining, and besides a portrayal of Rio de Janeiro at the beginning of

the 19th century, he details the nature and impact of gold and diamond mining in Minas Gerais at the end of the colonial period. His descriptions are among the best we have of these important economic activities.

63 **Accounts of nineteenth-century South America. An annotated checklist of works by British and United States observers.**
Bernard Naylor. London: Athlone Press, 1969. 80p. (University of London Institute of Latin American Studies Monographs, no. 2).

Naylor presents an invaluable and detailed listing of travellers' tales. Material on Brazil is listed for the periods 1800-30, 1830-70 and 1870-1900. The volume is an essential source for finding the early English accounts of Brazil. In addition to the British and American material, a brief appendix lists some key translated works. Although primarily a bibliographic source, this publication also includes useful brief annotations on the travellers.

64 **Richard Spruce (1817-1893): botanist and explorer.**
Edited by M. R. D. Seaward, S. M. D. Fitzgerald. Kew, United Kingdom: Royal Botanic Garden, 1996. 360p. maps. bibliog.

This collection of essays was published to commemorate the centenary of the death of Richard Spruce, one of the most important but less well-known Amazon explorers. His travels ranged beyond Brazil and he was much involved in the removal of cinchona and rubber from the region, in the interests of the British Empire. He spent fifteen years (1849-64) in Amazonia, collecting many plants new to science. The contributors to the book detail many aspects of his activities, but also set his work into a modern context. The bibliographical guides are useful not only on Spruce, but on other travellers of the period.

65 **Mato Grosso: last virgin land.**
Anthony Smith. London: Michael Joseph, 1971. 288p. maps.

A popular account of the 1967-69 Royal Society/Royal Geographical Society expedition to Mato Grosso, which worked close to the Belém-Brasília highway, which opened up the eastern margins of Amazonia in the late 1950s. The book summarizes the expedition's activities in biology, medicine, and rural development and includes some excellent photographs of wildlife, the impact of forest clearance, and expedition activities.

66 **Explorers of the Amazon.**
Anthony Smith. New York; London: Viking, 1990. 344p. maps.

This is a popular summary of the Amazon travels of ten major explorers, including Cabral, Francisco de Orellana – who made the first navigation of the river in 1541-42, Pedro de Teixeira – who secured most of the river for the Portuguese in 1638, and Richard Spruce.

67   **A narrative of travels on the Amazon and Rio Negro.**
Alfred Russel Wallace, with an introduction by H. Lewis McKinney.
New York: Dover Publications Inc., 1972. 364p. map.
Wallace travelled to the Amazon with H. W. Bates, who wrote *The naturalist on the River Amazons* (see item no. 55) in 1848. However, after a brief period of insect collecting together, they separated, and Wallace collected mainly on the north bank tributaries of the Amazon. His account is a more straightforward narrative of his adventures than Bates's volume, but includes pioneering observations on the geology, vegetation, zoology and native peoples of the region.

Flora and Fauna

General

68 **Biogeography and ecology on South America.**
Edited by E. J. Fittkau, J. Illies, H. Klinge, G. H. Schwabe, H. Sioli.
The Hague, Netherlands: Junk, 1968. 2 vols. 946p. maps. bibliog.

In spite of its age, this remains probably the best comprehensive review of the physical environment of South America. Some papers are in German or Spanish, but many are in English. Volume 1 deals mainly with fauna, and Volume 2 with climate, soils, and people-environment linkages. The essays deal with the continent, rather than specific countries, but cover a very wide range of biological themes. There are, for example, essays on geology, beetles, insects, ground-water fauna, birds, and fish. The human dimension is explored in essays on native peoples, environmental change, native and introduced crops, and national parks. Although written before recent concerns for the Latin American environment, this collection provides a valuable benchmark study.

69 **South America's national parks. A visitor's guide.**
William C. Leitch.   Seattle, Washington: The Mountaineers, 1990.
288p. maps. bibliog.

This field guide contains a general introduction to the wildlife of South America and basic information for visitors as to the location, facilities and principal features of the national parks. Pages 115-59 deal with six of Brazil's parks – Iguaçu, Tijuca, Itatiaia, das Emas, Aparados da Serra and Amazonia.

70 **Key Environments: Amazonia.**
   Edited by Ghillean T. Prance, Thomas E. Lovejoy. Oxford; New
   York: Pergamon Press, 1985. 444p. maps.

An essential text on the Amazon environment, covering the climate, geology and soils, flora and fauna, and the impact of human activities. It is probably the most comprehensive collection of work on the regional environment, and will be of great interest to a range of specialists in the earth and natural sciences. However, in general it is not too technical to be read by anyone with an interest in the environment. Detailed chapter references are included.

Flora

71 **Footprints in the forest. Ka'apor ethnobotany – the historical
   ecology of plant utilization by an Amazonian people.**
   William Balée. New York: Columbia University Press, 1993. 396p.
   maps. bibliog.

A detailed account of the relationship between native peoples and their botanical environment, covering the use, cultivation, naming and classification of plants by a Tupí-Guaraní tribe in eastern Amazonia, and discussing Indian land use for food, fibres and medicines, and the impact of their activities on the forest. An appendix lists the species known to the Indians, their native names, and their uses. This volume has a specialist theme, but is of considerable botanical importance.

72 **Ecosystems of the world 13. Tropical savannas.**
   Edited by François Bourlière. Amsterdam; Oxford; New York:
   Elsevier Scientific Publishing Co., 1983. 730p. maps. bibliog.

A good review of the climate, soils and fauna of tropical grassland areas, intended for the botanist and biogeographer. Although it is a general text, it includes a specific chapter on tropical America which discusses the grasslands of central Brazil (p. 245-88).

73 **The geophysiology of Amazonia: vegetation and climate interaction.**
   Edited by Robert Earl Dickinson. New York; Chichester, United
   Kingdom: John Wiley, 1987. 526p. maps.

This volume consists of the collected papers of a conference held in 1985 in São Jose dos Campos, Brazil. It includes useful material on the climate of Amazonia, the biogeochemistry of the rainforest, and the negative environmental consequences of deforestation and dam-building.

74 **Collins photo guide: tropical plants.**
W. Lötschert, G. Beese, translated by Clive King. London: Harper
Collins, 1983. 256p. maps.

Intended more for the tropical plant enthusiast and traveller than the botanist, this is a
basic field guide which includes numerous Brazilian plants in a coverage of over 300
species. Plants are classified as ornamental or economic and generally listed by their
English names. Although broad in scope, the excellent photographs make it a useful
general introduction to tropical flora.

75 **In search of the flowers of the Amazon forests.**
Margaret Mee. Woodbridge, United Kingdom: Nonesuch Expeditions,
1988. 304p. map.

Provides an account of Margaret Mee's travels (1956-88) to Amazonia in search of
plants. She did not begin painting in the region until she was over forty years old, but
then made a number of expeditions. Mee and her work became somewhat symbolic of
the threat to the forest flora posed by development. This book is heavily illustrated
with reproductions of her botanical paintings.

76 **Tropical rainforests.**
Chris C. Park. London; New York: Routledge, 1992. 188p. maps.
bibliog.

Despite its general title, much of this volume's material, especially on forest
destruction and the forest peoples, relates to Brazil. Primarily a college text, of
particular interest to geographers and biologists, it also provides a sound scientific
introduction to the rainforest and the impacts of deforestation for the lay reader.

77 **Vegetation history of a site in the central Amazon basin derived**
from phytolith and charcoal records from natural soils.
Dolores Piperno, Peter Becker. *Quaternary Research*, vol. 45 (1996),
p. 202-09.

This research paper suggests that the forest cover in the Manaus area was not stable
during the Holocene period, but has been subject to vegetation change and burning
over the past 5,000-7,000 years in response to climatic drying.

78 **Sooretama. The Atlantic rain forest of Brazil.**
Francis Dov Por. The Hague, Netherlands: SPB Academic, 1992.
130p. map.

A very useful commentary on the coastal forests of Brazil, which discusses not only
the variety of the vegetation cover, but the geology and fauna of the area, and human
impacts upon the flora and fauna.

79 **The grasses of Bahia.**
S. A. Renvoiza. Kew, United Kingdom: Royal Botanic Garden, 1984.
302p. map.

This is a specialist botanical monograph which provides the first detailed description
of the grasses of Bahia, in northeast Brazil, by genera and species.

80 **Ecossistemas brasileiras/Brazilian ecosystems.**
Carlos Toledo Rizzini, Aldemar F. Coimbra Filho, Antônio Houaiss.
São Paulo, Brazil: Editora Index, 1988. 200p. maps. bibliog.
A beautifully produced bilingual description and photo-portrait of Brazil's ecosystems. As well as the various major forest and grassland ecosystems, it describes the more restricted forms of the coastal vegetation, the Pantanal region in southwest Brazil, and the distinctive buriti and babaçu palm woodlands. Although intended for the specialist botanist, this volume is a useful guide for anyone interested in Brazil's vegetation cover.

81 **Flora of the Picos das Almas, Chapada Diamantina, Bahia, Brazil.**
B. L. Stannard. Kew, United Kingdom: Royal Botanic Garden, 1996.
854p. maps. bibliog.
Although this is a specialized Kew monograph, it is important as a pioneer study of the distinct upland vegetation of part of northeastern Brazil. A bilingual introduction to the environment of the Picos das Almas mountain, which describes its geology and climate, the uses of its vegetation, and previous botanical work, will be of interest to any environmentalist. The main part of the work consists of a specialized flora, which describes the *cerrado* (savanna) and *campos rupestres* (mountain grassland) species to be found on the mountain.

82 **Biogeography and quaternary history in tropical Amazonia.**
Edited by T. C. Whitmore, G. T. Prance. Oxford: Clarendon Press, 1987. 214p. maps. bibliog.
This is a valuable account of recent work on tropical biogeography. A major concern of the volume is the idea of biological 'refugia' during times of climatic change, which provided areas in which forest species survived such fluctuations. It also provides an excellent review of the Quaternary history of the region, and of its soils, butterflies and birds, and early human activity.

Fauna

83 **The fishes and the forest: explorations in Amazonian natural history.**
Michael Goulding. Berkeley, California: University of California Press, 1980. 280p. maps. bibliog.
Examines large fish species in the River Madeira, and the relationship between fish and the aquatic ecosystem. The study also considers the impact of recent human activity in the region. It is copiously illustrated.

84 **Rio Negro, rich life in poor water. Amazonian diversity and food chain ecology as seen through fish communities.**
M. Goulding, M. Leal Carvalho, E. G. Ferreira. The Hague, Netherlands: SBP Academic Publisher bv., 1988. 200p. maps. bibliog.

The Rio Negro, a major tributary of the Amazon, contains one of the richest and most colourful freshwater fish faunas in the world. This study deals with the river environment, the food chain ecology of its fish population, and the diversity of species. Appendices list plant and animal species of the river, making the material of interest to biologists as well as ichthyologists.

85 **Latin America: insects and entomology.**
Charles L. Hogue. Berkeley, California; London: University of California Press, 1993. 536p. maps.

This is an entirely systematic study, but since insects do not respect political boundaries, any interested entomologist will find reference to common and notable insects which occur in Brazil. The work provides a substantial general introduction to the continent's insect life, and then deals systematically with major groups, for example, moths and butterflies, beetles, and aquatic insects. Each entry is accompanied by a short bibliographical note, and there is a useful chapter on research agencies involved in entomological work.

86 **Observations on birds of southeastern Brazil.**
Margaret H. Mitchell. Toronto, Canada: University of Toronto Press, 1957. 258p. maps. bibliog.

Presents an ornithologist's diary of sightings, but one which provides an accessible record of the bird life of southeast Brazil, accompanied by details of locales where species have been observed. The volume contains an annotated list of over 280 birds from Rio de Janeiro, Minas Gerais, São Paulo, southern Mato Grosso and western Paraná.

87 **Size structure of illegally harvested and surviving caiman *Caiman crocodilus yacare* in Pantanal, Brazil.**
G. Mourão, Z. Campos, M. Coutinho, C. Abercrombie. *Biological Conservation*, vol. 75 (1996), p. 261-65.

This caiman (Brazilian alligator), although nominally a protected species, is hunted for its skin. The evidence of the research presented in this article suggests that hunters tend to take large, male animals, though there has been some variation in the numbers killed due to fluctuating world fashion for alligator leather.

88 **Amazon parrots.**
Paul R. Paradise. Neptune, New Jersey; Reigate, United Kingdom: TFH Publications, 1979. 94p.

This is a book for bird-keepers interested in parrots. The Amazon Parrot genus occurs throughout Central and South America, and this book provides a listing and description of species and their habitats, including those found in Brazil. It also gives details of the training, feeding and diseases of captive birds.

89 **Effects of hunting in western Amazonian primate communities.**
     Carlos A. Peres. *Biological Conservation*, vol. 54 (1990), p. 45-59.
A research study of the impact of subsistence hunting on monkeys, this paper
concludes that such hunting tends to adversely affect the larger species.

90 **Marsh deer *Blastocerus dichotomus* population estimate in the
     Paraná River, Brazil.**
     Laurenz Pinder. *Biological Conservation*, vol. 75 (1996), p. 87-91.
A study of the largest South American deer, which has been decreased in number by
disease, hunting, and habitat reduction. The survey is of an area on the São Paulo-
Mato Grosso do Sul border, threatened by flooding from a dam. It suggests that
translocation of herds away from flooded areas is not a real solution, and recommends
the protection of surviving wildlife habitats from development.

91 **A conservation plan for the jaguar *Panthera onca* in the Pantanal
     region of Brazil.**
     Howard B. Quigley, Peter G. Cranston. *Biological Conservation*,
     vol. 61 (1992), p. 149-57.
The Pantanal in southwest Brazil is one of the world's largest seasonally flooded
areas, with a distinct ecosystem. It contains a small national park, but the jaguar
population is not numerous and is threatened by development schemes. This paper
proposes the creation of larger reserves to protect the animals.

92 **Aves do Brasil.** (Birds of Brazil.)
     Augusti Ruschi. São Paulo, Brazil: Editora Rios, 1979. 336p. bibliog.
A wide-ranging bilingual study of ornithology, which discusses the origin of birds in
Brazil, their description and classification, and life cycle. The volume contains essays
on the place of birds in religion and art, and as food, and on rare species and
conservation. The main text is in English and Portuguese, but the detailed description
of the twenty-two orders and eighty-five families of Brazilian birds is in Portuguese
only. However, the scientific, popular Brazilian, and English names of each species
are provided, making it a basic work of reference for the tropical ornithologist.

93 **Marmosets and tamarins. Systematics, behaviour and ecology.**
     Edited by Anthony Rylands. New York; Oxford: Oxford University
     Press, 1993. 396p. maps. bibliog.
This is a highly specialized zoological study, but marmosets and tamarins are
important primate species in Latin America, especially in Amazonia and southeast
Brazil. Although essentially a text for those interested in primates, the book may be of
interest to others interested in forest wildlife and its conservation. Many species are
threatened by clearance of their forest habitats, and some are subject to conservation
operations.

94 **Primate species richness in relation to habitat structure in Amazonian rainforest fragments.**
Lin Schwarzkopf, Anthony Rylands. *Biological Conservation*, vol. 48 (1989), p. 1-12.
The process of deforestation in Amazonia leaves behind patches of forest of varying size. This study examines the factors influencing the ability of primates to survive in such areas.

95 **Birds in Brazil: a natural history.**
Helmut Sick, translated by William Betton. Princeton, New Jersey: Princeton University Press, 1993. 704p. and numerous unnumbered plates. maps. bibliog.
A definitive work of reference, which provides a history of ornithology in Brazil and discusses conservation issues. Its substance, however, is a comprehensive and well-illustrated listing and commentary on Brazilian birds, by order and family.

Environmental issues

96 **A desordem ecológica na Amazônia.** (Ecological disorder in Amazonia.)
Edited by Luis E. Aragón. Belém, Brazil: Associação de Universidades Amazônicas, 1991. 488p. maps.
A collection of papers, in Portuguese or English, dealing with a range of environmental issues, including: development and conservation; man and his habitat; the use and abuse of Amazonia; and the international implications of Amazon development.

97 **Environmental aspects of Brazil's economic development.**
W. Baer, C. C. Mueller. *Luso-Brazilian Review*, vol. 31 (1995), p. 83-101; vol. 32 (1996), p. 21-42.
This two-part study provides a comprehensive review of the environmental impacts of Brazil's economic development. It offers a long perspective on the history of resource exploitation, and detailed commentary on the impact of industrialization in fostering industrial and urban pollution and urban poverty. Also discussed is the impact of agriculture and deforestation. Part I includes the bulk of the text, notes, and bibliography; Part II contains the remainder of the text and tables. Given its summary character, this work is of interest to biologists, conservationists, and to economists interested in the adverse consequences of the development process.

98 **Conservation in Amazonia.**
Suzanne W. Barrett. *Biological Conservation*, vol. 18 (1980),
p. 209-35.
A useful early review of Brazil's attempts to provide protection for plants and
animals, which can be viewed as a benchmark for later responses to environmental
destruction. It observes that the earliest national parks and reserves were established
on the periphery of the region, with the consequence that the areas of richest diversity
were left unprotected.

99 **Brazilian policies that encourage deforestation in the Amazon.**
Hans P. Binswanger. *World Development*, vol. 19 (1991), p. 821-29.
Presents a helpful examination of financial policies applied in the development of
Amazonia, through general and special taxes, agricultural credit, and land allocation
schemes. It is suggested that all of these incentives accelerate deforestation and
increase the size of landholdings, to the detriment of the rural poor.

100 **Amazonia and Siberia. Legal aspects of the preservation of the
environment and development in the last open spaces.**
Edited by Michael Bothe, Thomas Kurzidem, Christian Schmidt.
London; Boston, Massachusetts; Dordrecht, Netherlands: Graham &
Trottman, 1993. 356p.
Amazonia and Siberia are a seemingly improbable pairing, but this book forms part of
an international series on environmental law and policy, and these areas can be seen as
two of the world's surviving wildernesses. The volume includes discussion of
development in Amazonia, problems of mercury poisoning, and Brazilian
environmental law.

101 **Amazonian conservation in a changing world.**
Mark B. Bush. *Biological Conservation*, vol. 76 (1996), p. 219-28.
Consitutes a very important review of appropriate areas to be protected in order to
sustain biodiversity in Amazonia. It includes some discussion of the implications of
possible climatic changes which might occur as a result of deforestation.

102 **Brazilian perspectives on sustainable development of the Amazon
region. Man and the biosphere series 15.**
Edited by M. Clüsener-Godt, I. Sachs. Paris: UNESCO, 1995. 312p.
This is a highly significant study, since most of the debate surrounding the
consequences of the development of Amazonia comes from outside Brazil, and is
generally hostile and lacking in perspective as to why Brazil has pursued its strategies
for developing Amazonia. This volume brings together work by Brazilian scholars,
researchers and resource managers. Its thirteen chapters cover the physical
environment of climate, hydrology, biology and ecological diversity, and the use of
the region for forestry, mining, agriculture, and fishing.

103 **The shifting middle ground: Amazonian Indians and eco-politics.**
Beth A. Conklin, Laura R. Graham. *American Anthropologist*,
vol. 97 (1995), p. 695-710.

An interesting and thoughtful paper on Indian responses to First World concerns for
their environment, suggesting that even sympathetic 'outsiders' tend to see the Indians
as a uniform group, ignoring their cultural diversity. It suggests that there are conflicts
emerging over the representation of Indians and environmental issues, in which the
'Indian' and the 'environment' become a simplified and overlapping 'cause' for
outsiders. The perceptions and aspirations of the Indian groups may be much more
complex and diverse.

104 **With broadax and firebrand: the destruction of the Brazilian
Atlantic forest.**
Warren Dean.   Berkeley, California; London: University of California
Press, 1995. 482p. maps.

This is a first-rate environmental history, which catalogues the early emergence of
'environmental issues' through the clearance of the coastal forest by the Portuguese. It
also suggests, contrary to conventional wisdom, that the native peoples may have
significantly modified the forest prior to the arrival of the Europeans.

105 **Ecology and land management in Amazonia.**
Michael J. Eden.   London; New York: Belhaven, 1990. 270p. maps.
bibliog.

Examines the environmental history and contemporary use of the whole of Amazonia,
ranging beyond Brazil, to include material from Peru, Colombia, Venezuela, and the
Guianas. The study provides an excellent discussion of the conflict between development and conservation. Analysis of the latter theme includes national parks and
integrated land management schemes.

106 **Amazon conservation in the age of development. The limits of
providence.**
Ronald A. Foresta.   Gainesville, Florida: University of Florida Press,
1991. 366p. maps. bibliog.

In the plethora of 'green' literature generated by Brazil's advance on the forest, this is
a balanced overview of Amazon development, and of the efforts at conservation,
which is set into the context of science, developmentalism and international capital.
Such a considered, thoughtful approach is rare.

107 **Amazon jungle: green hell to red desert?**
R. J. A. Goodland, H. S. Irwin.   Amsterdam; Oxford; New York:
Elsevier Scientific Publishing Co., 1975. 156p. maps. bibliog.

Goodland and Irwin produced the first significant commentary on the potential
environmental consequences of Brazil's advance into Amazonia in the 1970s. Beyond
its pioneering role, the volume remains a good introduction to the region and the
environmental issues raised by its development. Useful listings of plant, bird, animal
and fish species, and of Indian tribes, are included. The book's bibliography is an
important record of material published before 1975.

108   **The fate of the forest. Developers, destroyers and defenders of the Amazon.**
      Susanna Hecht, Alexander Cockburn.   London; New York: Verso, 1989. 266p. maps. bibliog.
Offering a greenish perspective on the experience of Amazonia, this book provides a brief description of the region and a history of its exploitation. It is largely concerned with the recent effects of government policy, developers, and the activities of those seeking to protect the forest. A series of appendices contain interviews with individuals from the latter group.

109   **Change in the Amazon basin. vol. 1 Man's impact on forests and rivers; vol. 2 The forest after a decade of colonisation.**
      Edited by John Hemming.   Manchester, United Kingdom: Manchester University Press, 1985. 2 vols. maps. bibliog.
The proceedings of a major symposium held in Manchester a decade after Brazil's new advance into the Amazon, this collection brings together the work of numerous experts. The two volumes cover a wide range of consequences for the natural environment, and the process and patterns of settlement and development. Included in the second volume are some useful commentaries on the progress of colonization schemes.' Discussion is not limited to the Brazilian Amazon, so there are some valuable comparative insights into exploitation of the western margins of the basin.

110   **Amazonia. Man and culture in a counterfeit paradise.**
      Betty J. Meggers.   Chicago: Aldine Publishing Co., 1971. 182p. maps. bibliog.
An early contribution to debates about Amazonian development, this study focuses on aboriginal adjustment to environment. It is intended for an undergraduate audience, but provides a good introduction into the way in which different groups use the environment. Its perspective is towards a harmonious balance between nature and native, and concern for the impact of development.

111   **Fight for the forest. Chico Mendes in his own words.**
      Chico Mendes, translated by Chris Whitehouse.   London: Latin American Bureau, 1989. 96p. maps. bibliog.
Mendes was the leader of the rubber tappers union and an advocate of forest protection. Following his assassination in 1988, he became a folk hero for the Green movement. This is the story of his mobilization of the tappers.

112   **Tropical deforestation, land degradation and social lessons from Rondônia, Brazil.**
      Brent H. Millikan.   *Latin American Perspectives*, vol. 19, no. 1 (1992), p. 45-72.
A good review of the impact of frontier advance in western Amazonia, covering deforestation, land degradation, the failure of small-farmer colonization schemes, and the wider issues raised by spontaneous migration to the frontier.

113   **The burning season: the murder of Chico Mendes and the fight for the Amazon rain forest.**
Andrew Revkin. London: Collins, 1990. 318p.
Presents a popular biography of a symbolic figure in the controversy over Amazonia, accompanied by a basic history of the exploitation of the region.

114   **The ecologist movement in Brazil (1974-86): from environmentalism to eco-politics.**
Eduardo J. Viola. *International Journal of Urban and Regional Research*, vol. 12 (1988), p. 211-28.
This is a useful broad survey of the environmental impact of Brazil's economic development, and the emergence of active responses to it, which culminated in the formation of a Green Party in 1986.

Archaeology and Prehistory

115   **Dating the first American.**
       P. Bahn.   *New Scientist*, vol. 131, no. 1778 (1991), p. 26-28.
Discusses the evidence of charcoal, tools, and rock paintings for a very early settlement site in the New World, located at Pedra Furada, in the northeastern state of Piauí.

116   **50,000 year old Americans at Pedra Furada.**
       P. Bahn.   *Nature*, vol. 362 (1993), p. 114-15.
The Pedra Furada site is very controversial, since it pushes back the date of human occupation in the New World to beyond 30,000 BP (against a North American view that the earliest settlement of the Americas was circa 15,000-12,000 BP). This is a sympathetic account of the research at Pedra Furada, on the basis of charcoal and pebble tool evidence.

117   **Brasil nas vesperas do mundo moderno.** (Brazil at the dawn of the
       modern world.)
       Edited by Jill R. Dias.   Lisbon: Comissão Nacional para as
       Comemorações dos Descobrimentos Portugueses, 1992. 262p. maps.
       bibliog.
Produced to commemorate the Portuguese contribution to the 'discovery' of the New World, this is a very important addition to the scholarship of the era of contact. The volume spans prehistory and history (in a European sense), but provides a series of valuable essays on the prehistory of Amazonia, and European perceptions and representations of the Indians. Its coverage extends into the 18th century, to examine issues of conflict, slavery and miscegenation. Although the text is in Portuguese, the book contains a rich collection of early drawings and maps, and photographs of surviving artefacts. These, together with a bibliography which contains both Portuguese and English material, will make it of use to the archaeologist and ethnologist.

118   **The chronology of the New World: two faces of one reality.**
       N. Guidon, B. Arnaud.   *World Archaeology*, vol. 23 (1991),
       p. 167-78.

Provides a useful summary of the evidence which points to a very early date of human occupation for the archaeological site at Pedra Furada. This paper supports the controversial early date (beyond 30,000 BP) of human settlement in the Americas.

119   **The Indians of Brazil in 1500.**
       John Hemming.   In: *Cambridge history of Latin America. Vol. 1.*
       Edited by Leslie Bethell. ' Cambridge, United Kingdom; New York:
       Cambridge University Press, 1984, p. 119-43.

A very useful historical geography of the Indian population at contact. There were four main language groups at that time – Tupi, Gê, Carib and Arawak – and this chapter describes their distribution in Brazil, and the nature of their societies and cultures. It makes effective use of the observations of the early European explorers.

120   **Advances in Brazilian archaeology, 1935-85.**
       Betty J. Meggers.   *American Antiquity*, vol. 50 (1985), p. 364-73.

Probably the best general introduction to the field of archaeology in Brazil, this paper outlines the modest level of research to date. It points out the particular obstacles to archaeological work, which are due to the limited range of materials available for study. For example, the pre-colonial societies lacked stone buildings, metal goods, or elaborate artefacts, and the forest environments have impeded archaeological research. However, as some of the more recent papers listed in this bibliography (qq.v.) indicate, knowledge of the scale and breadth of Indian culture is being extended.

121   **The prehistory of Amazonia.**
       Betty J. Meggers.   In: *People of the tropical rain forest.*   Edited by
       Julie S. Denslow, Christine Padoch.   Berkeley, California; London:
       University of California Press, 1988, p. 53-62.

A useful summary of the nature of Amazon settlement at contact, when Europeans reported a numerous population. The paper comments on the lack of durable artefacts to provide archaeological evidence, but suggests that there was human occupation of east and south Amazonia by 12,000 BP.

122   **On a Pleistocene human occupation at Pedra Furada, Brazil.**
       D. J. Meltzer, J. M. Adovasio, T. D. Dillehay.   *Antiquity*, vol. 68
       (1994), p. 695-714.

This paper is critical of the early date ascribed to the Pedra Furada site, and the interpretation of its artefacts. A dating of the oldest materials to 48,000 BP would make it the earliest known human site in the Americas, which is difficult to reconcile with other evidence, and with current ideas as to the arrival of people in the Americas.

123 **8th millennium pottery from a prehistoric shell midden in the Brazilian Amazon.**
A. Roosevelt, R. A. Housley, M. Imazio da Silveira, S. Maranca, R. Johnson. *Science*, vol. 254 (1991), p. 1621-24.

Discusses the earliest pottery yet found in the Western Hemisphere, from a shell midden near Santarém on the lower River Amazon. Evidence from shells, pottery, and charcoal date the existence of human occupation there to around 8-7,000 BP, as part of a fishing community. The paper argues that current evolutionary scenarios of settlement, which are based on negative evidence from little-researched but extensive tropical lowlands, are unsatisfactory. It suggests that 'absence of evidence', because of the lack of research in difficult environments, should not be used to assert that these areas were occupied late and by very simple societies. The authors argue that evidence such as that of the Santarém midden suggests that there was early settlement in the riverine environments of Amazonia.

History

General

124 The Cambridge history of Latin America.
Edited by Leslie Bethell. Cambridge, United Kingdom; New York: Cambridge University Press, 1984- . Vols. I-X.

This multi-volume series is a comprehensive study of the history of the continent. It provides many contextual essays, as well as covering specifically Brazilian topics (described elsewhere in the bibliography), and extensive bibliographical essays. The series brings together scholarship of the highest order, and though intended primarily for academic historians, the essays are an essential source of reference for anyone interested in Brazilian (or Spanish American) history.

125 A documentary history of Brazil.
Edited by E. Bradford Burns. New York: Alfred A. Knopf, 1966. 400p.

An important reference source of documentary material relating to Brazil's history. Arranged under the colonial, imperial and republican periods, the material includes over eighty documents which illuminate key points in the country's history. They range from the record of the first sighting of the country in 1500 to the declaration of independence in 1822, the law abolishing slavery in 1888 and the suicide letter of President Vargas in 1945.

126 A history of Brazil.
E. Bradford Burns. New York: Columbia University Press, 1980. 2nd ed. 580p. bibliog. maps.

The most accessible comprehensive history of Brazil, this volume covers the period from pre-colonial times to the height of the military régime in the 1970s. It provides a wide-ranging introduction to political, economic, social and cultural history. Although primarily a university text, the book's style makes it accessible to anyone interested in Brazil's history. A useful chronology of significant dates is included.

127 **Documentos historícos Brasileiras.** (Brazilian historical documents.)
Lydinéa Gasman. Rio de Janeiro, Brazil: FENAME, 1976. 302p. bibliog.

Comprises a collection of documents on Brazil's history from the colonial period to 1967. A useful introduction to the nature of Brazilian documentary sources is followed by text which is divided into the colonial, imperial and republican periods, and includes material on the discovery, slavery, the end of the Empire, the Vargas years, and planning documents of the post-war years. For all three periods, material is also provided on literature and music, etc.

128 **A century of Brazilian history since 1865.**
Edited by Richard Graham. New York: Alfred A. Knopf, 1969. 238p. bibliog.

This is a collection of essays on the Empire and Old and New Republics, by Brazilian and foreign writers. Topics include slavery, the Vargas years, and the activities of the Left from 1945-64. Different perspectives are presented on a number of these themes, making the volume a stimulating source. Thus, there are contrasting views of the Emperor Pedro II and President Vargas, on the nature of slavery, and on the significance of the War of 1865-70 as interpreted by Brazilian, Paraguayan and Argentinian participants.

129 **Historical dictionary of Brazil.**
R. M. Levine. Metuchen, New Jersey; London: Scarecrow Press Inc., 1979. 298p. bibliog.

An invaluable and wide-ranging 'dictionary' of the history of Brazil, covering topics including people, events, politics, high and popular culture, food and slang. It is a very useful source of short references on Brazil's past.

130 **A propos de l'histoire de l'historiographie brésilienne.** (Concerning the history of Brazilian historiography.)
Guy Martiniere. *Cahiers des Amériques Latine*, vol. 14 (1992), p. 119-48.

This is a very good review of historical research on Brazil, particularly the work done by Brazilian historians. It is a helpful background source for researchers.

131 **A pesquisa histórica no Brasil.** (The historical study of Brazil.)
José Honorio Rodrigues. São Paulo, Brazil: Companhia Editora Nacional, 1982. 4th ed. 306p.

Although a little dated, this is still an important source providing a review of Brazilian historical studies. Its persisting value derives from its extensive survey of sources for historical study, not only in Brazilian public sources, archives and journals, but in the archives of most European and Latin American countries, and elsewhere.

132 **The historiography of Brazil, 1889-1964.**
Thomas E. Skidmore. *Hispanic American Historical Review*, vol. 55
(1975), p. 716-48; vol. 56 (1976), p. 81-109.
A very useful review of work published from 1957-72 on the Old and New Republics,
which identifies the main themes of Brazil's recent history and the literature on it.
Besides discussing these broad periods, the article also deals with economic history,
foreign relations, and the states.

133 **Brazil: 500 years of history.**
L. Vasconceles, V. Curry. *International Social Science Journal*,
vol. 134 (1992), p. 473-86.
Provides a brief but useful review of the main phases of Brazilian history, and also
raises interesting questions on the country's need to modernize.

The colonial period (1500-1822)

134 **Royal government in colonial Brazil, with special reference to the
administration of the Marquis of Lavradio, Viceroy, 1769-79.**
Dauril Alden. Berkeley, California: University of California Press,
1968. 546p. map. bibliog.
Despite its age, this remains one of the best detailed studies of the colonial
administration of Brazil. It deals with the period 1769-79, and the need for the viceroy
to secure the colonial territory and encourage its development. The volume is an
invaluable source on the nature of the colonial administration at various levels.

135 **Late colonial Brazil, 1750-1808.**
Dauril Alden. In: *Cambridge history of Latin America. Vol. II.*
Edited by Leslie Bethell. Cambridge, United Kingdom; New York:
Cambridge University Press, 1984, p. 601-60. bibliog.
This is a detailed survey of the late-colonial period, which places strong emphasis on
demography and the agricultural economy. It suggests that after the decline of the
18th-century gold boom, the colony returned to an export economy based on
established crops such as sugar and tobacco, but also began to develop cotton, rice and
other export crops. A detailed account of activity in these products is provided, which
makes effective use of such sources as are available. Also included is a careful tracing
of population growth during the period.

136 **Portugal: a pioneer of the north/south dialogue.**
Luís Filipe Barreto. Lisbon: Imprensa Nacional, 1988. 166p. maps.
bibliog.
Presents a trilingual (English, French and Portuguese) study of the Portuguese empire,
which contains a wealth of maps and pictures from the period, and extracts from

contemporary narratives. The volume deals with the cultural context of the discoveries, in terms of science, navigation, technology, and aspects of the geography and anthropology of the new lands. It provides a useful popular introduction to Portuguese expansion.

137 **Colonial Brazil.**
Edited by Leslie Bethell. Cambridge, United Kingdom; New York: Cambridge University Press, 1987. 398p. maps. bibliog.

Bringing together essays on colonial Brazil from the first two volumes of the *Cambridge history of Latin America* (q.v.), this paperback is intended for the student market. The essays included cover the Indians, early Portuguese settlement, and the colonial economy and political development.

138 **The Dutch in Brazil, 1624-1654.**
C. R. Boxer. Oxford: Clarendon Press, 1957. 336p. maps. bibliog.

Remains the definitive study of the thirty-year occupation of northeast Brazil by the Dutch. The volume deals with the background of Dutch imperialist designs, their early forays against Brazil, 1624-29, and the process of conquest, 1630-36. Containing very detailed discussion of the governorship of Johan Maurits (1637-44), and the nature of Dutch society and economic activity, the work also covers the revolts against Dutch rule and the process of reconquest. Biographies of the leading Dutch and Portuguese personalities are provided.

139 **The golden age of Brazil, 1695-1750.**
C. R. Boxer. Berkeley, California; London: University of California Press, 1962. 444p. maps. bibliog.

This work endures as a classic and essential study of the economic peak of the colonial period. Though its dominant theme is a detailed portrait of the Brazilian gold rush and its consequences, it also explores the patterns of development in the remainder of the country. Providing much detail on the economy and society of the gold mining region of Minas Gerais, the volume is also a good source on sugar in the Northeast, cattle ranching in the interior, and the activities of missionaries in Amazonia. Although scholarly, the text is eminently readable.

140 **The Portuguese seaborne empire, 1415-1825.**
C. R. Boxer. London: Hutchinson and Co., 1969. 426p. maps. bibliog.

For anyone interested in the broader context of colonial Brazil, this is an essential reference work. It describes the evolution and nature of the Portuguese empire in Africa, Asia, and Brazil over the period 1415-1825. In discussing the 'characteristics of empire' the volume examines trade, colonial organization, the missions, race, and colonists.

141 **Dialogues of the great things of Brazil.**
Ambrósio Fernandes Brandão (attrib.), translated by Frederick H. Hall,
William F. Harrison, Dorothy W. Welker. Albuquerque, New
Mexico: University of New Mexico Press, 1987. 396p. map. bibliog.

The dialogues are a collection of commentaries made by a late-16th-century visitor to
northeast Brazil, and portray perceptions of the country as recorded by a Portuguese
businessman circa 1618. A fascinating contemporary source, they describe the
settlement of the country, the climate and diseases, the production of dyewood, sugar
and other commodities, and the flora and fauna.

142 **The Portuguese settlement of Brazil, 1500-1580.**
H. B. Johnson. In: *Cambridge history of Latin America. Vol. I.*
Edited by Leslie Bethell. Cambridge, United Kingdom; New York:
Cambridge University Press, 1984, p. 249-86.

Providing a good outline of the tentative early years of colonization, this covers: the
early exploration of Brazil; the first attempts to administer it by concessionary
captaincies (1534-48); and the establishment of royal control, based in Salvador, from
1549.

143 **Portuguese Brazil. The king's plantation.**
James Lang. New York; London: Academic Press, 1979. 268p. map.
bibliog.

The theme of this study is the nature of the relationship between Brazil and the
metropolitan power, and the way in which Portugal benefitted from the taxation of a
sequence of Brazilian products – sugar, gold, and tobacco – as well as the slaves
essential for their exploitation. It explores the evolution of this export economy, and
the nature of Portuguese colonial control. The author suggests that the export of these
commodities was an essential factor in the colonial development of Brazil; this book
not only argues the case, but provides a very good portrait of that economy.

144 **Portugal and Brazil: imperial re-organization, 1750-1808.**
Andrée Mansuy-Diniz Silva. In: *Cambridge history of Latin America.
Vol. I.* Edited by Leslie Bethell. Cambridge, United Kingdom; New
York: Cambridge University Press, p. 469-508. map. bibliog.

A useful survey of late-colonial territorial expansion, administrative change and
economic restructuring. This chapter details the evolving political geography of the
country, as its boundaries were expanded and defined, and colonial administration was
strengthened. The role of the Marquis of Pombal, the Portuguese prime minister for
much of the period, in shaping the late-colonial economy, is well described.

145   **Portugal and Brazil: political and economic structures of empire, 1580-1750.**
Frédéric Mauro.   In: *Cambridge history of Latin America. Vol. I.*
Edited by Leslie Bethell.   Cambridge, United Kingdom; New York: Cambridge University Press, 1984, p. 441-68.

Between 1580 and 1640 Portugal and its empire were part of a joint kingdom with Spain, and this essay details the implications for the way in which the political structure and economy of Brazil evolved during this period. It also contains detailed discussion of the development of the early export commodities – sugar, tobacco and gold.

146   **Conflicts and conspiracies: Brazil and Portugal 1750-1808.**
Kenneth R. Maxwell.   Cambridge, United Kingdom: Cambridge University Press, 1973. 290p. map. bibliog.

This is a scholarly monograph on an important phase in relations between Brazil and Portugal, during which Portuguese colonial policy, especially under the Marquis of Pombal (1750-77), changed. The new social and economic circumstances prompted rebellion in Minas Gerais in 1789, and this forms the main focus of the study. Although this *Inconfidência* (revolt) was unsuccessful, it is generally seen as an early stage of the movement towards Brazilian independence.

147   **The bandeirantes. The historical role of the Brazilian pathfinders.**
Edited by Richard M. Morse.   New York: Alfred A. Knopf, 1965. 216p. map. bibliog.

The *bandeirantes* (literally flag-bearers), based in São Paulo, were exploring pioneers who opened up much of interior South America and secured territory for Portugal. Morse provides an excellent introductory essay to a valuable collection of papers on their activities.

148   **New Iberian world. A documentary history of the discovery and settlement of Latin America to the early seventeenth century. Volume 5. Coastlands, rivers and forests.**
Edited by John H. Parry, Robert G. Keith.   New York: Times Books & Hector & Rose, 1984. 572p.

This volume provides a collection of original documents on the exploration and settlement of the coast (p. 1-140), and the navigation and exploration of the Amazon (p. 175-245).

149   **Colonial Brazil: the gold cycle, c.1690-1750.**
A. J. R. Russell-Wood.   In: *Cambridge history of Latin America Vol. II.*   Edited by Leslie Bethell.   Cambridge, United Kingdom; New York: Cambridge University Press, 1984, p. 547-600. bibliog.

A detailed study of the administration, economy and society of the gold rush area of Minas Gerais. It provides a comprehensive account of the nature and organization of gold mining, the attempts by the crown to secure its one-fifth share, and the efforts of the miners to circumvent payment of this.

150 **A world on the move: the Portuguese in Africa, Asia, and America, 1415-1808.**
A. J. R. Russell-Wood. Manchester, United Kingdom: Carcanet Press, 1992. 290p. maps. bibliog.

Provides a useful and elegant contextual study of the Portuguese colonial expansion, dealing with navigation, and the movement of people, goods and ideas to new worlds.

151 **Ports of colonial Brazil.**
A. J. R. Russell-Wood. In: *Atlantic American societies*. Edited by Alan L. Karras, J. R. McNeil. London: Routledge, 1992, p. 174-211. map. bibliog.

Outlines the maritime nature of the Portuguese colony. Links between the colony and the metropolitan power were clearly essential. This essay considers trans-Atlantic shipping, the relationships between the ports and their hinterlands, and provides a detailed account of the key colonial ports of Salvador and Rio de Janeiro.

152 **Society and government in colonial Brazil, 1500-1822.**
A. J. R. Russell-Wood. Aldershot, United Kingdom; Brookfield, Vermont: Variorum, 1992. 337p.

A collection of papers from the period 1967-91 by a distinguished historian of Brazil. They cover a variety of topics, including the lay brotherhoods in the Church, women in colonial society, and portraits of a number of important figures from the period.

153 **The world encompassed. The first European maritime empires c.800-1650.**
Geoffrey V. Scammell. London: Methuen University Paperback, 1987. 538p. maps. bibliog.

This book provides a general context to European imperialism, which gives a useful setting for examining the colonial experience of Brazil. Chapter 5 (p. 225-300) deals specifically with Portugal, outlining the process of imperialism, and the maritime technology by which it was implemented.

154 **Colonial Brazil, c.1580-c.1750: plantations and peripheries.**
Stuart B. Schwartz. In: *Cambridge history of Latin America. Vol. II*. Edited by Leslie Bethell. Cambridge, United Kingdom; New York: Cambridge University Press, 1984, p. 423-99. maps. bibliog.

A comprehensive survey of the economy and society of the northeastern sugar region, this provides a detailed and scholarly account of the nature of the plantation economy, which describes output, production methods, the importance of slavery, and the associated production of tobacco, cattle and manioc. The study also refers to the tentative efforts to develop São Paulo and eastern Amazonia, and the early growth of towns.

155 **Sugar plantations in the formation of Brazilian society. Bahia 1550-1835.**
Stuart B. Schwartz. Cambridge, United Kingdom; New York: Cambridge University Press, 1985. 616p. maps. bibliog.

This is a detailed historical monograph on one of the key areas of the colonial sugar industry in Brazil, which explores the nature of the plantation economy, its technology, its dependence on slavery, and the relations between masters and slaves. As a research study this is a book for the specialist historian, both as an extensive survey of the sugar economy, and as a meticulous piece of scholarship.

156 **The formation of a colonial identity in Brazil.**
Stuart B. Schwartz. In: *Colonial identity in the Atlantic world, 1500-1800.* Edited by Nicholas Canny, Anthony Pagden. Princeton, New Jersey; Guildford, United Kingdom: Princeton University Press, 1987, p. 15-50.

Tracing the development of Brazil from 1500 to circa 1810, this is an important study of the factors shaping the emergence of collective identity in colonial Brazil, which suggests that the emergence of national consciousness needs to be understood within the context of the country's politics and society. It also argues that, beside the emergence of such identity as chronicled by the literate colonial aristocracy, there may have been a feeling of distinctiveness among the non-literate mestizo and mulatto population.

157 **The histories of Brazil of Pero de Magalhães.**
Translated by John B. Stetson. New York: Cortes Society, 1922. 266p.

Comprises a facsimile and translation of a late-16th-century account of Brazil. It offers an interesting contemporary perception of the new land, which describes its inhabitants and wildlife, and contains brief descriptions of the captaincies, which were the first administrative units employed by the Portuguese.

158 **Pero Vaz de Caminha: the voice of the Luso-Brasilian chronicle.**
Jerry M. Williams. *Luso-Brazilian Review*, vol. 28, no. 2 (1991), p. 59-72.

Vaz de Caminha was the notary on the voyage which discovered Brazil. His report described the land, the character of the people, and the first contact between Europeans and Brazil. This article provides a critical appraisal of Caminha's attempts to describe what he saw.

Independence and Empire (1822-89)

159 **Brazil. The forging of a nation, 1798-1852.**
Roderick J. Barman.   Stanford, California: Stanford University Press,
1988. 334p. maps. bibliog.

This political history of the emergence of the nation-state of Brazil examines the
gradual evolution of a national identity in the late-18th century, and the way it took on
a more precise definition after 1808.

160 **The independence of Brazil.**
Leslie Bethell.   In: *Cambridge history of Latin America. Vol. III.*
Edited by Leslie Bethell.   Cambridge, United Kingdom; New York:
Cambridge University Press, 1985, p. 157-96. map. bibliog.

A comprehensive and detailed survey of the period circa 1750-1823, which covers the
background to, and securing of, independence.

161 **Brazil from independence to the middle of the nineteenth century.**
Leslie Bethell, José Murilo de Carvalho.   In: *Cambridge history of
' Latin America. Vol. III.*   Edited by Leslie Bethell.   Cambridge,
United Kingdom; New York: Cambridge University Press, 1985,
p. 679-746. map. bibliog.

As with item no. 160, this is a detailed account of a period of Brazilian history,
covering political, economic and social change. It contains some interesting discussion
of Brazil's ambivalence over the ending of slavery, but also of the beginnings of
European immigration, which was to provide an alternative labour source to the
slaves.

162 **Brazil: empire and republic, 1822-1930.**
Edited by Leslie Bethell.   Cambridge, United Kingdom; New York:
Cambridge University Press, 1989. 354p. maps. bibliog.

This is a paperback collection of essays from the *Cambridge history of Latin America*
(q.v.), aimed at the student market. They deal with independence, the Empire period,
and the economy, society and politics of the Old Republic.

163 **The independence of Brazil.**
Roderick Cavaliero.   London; New York: British Academy Press,
1993. 232p. bibliog.

A survey of the events leading up to Brazil's declaration of independence in 1822. The
volume includes discussion of Britain's role in securing Portugal's acquiescence to the
loss of the colony. It makes some use of the commentaries of contemporary travellers.

164 **A presença Britânica no Brasil (1808-1914)/The British presence in Brazil (1808-1914).**
Elizabeth de Fiore, Ottaviano de Fiore. São Paulo, Brazil: Editora Paubrasil, 1987. 156p. bibliog.
This is a lavishly produced, bilingual, coffee-table book which explores the major role played by Britain in 19th-century Brazil. The volume deals with the securing of independence, exploration, railway building, and urbanization, and contains case-studies of some key British figures such as Henry Koster, Henry Bates, Richard Burton and Maria Graham. The numerous paintings and early photographs it reproduces are of considerable interest.

165 **Brazil from the middle of the nineteenth century to the Paraguayan War.**
Richard Graham. In: *Cambridge history of Latin America. Vol. III.* Edited by Leslie Bethell. Cambridge, United Kingdom; New York: Cambridge University Press, 1985, p. 746-94. bibliog.
Appraises an important period of economic and political change in Brazil. Providing a thorough review of the development of the coffee economy and of other crops, the essay draws attention to the dependence of these agricultural activities on slave labour, but also indicates the beginning of moves towards emancipation. Other key issues which emerged during this period were the building of the railways, the involvement of British and American capital in the economy, and the beginnings of urbanization; all of these topics are well summarized here.

166 **The Great Drought and elite discourse in Imperial Brazil.**
Gerald M. Greenfield. *Hispanic American Historical Review*, vol. 72 (1992), p. 375-400.
The period 1877-79 saw a major drought in northeast Brazil, with much damage to life and property. This prompted debate about Brazil's destiny, the problems of agricultural productivity, and the backwardness of the *sertanejos* (inhabitants of the interior). The author suggests that the élite saw the crisis not as the product of the natural environment or poverty, but of lazy peasants and indolent landowners.

167 **Empire in Brazil. A New World experiment with monarchy.**
C. H. Haring. Cambridge, Massachusetts: Harvard University Press, 1966. 182p. bibliog. map.
This is an interesting exploration of Brazil's retention of a monarchy, with a member of the Portuguese royal family, Dom Pedro, as emperor after independence. The study also offers insights into the debate about the ending of slavery, and the links between abolition and the fall of the monarchy. Royal support for abolition antagonized the old slave-owning, landed class, who then joined the republican movement.

168　**Dom Pedro. The struggle for liberty in Brazil and Portugal, 1798-1834.**
Neill MacCauley.　Durham, North Carolina: Duke University Press, 1986. 362p. bibliog. maps.
Provides a very detailed study, particularly of the Portuguese court's period of exile in Brazil, and the role of Dom Pedro, as Prince Regent, in Brazil's declaration of independence. The account contains much detail of court life in Rio de Janeiro.

169　**In pursuit of honor and power: noblemen of the Southern Cross in nineteenth-century Brazil.**
Eul-Soo Pang.　Tuscaloosa, Alabama; London: University of Alabama Press, 1988. 342p. map. bibliog.
During the Empire period (1822-89), over 1,000 titles were awarded in order to create a small noble élite. These titles, which were life peerages only, were awarded to key figures among landowners, politicians, the military, the Church and intellectuals. This study examines the regional, social and economic origins of this nobility.

170　**From colony to nation. Essays on the independence of Brazil.**
Edited by A. J. R. Russell-Wood.　Baltimore, Maryland; London: Johns Hopkins University Press, 1975. 268p.
These eight essays by American and Brazilian historians cover the fifty-year period leading to Brazilian independence in 1822. In addition to providing the broad background to the independence movement, they explore the political, social and cultural contexts within which it occurred.

171　**The Brazilian Empire: myths and histories.**
Emilia Viotti da Costa.　Chicago; London: University of Chicago Press, 1985. 288p. map.
The focus of this book is on the role of élite groups in shaping the economic, social and political evolution of Brazil in the 19th century. Although it consists of a set of essays, the volume provides a seamless portrait of major themes relating to liberalism, the control of land, labour organization, race, and urbanization. It represents a stimulating commentary on this period.

The Old Republic (1889-1930)

172　**The family in Bahia, Brazil, 1870-1945.**
Dain E. Borges.　Stanford, California: Stanford University Press, 1992. 422p. map. bibliog.
Though in essence a case-study, this is a useful guide to élite family organization in Brazil during a period of social change. With the emergence of an urbanizing economy, there was some shift from patriarchal to more nuclear family structure. The account discusses issues of home, health, religion and politics.

173 **The bandit king: Lampião of Brazil.**
Billy Jaynes Chandler. College Station, Texas; London: Texas
A & M University Press, 1978. 262p. bibliog.
Banditry has an important role in the history of interior Brazil. Lampião (1897-1938)
is probably the most famous or notorious of the bandits of the Northeast. This well-
documented study sets the context and provides a straightforward biography of a
20th-century rural bandit.

174 **Millenarian vision, capitalist reality: Brazil's Contestado rebellion,
1912-1916.**
Todd A. Diacon. Durham, North Carolina: Duke University Press,
1991. 200p. map. bibliog.
An interesting portrait of conflict in the interior of Santa Catarina between religiously-
inspired peasants on one hand, and the State, local bosses, and a foreign railroad
company on the other. The settlers came into conflict with the railroad's plan to
establish agricultural colonies along its route. This account provides a good description of the settlement of the interior of southern Brazil, and of railway development.

175 **Bringing the countryside back in: a case study of military
intervention as State building in the Brazilian Old Republic.**
Todd Diacon. *Journal of Latin American Studies*, vol. 27 (1995),
p. 569-92.
This paper is in part a summary version of item no. 174, but it focuses particularly on
lessons learned by the military about rural Brazil.

176 **Coffee, contention, and economic change in the making of modern
Brazil.**
Mauricio A. Font. Oxford; Cambridge, Massachusetts: Blackwell,
1990. 352p. bibliog.
Coffee dominated the Brazilian economy from the late-19th century until the 1930s,
and coffee *fazendeiros* (plantation owners) exercised considerable political influence.
This study explores the social organization of the coffee economy, with discussion of
the role of small and large landowners, and the involvement of planters in the
revolution of 1930.

177 **Pernambuco in the Brazilian federation, 1889-1937.**
Robert M. Levine. Stanford, California: Stanford University Press,
1978. 236p. maps. bibliog.
This is one of three studies with a common format on the regional dynamics of the
Old Republic (see also item nos. 182 and 186). They each portray the nature of a
significant part of the country, and explore its links to events on the national stage.
This volume contains a discussion of part of the Northeast, describing its society and
economy, and its politics and politicians. It provides a contrast with the other two
volumes in that Pernambuco was rather stagnant in this period, compared to the
dynamism of São Paulo and Minas Gerais.

178 **The centenary of Brazil's republican revolution.**
Edited by Robert Levine, Steven Topik. *The Americas*, vol. 48, no. 2
(1991), p. 131-278.

Dealing with the centenary of the establishment of the Brazilian Republic, this special
issue of *The Americas* contains contributions which examine its emergence from
different perspectives. The editors suggest that this period caused major ideological
debates in Brazil, and brought new social interests on to the political scene. One
contribution argues that the founding fathers of the republic had in fact quite varied
visions, variously representing the goals of the military, the emerging urban-middle
class, and the rural oligarchy. Other essays use the Canudos revolt (1893-97) to
explore popular responses to the new régime, and assess the residual monarchism in
the Southeast. A thoughtful concluding essay draws these varied strands together, and
suggests that, in common with other key phases in Brazilian history, the creation of
the republic largely excluded the mass of the population. Collectively, these essays
comprise an excellent review of a transforming moment in Brazilian history.

179 **Vale of tears: revisiting the Canudos massacre in northeastern
Brazil, 1893-1897.**
Robert M. Levine. Berkeley, California: University of California
Press, 1992. 352p. bibliog.

The millenarian movement at Canudos in the interior of Bahia in the 1890s was led by
a religious mystic, Antônio Conselheiro. It was suppressed by the federal government
in 1897, after a protracted campaign. This bloody event in Brazilian history, in which
its significance for the rebels, the local and national élite, the military, and the clergy,
is explored. It provides an excellent portrait of the interior Northeast.

180 **Politics and parentela in Paraíba. A case study of family-based
oligarchy in Brazil.**
Linda Lewin. Princeton, New Jersey: Princeton University Press,
1987. 498p. maps. bibliog.

A useful study of regional politics in the Old Republic, in which a small élite
determined the political fortunes of the state. The *parentela*, or extended family,
formed the political and economic élite. In this case a member of one of these
families, Epitácio Pessoa, served as president of Brazil, from 1919-22.

181 **Rio Grande do Sul and Brazilian regionalism, 1882-1930.**
J. L. Love. Stanford, California: Stanford University Press, 1971.
312p. bibliog.

It is argued that in the Old Republic the states were important in the absence of
national political parties. Powerful states were able to exercise considerable influence
in national politics. In the case of Rio Grande do Sul, this led to a revolt against the
federal government, 1893-95, and to the rise of Getúlio Vargas in the 1920s. This
volume outlines the internal growth of the state from 1882-1905, and its influence on
national politics from 1900-30.

182 **São Paulo in the Brazilian federation, 1889-1937.**
J. L. Love. Stanford, California: Stanford University Press, 1980.
398p. bibliog.

An important examination of São Paulo as it began to emerge as a major force in the economy and politics of Brazil. As with its companion volumes (see item nos. 177 and 186), its format explores economic and political developments within the state, and links them to national events. In the case of São Paulo, the emergence of a political and economic élite from the coffee boom was of much significance, both locally and nationally.

183 **The Canudos War in history.**
Lori Madden. *Luso-Brazilian Review*, vol. 30, no. 2 (1993), p. 5-22.

The 1897 Canudos War was an important event in the history of the Northeast, involving the repression of a millenarian movement in the interior of Bahia. The paper explores a number of important themes: the issue of environmental determinism, religious fanaticism, the mentality of the *sertanejos* (inhabitants of the interior), and the role of social reform movements. It considers the events from military, intellectual, social-science, and Marxist, perspectives.

184 **Brazil 1870-1914 – the force of tradition.**
José Murilo de Carvalho. *Journal of Latin American Studies*, vol. 24, Quincentenary supplement (1992), p. 145-62.

This is a useful summary paper of the period which saw the end of Empire and the creation of a republic. However, it argues that the modernizing which took place in Brazil around the turn of the century was still contained within a rural, patriarchal framework.

185 **The political economy of the Brazilian state, 1889-1930.**
Steven C. Topik. Austin, Texas: University of Texas Press, 1987.
242p. map. bibliog.

Offers a counter to the standard view that *laissez-faire* dominated the economy of Brazil in this period. It suggests instead that the State had considerable involvement in key areas such as railways, shipping, ports, banks, industrial development and the coffee economy.

186 **Minas Gerais in the Brazilian federation, 1889-1937.**
John D. Wirth. Stanford, California: Stanford University Press, 1977.
322p. map. bibliog.

As with its parallel volumes (see item nos. 177 and 182), this study explores the economy and society of Minas Gerais, its politics and politicians, and the contribution it made to national events. In the Old Republic, Minas Gerais, along with São Paulo, played a major role in national politics. The two states dominated Brazilian politics in the early 20th century.

The New Republic (1930-64)

187 **Juscelino Kubitschek and the development of Brazil.**
Robert J. Alexander. Athens, Ohio: Ohio University Center for
International Studies, 1991. 438p. map. bibliog. (Latin American
Series 16).

Juscelino Kubitschek (1902-76) was President of Brazil from 1956-61, and a key
figure in state and national politics from 1951-64. He was responsible for the
economic boom of the late 1950s and for the construction of Brasília. Though this is a
biography of his life, it concentrates on the achievements of the presidential years. It
is a well-written study, and a knowledge of the Kubitschek years is important for
understanding modern Brazilian politics and economic development.

188 **Power and the ruling classes in northeast Brazil: Juazeiro and
Petrolina in transition.**
Ronald H. Chilcote. Cambridge, United Kingdom; New York:
Cambridge University Press, 1990. 386p. bibliog.

This is a detailed study of power structures in two towns in the interior Northeast. It
identifies the powerful figures in the communities, their roles in local politics and
economic activities, and the opinions they hold. Although it is a specialist study, the
book offers an insight into the nature of traditional local politics in Brazil which the
interested general reader would also find useful. It is based on research undertaken in
the late 1960s and early 1980s.

189 **Unrest in Brazil: political-military crises, 1955-1964.**
J. W. F. Dulles. Austin, Texas: University of Texas Press, 1970.
449p. maps. bibliog.

The value of this study lies in its detailed portrait of Brazilian politics in the late
1950s, and its comprehensive analysis of the overthrow of the Goulart presidency
(1961-64) by the military in 1964. Goulart's period of office had been marked by
deteriorating economic conditions, and an increasing shift to the Left, which became
unacceptable to the armed forces.

190 **Brazilian Communism, 1935-1945. Repression during world
upheaval.**
J. W. F. Dulles. Austin, Texas: University of Texas Press, 1983.
290p.

A detailed history of the Brazilian Communist Party and other leftist movements from
the abortive coup by the Party against President Vargas in 1935, until 1945. During
this time the Left was subject to severe repression. As a meticulous analysis of the
internal structures of the Left, and of relations with the State, this volume would be of
particular interest to political historians.

191 **The São Paulo Law School and the anti-Vargas resistance (1938-1948).**
J. W. F. Dulles. Austin, Texas: University of Texas Press, 1986.
262p.

Dulles describes the Law School of São Paulo as 'the most conscientious democratic redoubt' during the period of President Vargas' *Estado Novo* (New State) dictatorship. This is a detailed portrait of student resistance to the régime.

192 **Carlos Lacerda: Brazilian crusader. Vol. I The years 1914-1960.**
J. W. F. Dulles. Austin, Texas: University of Texas Press, 1991.
494p. maps. bibliog.

Lacerda was a major figure in Brazilian politics from 1950-68, though it is perhaps questionable whether his early life merits such a substantial tome. Initially a campaigning journalist opposed to President Vargas, he became a federal deputy and governor of Guanabara (the city-state of Rio de Janeiro), 1960-65.

193 **The populist gamble of Getúlio Vargas in 1945: politics and ideological transition in Brazil.**
John D. French. In: *Latin America in the 1940s: war and post-war transitions.* Edited by David Rock. Berkeley, California; London: University of California Press, 1994, p. 141-65.

Examines the moves made by Getúlio Vargas to secure his democratic election to the presidency after his dictatorship of 1930-45. There was suspicion of his intentions, and the military intervened to ensure a return to democracy. Vargas was elected president in 1951, but committed suicide in 1954.

194 **The overthrow of Getúlio Vargas in 1945: diplomatic intervention, defense of democracy, or political retribution?**
Stanley Hilton. *Hispanic American Historical Review*, vol. 67 (1987), p. 1-37.

A useful exploration of the controversy surrounding Vargas' deposition, involving the US Ambassador, the Brazilian military, and Vargas himself.

195 **Juscelino Kubitschek and the politics of exuberance, 1956-61.**
Sheldon Maram. *Luso-Brazilian Review*, vol. 27, no. 1 (1990), p. 31-46.

A review of President Kubitschek's career, personality, and achievements. The paper argues that it is impossible to understand this period of Brazilian history without reference to Kubitschek's personality and his policies.

196 **Juscelino Kubitschek and the 1960 presidential election.**
Sheldon Maram. *Journal of Latin American Studies*, vol. 24 (1992), p. 123-45.

This is an interesting exploration of the activities of Kubitschek to secure his return to the presidency in 1965, after his 1956-61 presidency.

197 **The Fundação Getúlio Vargas and the new Getúlio.**
Michael Weis. *Luso-Brazilian Review*, vol. 24, no. 2 (1987), p. 49-60.
Offers a major reappraisal of the Vargas era, based on archival material from the Fundação Getúlio Vargas (Getulio Vargas Foundation) and the Centre for Research and Documentation of Contemporary History (CPDOC). Vargas was the founder of the modern Brazilian State, but this paper re-examines his legacy after Brazil's return to democracy in 1985. A useful listing of the materials held by the FGV and CPDOC is included.

198 **The Brazilian revolution of 1930 and the aftermath.**
Jordan M. Young. New Brunswick, New Jersey: Rutgers University Press, 1967. 158p. map. bibliog.
1930 was a key point in the modern history of Brazil, marking the end of the Old Republic. It saw the end of the established dominance of São Paulo and Minas Gerais in national politics, and the rise of the Vargas régime. This study explores the advent of Getúlio Vargas, the years of his *Estado Novo* (New State), and his legacy for Brazilian politics up to 1964.

The military period (1964-85)

199 **Mission in mufti. Brazil's military regimes, 1964-1985.**
Wilfred A. Bacchus. New York; London: Greenwood Press, 1990. 166p. bibliog.
This is a good evaluation of the period of military rule – its system, policies and the issues faced by the military presidents. Exploring the aims and achievements of the military, especially with regard to economic goal, the study is structured round the periods in office of the five military presidents (Castelo Branco 1964-67, Costa e Silva 1967-69, Médici 1969-74, Geisel 1974-79 and Figueiredo 1979-85). It includes a list of acronyms and a chronology.

200 **Castello Branco: the making of a Brazilian president.**
J. W. F. Dulles. College Station, Texas; London: Texas A & M University Press, 1978. 488p. maps. bibliog.
A detailed biography of the career and political involvement of the first military president. Gen. (later Marshal) Humberto Castelo Branco had served in the army since 1918, and had fought in Italy with the Brazilian Expeditionary Force in the Second World War. His period of office (1964-67) was associated with the *linha dura* (hard line) against the perceived Communist threat to Brazil.

201 **President Castello Branco: Brazilian reformer.**
J. W. F. Dulles.   College Station, Texas; London: Texas A & M
University Press, 1980. 558p. bibliog.
A mammoth and sympathetic study of the three years of the Castelo Branco
presidency (1964-67). [Notwithstanding the title of these two volumes, the standard
spelling is Castelo Branco.]

202 **Brazil in the sixties.**
Edited by Riordan Roett.   Nashville, Tennessee: Vanderbilt
University Press, 1972. 434p. map. chapter bibliogs.
Mainly written by American scholars, this is a retrospective of the most turbulent
period in Brazil's recent history. It covers the unstable period of democracy from
1961-64, and the most repressive years of the military régime in the late 1960s.
Representing an invaluable survey of the period, it covers not only politics, but
economic strategies, social change as it affected the middle class, education and the
Catholic Church. The study also discusses trends in literature and the theatre. It
includes a listing of significant dates in the 1960s.

203 **Brazil in the seventies.**
Edited by Riordan Roett.   Washington, DC: American Enterprise
Institute for Public Policy Research, 1976. 120p.
In contrast to *Brazil in the sixties* (q.v.), this volume concentrates on Brazil's external
relations, especially with the United States, and on economic matters. Despite its title,
the study deals essentially with the period 1964-75.

204 **The political system of Brazil. Emergence of a 'modernizing'
authoritarian regime, 1964-1970.**
Ronald M. Schneider.   New York; London: Columbia University
Press, 1971. 432p.
An analysis of the early years of military rule from a political science perspective,
which looks at the background to military intervention, the nature of military
institutions, and the early years of authoritarian rule. It is a near-contemporary study
of this period of the régime, and includes a brief biography of the army leaders of
1964.

205 **The military in politics: changing patterns in Brazil.**
Alfred Stepan.   Princeton, New Jersey: Princeton University Press,
1971. 314p.
This is a study of the advance of the military in Brazilian politics from 1945, the
mechanisms of the 1964 'revolution', and the political problems faced by the military
régime up to 1968.

206   **Authoritarian Brazil. Origins, policies, and future.**
Edited by Alfred Stepan.   New Haven, Connecticut; London: Yale
University Press, 1973. 266p. bibliog.
In a sense this book is a sequel to item no. 205, but it draws upon the work of a
number of Brazilian and American scholars. The volume provides an appraisal of the
early years of military rule, in the 1960s, especially its economic activities, which saw
a period of economic dynamism and political repression.

The return to democracy (1985-)

207   **Brazil's economic and political future.**
Edited by Julian M. Chacel, Pamela S. Falk, David V. Fleischer.
Boulder, Colorado; London: Westview Press, 1988. 288p. bibliog.
A useful assessment of Brazil's prospects after the return to democracy in 1985. Its
essays explore economic issues and policy, debt, the emerging political structure,
elections from 1982 onwards, and foreign policy.

208   **Collor, corruption and crisis: time for reflection.**
Peter Flynn.   *Journal of Latin American Studies*, vol. 25 (1993),
p. 351-71.
A very good summary of the election, government, and downfall of President Collor
(1989-92).

209   **The political economy of Brazil: public policies in an age of
transition.**
Edited by Lawrence S. Graham, Robert H. Wilson.   Austin, Texas:
University of Texas Press, 1990. 304p.
This is a wide-ranging view of the circumstances leading to the return to democracy in
1985, and probably offers the best assessment of the problems and prospects for Brazil
in seeking to re-create a democratic system and deal with economic and social issues.
The study considers the institutional and historical background, and the legacy of the
authoritarian régime in the spheres of politics, the economy, and society. It also
contains essays on issues such as the frontier, urban growth and housing policy,
labour, and health.

210   **Brazil: the challenge of the 1990s.**
Maria D'Alva Kinzo.   London; New York: Institute of Latin
American Studies, University of London, 1993. 214p.
Providing a useful insight into key problems facing Brazil in the 1990s, this volume
deals with the economic issue of inflation, social concern with poverty, and the
complexities of the return to democracy.

211 **Political liberalization in Brazil: dynamics, dilemmas and future prospects.**
Edited by Wayne Selcher. Boulder, Colorado; London: Westview Press, 1986. 272p.

A valuable study of the period of return to democracy between 1977 and 1985. It outlines the phases leading up to the *abertura* (opening up) of the political system after two decades of military rule, and examines the role of political parties, the Church, labour unions, and the military in bringing this about. Although it was published soon after the end of authoritarian government, the volume concludes that a return to democratic development was sustainable by Brazil.

212 **The rise and fall of President Collor and its impact on Brazilian democracy.**
Kurt Weyland. *Journal of Interamerican Studies*, vol. 35, no. 1 (1993), p. 1-37.

In the light of the comment in item no. 211, the enforced resignation of President Collor in December 1992, on the basis of allegations of corruption, was a potential set-back for the fledgling democracy. This paper is a detailed examination of the circumstances of Collor's fall, and suggests that Brazil's new political structures were still fragile.

Economic History

213 **Essays concerning the socioeconomic history of Brazil and Portuguese India.**
Edited by Dauril Alden, Warren Dean. Gainesville, Florida: University Presses of Florida, 1977. 248p.

Despite its title, seven of the eight essays in this volume deal with Brazil. Its value, therefore, is not in imperial comparisons, but in its rather disparate coverage of Brazilian social and economic themes spanning the period from 1620 to 1920. The topics covered are aspects of the tobacco and coffee economies, female employment, urban improvements, military service, slavery, and immigrants. These are all dealt with in specialized essays, but together they provide interesting insights into 19th-century Brazil.

214 **The Brazilian diamond in contracts, contraband and capital.**
Harry Bernstein. Lanham, Maryland: University Press of America, 1986. 164p. bibliog.

This volume offers a detailed discussion of an important, but little-studied, product of the colonial economy of Brazil. Its principal concern is the role of Brazilian diamonds in the economies of Portugal, England and Holland during the period 1728-1850, but it does provide material on the development, finance and trade in diamonds.

215 **Proto-industrialisation in slave society: the case of Minas Gerais.**
Douglas Cole Libby. *Journal of Latin American Studies*, vol. 23 (1991), p. 1-35.

A broad discussion of the demographic characteristics of Minas Gerais, and the importance of the slave population. Of greater significance, however, is the evidence the paper produces for early industrial development in Minas Gerais. It describes the local conditions for early industrialization, especially the development of a cotton textile industry.

216 **L'histoire quantitative du Bresil de 1800 à 1930.** (The quantitative history of Brazil, 1800-1930.)
Colloques Internationaux du CNRS. Paris: CNRS (Centre National de la Recherche Scientifique), 1973. 488p.
Presents a disparate but very useful collection of thirty essays by Brazilian, European and American scholars, which draw upon quantitative data from Brazil's economic history. Topics covered include agriculture, early industrialization, inflation, foreign capital, trade, demography, and urban growth. Material is also included on the regional economies of the Northeast and Southeast. The majority of the essays relate to the 19th century, but there is some material on the colonial period, and on the 20th century.

217 **The industrialization of São Paulo, 1880-1945.**
Warren Dean. Austin, Texas; London: University of Texas Press, 1969. 264p. bibliog.
A scholarly study of the rise of industrial activity in São Paulo, with reference to the contribution from coffee prosperity, and the origins of entrepreneurs. It identifies three phases in São Paulo's industrialization: the emergence of an entrepreneurial class, 1880-1914; industrial growth, 1914-30; and the evolving relationship between industrialists and the State, 1920-45.

218 **Brazil and the struggle for rubber.**
Warren Dean. Cambridge, United Kingdom; New York: Cambridge University Press, 1987. 234p.
This is an interesting and detailed study of Brazil's efforts to establish plantation rubber after the loss of its monopoly of natural rubber production to the plantations of Asia. It is a very scholarly but readable account of the end of the rubber boom, which demonstrates that the problems encountered in trying to develop plantation rubber production in Amazonia were largely environmental. The book is unusual in combining conventional socio-economic themes in history with some detailed commentary on ecological matters.

219 **Business imperialism and British enterprise in Brazil: the St. John d'el Rey Mining Company, Limited, 1830-1860.**
Marshall C. Eakin. *Hispanic American Historical Review*, vol. 66 (1986), p. 697-741.
A very detailed study of a major, and highly profitable, British gold mine in Brazil, which covers the organization of the company and the nature of its activities.

220 **British enterprise in Brazil: the St. John d'el Rey Mining Company and the Morro Velho gold mine, 1830-1960.**
Marshall C. Eakin. Durham, North Carolina; London: Duke University Press, 1989. 336p. maps. bibliog.
This is the book-length version of item no. 219. It is based on detailed archival work, and portrays the company, the mining technology, and the mining town of Nova Lima. The company made use of slaves until 1888, but also sustained a community of British miners. The book represents a very thorough piece of research in economic history,

but it also has more general interest because the St. John d'el Rey company was one of the most important British investments in Brazil.

221 **External constraints on economic policy in Brazil, 1889-1930.**
Winston Fritsch. London: Macmillan; Pittsburgh,
Pennsylvania: University of Pittsburgh Press, 1988. 266p. bibliog.
An exploration of economic policy in the heyday of Brazil's export economy during the period of the Old Republic. Suggesting that traditional explanations of policy being conducted only in the interests of coffee producers are too simplistic, the study argues that policy was as much shaped by external factors such as the First World War, and post-1918 booms and slumps.

222 **The economic growth of Brazil. A survey from colonial to modern times.**
Celso Furtado, translated by Ricardo W. de Aguiar and Eric C.
Drysdale. Berkeley, California: University of California Press, 1963.
286p.
Furtado was an economic planner and government minister in Brazil in the 1950s and early 1960s. His book still provides a useful introduction to the country's economic history, which sets its various phases into the contexts of slave labour, the emergence of wage labour, and the growth of an industrial system. Written for the non-specialist in economic matters by a leading practitioner, the volume offers a very readable account of Brazil's economic development.

223 **Diagnosis of the Brazilian crisis.**
Celso Furtado, translated by Suzette Macedo. Berkeley, California: University of California Press, 1965. 168p.
Written just prior to the 1964 military coup in Brazil, this volume offers a left-wing interpretation of Brazil's economic growth, and of the economic difficulties which arose in the early 1960s. Given Furtado's direct involvement as a planner and politician in this period, it offers an 'insider's' view of events. Of particular importance is the book's commentary on the problems of the impoverished Northeast, where Furtado had served as director of the regional development agency. Although in essence a historical study, this volume provides a good portrait of a turbulent time in Brazil's economic development, and the author's direct involvement makes it a work of record.

224 **Britain and the onset of modernization in Brazil, 1850-1914.**
Richard Graham. Cambridge, United Kingdom; New York:
Cambridge University Press, 1968. 386p. maps. bibliog.
Britain had a major role in Brazil's economic development in the late-19th century, especially in railway-building, urban services and commerce. The country also had significant influences on Brazil's social and political ideas. This study is a careful appraisal of these economic activities, and of the waning of British influence after 1900. It remains the standard work on the topic.

225 **Household economy and urban development: São Paulo 1765-1836.**
Elizabeth Anne Kuznesof. Boulder, Colorado; Westview Press, 1986.
216p. maps. bibliog.
This is a very detailed but fascinating monograph on the development of the town of
São Paulo. The town grew in response to the emergence of a market economy, which
was encouraged by an élite who stimulated the building of roads, markets, warehouses
and ports, in order to expand the production of sugar and coffee. In addition to
exploring these developments, the book also provides insights into changes in society,
kinship and the household.

226 **British preeminence in Brazil. Its rise and decline.**
Alan K. Manchester. New York: Octagon Books, 1972. 372p.
bibliog.
Originally published in 1933 (Chapel Hill, North Carolina: University of North
Carolina Press. 372p.), this remains a valuable study of the way in which Great Britain
came to dominate newly-independent Brazil. Its perspective is primarily that of the
latter's importance to the British economy, and the consequent British involvement in
the economic and political affairs of Brazil. The major themes dealt with are: the
benefits which Britain secured for assisting the Portuguese Court to escape to Brazil
from the Napoleonic invasion of Portugal in 1808; British constraints on Portuguese
designs on the territory which was to become Uruguay; and attempts to stop the slave
trade.

227 **Viscount Mauá and the Empire of Brazil: a biography of Irineu
Evangelista de Sousa, 1813-89.**
Anyda Marchant. Berkeley, California: University of California
Press, 1965. 292p.
Mauá was a key figure in the economic development of Brazil in the 19th century. He
was one of the country's first entrepreneurs, and this biography chronicles his
pioneering involvement in banking, railways, shipping and industrialization.

228 **La préindustrialisation du Brésil. Essais sur une économie en
transition, 1830/50-1930/50.** (The preindustrialization of Brazil.
Essays on an economy in transition, 1830-50 – 1930-50.)
Edited by Frédéric Mauro. Paris: Centre National de la Recherche
Scientifique, 1984. 360p.
This collection of French and Portuguese essays covers a wide range of topics, with
the process of industrialization before 1920 being a major theme. The volume also
discusses the origins of capital and labour, and includes a series of regional case-
studies. Several of the latter relate to the Northeast, which is not usually regarded as
being at the forefront of Brazil's modernization.

229 **The colonial background to modern Brazil.**
Caio Prado Junior, translated by Suzette Macedo. Berkeley,
California: University of California Press, 1969. 530p.
A classic study of the economic history of colonial Brazil. Its focus is on the
economic areas of agriculture, pastoralism, mining, subsistence activities and craft

industries, but it also usefully explains the context of the evolution of settlement and the political and social organization of the colony. The book remains an essential background source for understanding Brazil's economic development. The author's view is that modern Brazil can only be understood by reference to the nature of its economic circumstances at the end of the colonial period.

230   **Business interest groups in nineteenth-century Brazil.**
Eugene W. Ridings.   Cambridge, United Kingdom: Cambridge University Press, 1994. 378p. map. bibliog.

As much a political as an economic history, this book explores the role of business groups in seeking Brazilian development in the period 1834-1900. It highlights their activities in securing government assistance for: industry, regional interests in coffee and sugar, and improvements in transport and the emerging cities.

231   **Vassouras. A Brazilian coffee county, 1850-1890.**
Stanley J. Stein.   New York: Atheneum, 1976. 316p. map. bibliog.

Stein's book remains one of the best studies of the coffee era. It explores the rise and fall of the coffee economy in the Paraíba Valley, one of the earliest areas of production. Chronicling the dependence of the plantations on slave labour, the volume details not only the plantation economy, but the lives of freemen and slaves. The Paraíba coffee economy declined as a result of environmental factors and the abolition of slavery, both of which are examined here.

232   **Sugar and the underdevelopment of Northeastern Brazil, 1500-1970.**
Kit Sims Taylor.   Gainesville, Florida: University of Florida Social Sciences Monograph 63, 1978. 170p. maps. bibliog.

Sugar has been a key element of the economy of the coastal Northeast since colonial times. This concise but comprehensive study traces its historical development and its close association with slavery, and the 20th-century circumstances of land ownership, political disturbance and attempts at agrarian reform. Although brief, this book probably remains the best overview of the role of sugar in the economy and society of the Northeast.

233   **The evolution of the economic role of the Brazilian State, 1889-1930.**
Steven Topik.   *Journal of Latin American Studies*, vol. 11 (1979), p. 325-42.

Presents a case for the early involvement of the State in the economy, which is argued as having intervened to facilitate the agricultural export sector. Major areas of concern to the State were banking, exchange control, and the railways.

234 **The State's contribution to the development of Brazil's internal economy, 1850-1930.**
Steven Topik. *Hispanic American Historical Review*, vol. 65 (1985), p. 203-28.
Examines State involvement in the internal economy, particularly with regard to monetary policy, taxation, and spending on industrial development and railways.

235 **The Amazon rubber boom, 1850-1920.**
Barbara Weinstein. Stanford, California: Stanford University Press, 1983. 356p. maps. bibliog.
This is a very thorough study of the rise and fall of rubber production, based firmly on the internal experiences of Amazonia. It is probably the best academic account, as opposed to the numerous and often exaggerated popular versions, of this lively period in Brazil's economic history.

236 **White gold. The diary of a rubber cutter in the Amazon, 1906-1916.**
John C. Yungjohann, edited by Ghillean T. Prance. Oracle, Arizona: Synergetic Press, 1989. 104p. map.
An interesting first-hand diary of the rubber boom in its heyday, by an American in the Acre region. It represents an unusual perspective, as most of the tappers attracted to the region were impoverished and illiterate migrants from the Northeast.

Population

237 **After the mining boom: demographic and economic aspects of slavery in Mariana, Minas Gerais, 1750-1808.**
Laird Bergad. *Latin American Research Review*, vol. 31, no. 1 (1996), p. 67-97.
Although this is a very detailed study of colonial demography, it is of considerable value because of its extensive bibliography on slavery in Minas Gerais.

238 **Demographic change in a post-export boom society: the population of Minas Gerais, Brazil, 1776-1821.**
Laird Bergad. *Journal of Social History*, vol. 29 (1996), p. 895-932.
The economy of Minas Gerais was dependent on slaves, and they remained important after the economy shifted from the export of gold to more local agro-pastoral activities. This article uses four censuses from the period 1776-1821 to trace population trends. It is of interest because of its methods and data.

239 **La population du Brésil.** (The population of Brazil.)
Comité International de Coordination des Recherches nationales en Démographie (CICRED). Gap, France: CICRED, 1975. 214p. bibliog.
Produced for World Population Year, organized by the United Nations, this remains a useful comprehensive survey of Brazil's population. It covers demographic history before the first census of 1872, and from 1872-1970. The study discusses: the elements of growth; the composition of population by religion, colour, education, marital status and income; rural-urban patterns; and employment.

240   **Marx and Malthus in northeast Brazil. A note on the world's largest class difference in fertility and its recent trends.**
H. E. Daly. *Population Studies*, vol. 39 (1985), p. 329-38.
This paper argues that the benefits of economic growth in the Northeast are not diffusing through society, because of the rapid growth of the lower income population. Though fertility rates fell in the 1970s, class differences are still very large by international standards – of the order of five children between the top and bottom economic class – so that demographic differences offset any income improvement.

241   **Migration in Brazil: research during the 1980s.**
Cyrus B. Dawey, III.   In: *Benchmark 1990.*   Edited by Tom L.
Martinson.   Auburn, Alabama: Conference of Latin Americanist
Geographers, 1992, p. 109-16.
The text of this article is brief, touching upon migration to the cities and to Amazonia. The bibliography, however, is a valuable guide to recent work in English and Portuguese.

242   **The native population of the Americas in 1492.**
Edited by William Denevan.   Madison, Wisconsin: University of
Wisconsin Press, 1992. 2nd ed. 354p. bibliog.
Attempts to calculate the population of both continents before the 'Discovery'. The volume contains discussion of the aboriginal population of Amazonia (p. 205-34), with a detailed commentary on environmental habitats. The population for Amazonia is estimated at 6.8 million, as against earlier estimates of circa 2 million.

243   **Migration to the gold-mining frontier in Brazilian Amazonia.**
Brian J. Godfrey.   *Geographical Review*, vol. 82 (1992), p. 458-69.
This paper argues that small-scale gold-mining has been important in the regional economy, and has attracted migrants and encouraged urbanization.

244   **Changing Brazilian families and the consequent need for public policy.**
Ana Maria Goldani.   *International Social Science Journal*, vol. 126
(1990), p. 523-37.
A study of how the family has changed in Brazil, and of possible new public strategies to meet it. The traditional notion has been of a patriarchal family, in which the woman's role is essentially domestic. Changes in this pattern were recognized in the 1970s and acknowledged in the 1988 constitution, where the family was still seen as the foundation of society, but no longer patriarchal and dependent on legal marriage. The paper includes a range of data on family structure, including female-headed households and fertility patterns.

245 **The Prados of São Paulo, Brazil: an elite family and social change, 1840-1930.**
Darrell E. Levi. Athens, Georgia; London: University of Georgia Press, 1987. 284p. map. bibliog.

This is an example of the application of 'new family history' techniques to Brazil. It is a qualitative study of the institution of the family in a period of rapid social change. The author acknowledges that there is a class bias in the analysis because of its dependence on the surviving wills and letters, etc., of an affluent Paulista family, but this is nevertheless an important pioneer study.

246 **Migrants to Amazonia: spontaneous colonization in the Brazilian frontier.**
Judith Lisansky. Boulder, Colorado; London: Westview Press, 1990. 176p. maps. bibliog.

Although this is a case-study of a single settlement in southeast Amazonia, it provides a good portrait of the experience of migrants to the frontier. The volume focuses on spontaneous migrants, outside the official colonization schemes, who came mainly from the Northeast, and assesses the problems posed for such migrants by national planning policies and by large cattle ranches which developed on the frontier. It describes the experience of small farmers in production and marketing, and the economic, social and institutional strategies which they developed to survive. The original fieldwork was carried out in 1978-79, but the author comments that a return visit in 1987 recorded neither success nor failure. There were, however, grounds for optimism as to the future of the migrants, as the cattle economy had declined, but a range of smaller-scale agricultural activities had evolved.

247 **The politics of population in Brazil. Elite ambivalence and public demand.**
Peter McDonough, Amaury DeSouza. Austin, Texas; London: University of Texas Press, 1981. 178p. bibliog.

As the title implies, this book is not about population policies, but about the politics of population control. Based on sample surveys, it explores élite attitudes as to whether Brazil has a 'population problem' and, if so, what control strategies might be adopted. It concludes that various élites, in government, the Church, trades unions, and business, greatly underestimate popular desire for the provision of family planning services.

248 **The population of colonial Brazil.**
Maria Luiza Marcílio. In: *Cambridge history of Latin America. Vol. II.* Edited by Leslie Bethell. Cambridge, United Kingdom; New York: Cambridge University Press, 1984, p. 37-63. bibliog.

A useful demographic survey, which seeks to reconstruct the Indian, white and African population of the colony. It is of interest because of its discussion of the decline of the Indian population, and the growth of the European and African elements, and because of its attempts at demographic reconstruction from limited data.

249 **Brazil's fertility decline, 1965-95: a fresh look at key factors.**
G. Martine. *Population and Development Review*, vol. 22 (1996),
p. 47-75.
Brazil experienced a spectacular drop, of over fifty per cent, in its fertility rate
between 1970 and 1990, and the annual rate of population growth declined from 2.8
per cent in the 1960s to 1.5 per cent in the 1990s. This paper provides a very thorough
review of the factors involved, and of the position of government, the Church, and
women's groups on the population issue.

250 **Impacts of social research on policy formation: lessons from the
Brazilian experience in the population field.**
G. Martine, V. Faria. *Journal of Developing Areas*, vol. 23 (1988),
p. 45-62.
A useful review of population research and policy, especially as it relates to mortality,
fertility and migration.

251 **Population and economic development in Brazil, 1800 to the
present.**
Thomas W. Merrick, Douglas H. Graham. Baltimore, Maryland;
London: Johns Hopkins University Press, 1979. 386p. map. bibliog.
The essential text on the population of Brazil, this volume is a detailed demographic
history, which contains much data and analysis on many aspects of Brazil's
population. It deals with the principal demographic themes in a series of major
chapters. The demographic consequences of the abolition of slavery and the encouragement of European immigration in the late 19th century are counter-posed. The
changing population geography, in terms of regional growth, and rural-urban
migration, is explored in detail, as are the links between population, employment,
urbanization, and urban poverty. The volume also contains commentary on the basic
demographic variables of fertility and mortality, and some more speculative
discussion of development planning and population, and likely future demographic
trends. In sum, this is the basic reference work on the subject.

252 **Inequality and social mobility in Brazil.**
José Pastore, translated by Robert M. Oxley. Madison, Wisconsin:
University of Wisconsin Press, 1982. 194p. bibliog.
This study of the occupational mobility of heads of families is based on a large sample
survey. It indicates that, despite significant income inequalities, there is social
mobility in Brazil. It indicates that economic growth has resulted in a general, if slow,
increase in occupational status.

253 **From Minho to Minas: the Portuguese roots of the Mineiro family.**
Donald Ramos. *Hispanic American Historical Review*, vol. 73
(1993), p. 638-62.
A detailed but useful case-study of family history, which argues that the distinct
family structures of northern Portugal, particularly of a mobile male population, were
transported to the gold-fields of Minas Gerais in the 18th century.

254 **The population of Latin America.**
Nicolás Sánchez-Albornoz, translated by W. A. R. Richardson.
Berkeley, California; London: University of California Press, 1974.
300p. maps. bibliog.
Although this book does not have a specifically Brazilian section, there are numerous references to the country's demographic circumstances. It provides a very good demographic history of the continent from pre-Columbian times to the present, and includes discussion of the recent population 'boom', cityward migration, and predictions for the year 2000. In the latter regard, the 1971 projection was that Brazil would have a population of 215 million by the end of the century; a 1994 estimate is that it will reach only 172 million, a reflection of the slow-down in the demographic growth rate.

255 **The population of Latin America, 1850-1930.**
Nicolás Sánchez-Albornoz. In: *Cambridge history of Latin America.*
Vol. IV. Edited by Leslie Bethell. Cambridge, United Kingdom;
New York: Cambridge University Press, 1986, p. 121-52.
The importance of this essay lies in its concentration on major demographic issues of the period, particularly immigration. In the case of Brazil there was a substantial influx of Italian, Spanish and German immigrants. Issues of mortality, fertility and internal migration are also discussed.

256 **The demography of inequality in Brazil.**
Charles H. Wood, José Albert Magno de Carvalho. New York;
Cambridge: Cambridge University Press, 1988. 304p. map. bibliog.
Exploring the role of social, political and economic factors in the demographic practices of different social classes in various parts of Brazil, this study considers influences such as income levels and race upon life expectancy, family size, etc. Its examples come from São Paulo, the experiences of rural migrants, and the frontier.

Nationalities, Minorities and Migrants

General

257 **Race, gender and development in Brazil.**
Peggy Lovell. *Latin American Research Review*, vol. 29, no. 3
(1994), p. 7-36.
This academic paper examines the differential progress of white and Afro-Brazilian
men and women over the period 1960-80. The research indicates that although there
was some general gain in levels of well-being as a result of economic development,
women fared relatively less well than men, and Afro-Brazilians less than whites. In
addition to the evidence it offers of persisting economic inequity, the study provides a
good theoretical frame for the research, and a useful broad discussion about race
relations in Brazil.

258 **Brazil: anthropological perspectives. Essays in honor of Charles**
Wagley.
Edited by Maxine L. Margolis, William E. Carter. New York:
Columbia University Press, 1979. 444p. maps.
Comprising a somewhat disparate collection of essays in honour of a distinguished
anthropologist of Brazil, this volume nevertheless provides a valuable reader which
introduces a diversity of themes on people and society in Brazil. The coverage
encompasses: the major ethnic groups – Indian, African and immigrant; environmental
issues in terms of adaptations by Indians and modern settlers; social structure at the
contrasting scales of Indian villages and major cities; and an outline of the country's
political organization.

259 **Race and class in Brazil: historical perspectives.**
Thomas E. Skidmore. *Luso-Brazilian Review*, vol. 20, no. 1
(1983), p. 104-18.
Although this paper is over a decade old, it provides a very good survey of race issues
in Brazil since 1945, with emphasis on the work of major foreign scholars such as
Donald Pierson, Roger Bastide, Charles Wagley, and Marvin Harris. Offering a
helpful introduction to the theme of race in Brazil, and its literature, the study
discusses the general area of race relations and challenges the notion of Brazil as a
racial democracy.

260 **Residential segregation by skin color in Brazil.**
Edward E. Telles. *American Sociological Review*, vol. 57 (1992),
p. 186-97.
This is a statistical analysis of residential segregation in thirty-five metropolitan areas
of Brazil, using data from the 1980 census. It suggests that spatial segregation is
lowest within low-income groups and increases with income level. However, it also
shows a tendency for there to be a concentration of blacks and mulattos in lower
socio-economic classes and distinct urban areas. The paper discusses the implications
of these patterns for race relations.

261 **Rethinking race in Brazil.**
Howard Winant. *Journal of Latin American Studies*, vol. 24 (1992),
p. 173-92.
Despite being concerned only with white-black relations, this paper provides a useful
summary of ideas about race in Brazil in the 100 years since the abolition of slavery,
and of the experience of the black population in that period. It traces the main
theoretical work on race since emancipation, and identifies debates which have
emerged since Brazil's return to democracy, concerning racial inequality, and the
meaning of race.

Indians

262 **In favor of deceit: a study of tricksters in an Amazonian society.**
Ellen B. Basso. Tucson, Arizona: University of Arizona Press, 1987.
376p. maps. bibliog.
The prime interest of this study would be for anthropologists. It draws upon the oral
traditions of the Kalapalo indians of northern Mato Grosso to reveal Indian ideas
about their self-identity, society, history and relations with the world around them, and
includes substantial quotations from the Kalapalo tales.

263 **The last cannibals: a South American oral history.**
Ellen B. Basso. Austin, Texas: University of Texas Press, 1995.
320p. bibliog.
Oral communication is the key to Kalapalo representation of themselves and their
community, in the form of historical narratives, personal accounts, and myths. In this
study extensive use is made of nine stories to demonstrate Indian remembrance and
recording of their past. Together with item no. 262, this volume forms part of a
detailed portrait of a particular tribal group.

264 **Tribes of the Amazon basin 1972.**
Edwin Brooks, René Fuerst, John Hemming, Francis Huxley.
London: Charles Knight & Co., 1973. 202p. maps.
In the late 1960s there were substantial allegations of the abuse of Brazil's Indian
population. This report, compiled for the British-based Aborigines Protection Society,
is principally a record of visits to tribal groups and Indian posts, but also contains
useful commentary on the failings of Brazil's Indian Protection Service (SPI), and its
replacement by the National Indian Foundation (FUNAI). Although dated, this
provides a useful perspective on an ongoing issue in Brazil, namely the relationship
between the dominant society and native peoples.

265 **Yanomamo, the fierce people.**
Napoleon A. Chagnon. Fort Worth, Texas; London: Holt, Rinehart
and Winston Inc., 1983. 3rd ed. 224p. map. bibliog.
This book is important for two reasons. Firstly, it has come to be regarded as a model
anthropological study of a tribal society. Secondly, its three editions, of 1968, 1977
and 1983, chronicle the modification of Yanomamo society through recent contact
with Europeans, particularly the invasion of their land by gold prospectors. The work
deals with the Yanomamo's tribal environment, subsistence practices and settlement
patterns, myths, social organization, relations with other Indian groups and, latterly,
with the intrusion of Europeans. It also lists more than twenty films made by Chagnon
on aspects of Yanomamo life.

266 **The Wanano Indians of the Brazilian Amazon: a sense of space.**
Janet M. Chernela. Austin, Texas: University of Texas Press, 1993.
186p. maps. bibliog.
The Wanano inhabit the Uaupés basin of northwest Amazonia. The main focus of this
study is on their social organization and kinship structure, particularly the role of rank.
There is also a useful summary of the impact of European intrusion into the region.

267 **Victims of the miracle. Development and the Indians of Brazil.**
Shelton H. Davis. Cambridge, United Kingdom: Cambridge
University Press, 1977. 206p. maps. bibliog.
This was one of the earliest studies of the impact of post-1970 development on the
native peoples of Amazonia, and it affords a good review of policies towards the
Indians. The volume is particularly useful in its account of the policies adopted as part
of the frontier advance from 1970, though it is strongly critical of their impact upon
Indian society. Also discussed are some of the ecological impacts of development.

268   **Space-time of the Bororo of Brazil.**
      Stephen Michael Fabian.   Gainesville, Florida: University Press of
      Florida, 1992. 254p. maps. bibliog.
An exploration of the role of time and planetary space in a non-literate society. The
Bororo inhabit Mato Grosso, and this study examines the role which time plays in
their life cycle, and their use of diurnal, lunar and seasonal time. An appendix includes
Bororo designations of astronomic phenomena.

269   **Anxious pleasures: the sexual lives of an Amazonian people.**
      Thomas Gregor.   Chicago; London: University of Chicago Press,
      1985. 224p. map. bibliog.
A study of the sexual behaviour of the Mehinaku of the Xingú region. It explores the
meaning and context of sexuality, of gender symbols, and of sexual relations and
practices in a male-dominated society.

270   **Red gold. The conquest of the Brazilian Indians.**
      John Hemming.   London: Macmillan, 1978. 678p. maps. bibliog.
This is a massive study of the conquest and settlement of Brazil up to circa 1750. It
makes much use of contemporary sources to explore the settlement process, the
colonial economy, and the impact of conquest and development on the native peoples.
The volume's coverage is extensive, dealing with the various regions of the country,
and different phases of development. It is particularly effective in the discussion of
Amazonia, the gold-fields, and the slaving expeditions of the *bandeirantes*. An
interesting appendix is included, which lists modern tribal populations, and attempts
to estimate figures for the year 1500.

271   **Indians and the frontier in colonial Brazil.**
      John Hemming.   In: *Cambridge history of Latin America. Vol. II.*
      Edited by Leslie Bethell.   Cambridge, United Kingdom; New York:
      Cambridge University Press, 1984, p. 501-45.
Explores in some detail the impact of the Portuguese frontier on the native population
in various parts of Brazil from 1500-1700, with more general observations for the 18th
century. The study provides regional coverage of the adverse consequences of the
advance of the frontier, for the South, the Centre, the Northeast, and Amazonia. Dr.
Hemming suggests that the Indian population of Brazil fell by three-quarters during
the colonial period, and that the culture of the surviving groups was much diminished.

272   **Amazon frontier. The defeat of the Brazilian Indians.**
      John Hemming.   London: Macmillan, 1987. 648p. maps. bibliog.
Though ostensibly a sequel to *Red gold. The conquest of the Brazilian Indians* (item
no. 270), this similarly scholarly volume focuses much more on the fate of the Indians
in the period 1750-1910. Its wide use of contemporary travellers' tales also makes it
an important source on the exploration of Brazil. The book includes an extensive
appendix on such travellers. Despite its length and meticulous research, this is a well-
written and very readable account of the retreat of the Indians.

273 **Indians of Brazil in the twentieth century.**
Edited by Janice E. Hopper. Washington, DC: Institute for Cross Cultural Research, 1967. 258p. map. bibliog.
This book is important as a matter of record. It summarizes the distribution of Brazilian Indian groups in the first half of the century. The individual tribes are set into broad culture areas, and there is discussion of their culture and language, and of levels of contact with Europeans. There is a useful survey of ethnological work on the Indians in the 1950s, but the most significant part of the book is its listing of tribal groups and estimation of their numerical status.

274 **The Indian policy of Portugal in the Amazon region, 1614-1693.**
Mathias C. Kiemen. New York: Octagon Books, 1973. 216p. bibliog.
An important historical study, which explores: the role of Franciscan and Jesuit missions; Portuguese legislation concerning the Indians; and relations between Indians and Portuguese. It traces the history of early contact, and the slow, uncertain evolution of policy before 1680. At that date legislation placed the Indians under Jesuit tutelage, in an effort to protect them from the colonist demand for labour.

275 **Force and persuasion: leadership in an Amazonian society.**
Waud Kracke. Chicago; London: University of Chicago Press, 1978. 322p. maps. bibliog.
A specialized psychoanalytical and anthropological study of the patterns of leadership among the Kagwahiv of the Madeira River, and the relationships between leaders and followers.

276 **Dialectical societies. The Gê and Bororo of central Brazil.**
Edited by David Maybury-Lewis. Cambridge, Massachusetts; London: Harvard University Press, 1979. 340p. map. bibliog.
The Gê peoples have complex social structures, and this volume is important because it consists of comparative studies of different Gê groups and the Bororo. The study is based on fieldwork by a number of researchers in the 1960s, which sought to identify common strands and variations, especially in kinship patterns, between different tribal groups. It is, therefore, an important summary volume of a major body of study relating to Brazilian Indians.

277 **Women of the forest.**
Yolanda Murphy, Robert F. Murphy. New York: Columbia University Press, 1985. 2nd ed. 262p. bibliog.
Examines the place of women in the Munducurú tribe of the Tapajós valley. It is a society where women are formally inferior to men, and this study explores their lives, activities, and place in myth and symbolism.

278   **Amazonian Indians from prehistory to the present:
anthropological perspectives.**
Edited by Anna C. Roosevelt.   Tucson, Arizona; London: University
of Arizona Press, 1994. 422p. chapter bibliogs.

The main concern of this book is with change in Amazon culture and lifestyle.
Coverage extends beyond Brazil, but of the seventeen chapters, six deal with Brazilian
Indian groups, and there are a number of more general essays. Broad themes in the
work are the process of contact with Europeans and its consequences for Indian
society, ecology and cosmology. The general essays deal with health, demography,
diet, and subsistence, while specific topics include warfare, language, female status,
plant names and archaeological remains. It is a useful summary and comparative
volume.

279   **Nature and society in central Brazil: the Suya Indians of Mato
Grosso.**
Anthony Seeger.   Cambridge, Massachusetts; London: Harvard
University Press, 1981. 278p. maps. bibliog.

A specialist anthropological study, which deals with topics including kinship, life
cycle, tribal structure, myth, and the use of plants and animals.

280   **Handbook of South American Indians.**
Edited by J. H. Steward.   New York: Cooper Square Publishers, 1963.
8 vols. maps. bibliog.

Originally published in 1944 (Washington, DC: US Government Printing Office), this
series remains in many ways the standard reference in the field. The complete
collection provides a detailed portrait of the native population of South America.
Though some of the detail has been superseded by later scholarship, the work remains
a useful reference compendium. Brazil's coastal tribes are dealt with in Vol. I (p. 381-
574) and the Amazon tribes in Vol. III (p. 1-379). Vols. V and VI contain useful
comparative material on ethnology and anthropology, as well as information of
broader interest on the natural environment and wildlife.

281   **Bound in misery and iron: the impact of the Grande Carajás
Program.**
David H. Treece.   London: Survival International, 1987. 152p.
bibliog.

This is a very critical commentary on the human consequences of the Grande Carajás
regional development project, created in 1980. It provides a useful background and
summary of the main investors in this integrated agro-pastoral and industrial scheme,
but its main concern is the impact of the project on individual Indian tribes.

282   **Developments in the situation of Brazil's tribal populations from
1976 to 1982.**
Greg Urban.   *Latin American Research Review*, vol. 20, no. 1 (1985),
p. 7-20.

Although it covers only a short time-span, this paper is of interest because it deals
with a period when 'national economic interests' had come to predominate over the

concerns of the native peoples. The Indians were seen as an obstacle to Brazil's development goals. This article considers the role of FUNAI (the National Indian Foundation), the churches, and other groups concerned with the Indians. It also notes some emergence of a collective 'Indian' identity amongst the various individual tribes.

283 **Xingu. The Indians, their myths.**
Orlando & Claudio Villas Boas, translated by Susana H. Rudge.
London: Souvenir Press, 1974. 270p. maps.

This volume contains a brief study of the history of the Xingu peoples, but its fascination lies in its presentation of thirty Indian myths. These deal with Indian interpretations of the sun and moon, forest animals, death, and other aspects of their life and world-view. Among the tales are those concerning the first man, the origin of the sun and the moon, and of the rivers, the conquest of fire, and the end of the world.

284 **From the enemy's point of view: humanity and divinity in an Amazonian society.**
Eduardo Viveiros de Castro, translated by Catherine V. Howard.
Chicago; London: University of Chicago Press, 1992. 408p. maps. bibliog.

Presents a detailed ethnographic study of the Araweté Indians of Pará, which explores self-identity, divinity, shamanism and warfare. These issues are set in the frame of life cycle, family, subsistence, and the use of time and space.

285 **Native American cultures along the Atlantic littoral of South America, 1499-1650.**
Neil L. Whitehead. In: *The meeting of two worlds: Europe and the Americas, 1492-1650.* Edited by Warwick Bray. Oxford: British Academy, 1993, p. 197-231. bibliog.

A useful summary of coastal Indian society before the arrival of the Portuguese, and of the impact of the conquest. It attempts to portray both the European and the Indian perspectives on their contact. The other essays in the volume offer some comparisons in the form of the contact experiences of other parts of the Americas.

Slavery

286 **The *Quilombo* of Palmares: a new overview of a Maroon State in seventeenth-century Brazil.**
Robert N. Anderson. *Journal of Latin American Studies*, vol. 28 (1996), p. 545-66.

Quilombos were refuges created by escaped slaves. Palmares, on the border between Alagoas and Pernambuco, in the Northeast, was the most substantial of these. It lasted from circa 1606 to 1694. This paper examines previous work on the site, and provides considerable detail regarding its organization and activities. In addition, there is discussion of the significance of Palmares, and its last leader, Zumbi, for the contemporary Afro-Brazilian population.

287   **Persistence and decline: slave labour and sugar production in the Bahian Recôncavo, 1850-1888.**
B. J. Barickman. *Journal of Latin American Studies*, vol. 28 (1996), p. 581-633.

The use of African slaves was an integral part of the sugar economy of Brazil. After the end of the slave trade in 1850, and the moves towards abolition, plantations dependent on slave labour became increasingly vulnerable. This paper examines the experience of a major sugar area, adjacent to Salvador. It argues that the plantation owners' continued dependence on slaves right up to abolition in 1888 resulted in a decline in production and exports, in contrast to other parts of the Northeast, where there was earlier use of free labour. The paper contains much detail about the slave population and the organization of the plantations.

288   **The abolition of the Brazilian slave trade.**
Leslie Bethell. Cambridge, United Kingdom: Cambridge University Press, 1970. 426p. maps. bibliog.

A careful study of the British role in the abolition of the transatlantic trade in slaves, 1807-50, drawing heavily on British documents. Although Britain succeeded in having the trade in slaves to Brazil declared illegal in 1831, the author explains why the trade persisted for a further twenty years, and why the institution of slavery lasted until 1888. The book includes an appendix containing estimates of slave imports into Brazil, 1831-55.

289   **Slavery and social life: attempts to reduce free people to slavery in the sertão Mineiro, Brazil, 1850-1871.**
J. Bieber Freitas. *Journal of Latin American Studies*, vol. 26 (1994), p. 597-619.

After the ending of the slave trade, a market still existed in Brazil for slave labour. This paper deals with the consequences of this in the northern part of Minas Gerais state. It records the abduction into slavery of freedmen and women, and an illicit trade in such captives, especially during the 1860s. However, even at this early date, and thirty years before slavery was finally abolished, there were clear attempts to protect free blacks from abuse.

290   **The destruction of Brazilian slavery 1850-1888.**
Robert Edgar Conrad. Malabar, Florida: Kreiger Publishing Co., 1993. 2nd ed. 228p. map. bibliog.

There was a long gap between the abolition of the slave trade to Brazil in 1850, and the emancipation of slaves in 1888. After explaining the background to the trade and its abolition, this book explores the slow rise of emancipationism, and the rapid move towards the abolition of slavery, 1880-88. It includes numerous tables on the late-19th-century slave population.

291 **Children of God's fire. A documentary history of black slavery in
Brazil.**
Robert Edgar Conrad.   Princeton, New Jersey: Princeton University
Press, 1983. 516p. map. bibliog.
A major work of reference, this book complements item nos. 289-90. It brings
together documents from a wide range of Portuguese, Brazilian, English, and other
sources, to provide a detailed portrait of the slave trade, the slave experience on
plantations and in the towns, and the slave rebellions. The volume also discusses the
abolition movement, and the positions of the law and the Church regarding slavery.

292 **World of sorrow: the African slave trade to Brazil.**
Robert Edgar Conrad.   Baton Rouge, Louisiana; London: Louisiana
State University Press, 1986. 216p. maps. bibliog.
Slavery persisted until late into the 19th century in Brazil, because of its significance
to the economy, and external pressures were therefore an important factor in its final
demise. This study focuses on the period between 1810 and 1850, when the slave trade
was (in theory) partially or totally illegal. It also explores the importance of the
internal trade in slaves, as external sources were cut off.

293 **Slavery and beyond: the African impact on Latin America and the
Caribbean.**
Darién J. Davis.   Wilmington, Delaware: Scholarly Resources Inc.,
1995. 195p. bibliog.
This collection of essays contains a general survey of the demographic and cultural
impact of slaves, with two papers on Brazil, covering Afro-Brazilian ethnicity, and the
civil rights and political participation of Afro-Brazilian women. It also includes a
listing of films dealing with Afro-American topics.

294 **Slave life in Rio de Janeiro, 1808-1850.**
Mary C. Karasch.   Princeton, New Jersey: Princeton University Press,
1987. 422p. bibliog.
A detailed and comprehensive examination of slave life in what was the Brazilian
capital, covering the slaves' origins, living conditions, contribution to the urban
economy, and to music and religion. Of particular value is the inclusion of a wealth of
tables on demographic data, health and slave price, etc., and an appendix on the
African origins of the slaves.

295 **African slavery in Latin America and the Caribbean.**
Herbert S. Klein.   New York; Oxford: Oxford University Press, 1986.
312p. bibliog.
Offers a useful contextual study of the general rise and nature of slavery in Latin
America. The volume provides commentary on slavery in the Caribbean, Spanish
America and Brazil, covering slave life, rebellion and emancipation.

296   **Freedmen in slave economy: Minas Gerais in 1831.**
Herbert S. Klein, Clotilde Andrade Paiva. *Journal of Social History*,
vol. 29 (1996), p. 933-62.
This study indicates that freed slaves rapidly became economically mobile, and as
early as 1831 were important, competitive, and integrated members of rural society.

297   **Background to rebellion: the origin of Muslim slaves in Bahia.**
Paul E. Lovejoy. *Slavery and Abolition*, vol. 15 (1994), p. 150-80.
A rare attempt to explore the identity of the slave population, using data from records
of 19th-century revolts. The paper explores the conception of ethnicity among the
slaves, and the role of religion – specifically Islam – in giving them a sense of identity
and community.

298   **The transition from slavery to migrant labour in rural Brazil.**
Nancy Priscilla Naro. *Slavery and Abolition*, vol. 15 (1994),
p. 183-96.
Despite its title, this is largely a detailed study of slavery on the coffee plantations of
the Paraíba Valley.

299   **To be a slave in Brazil, 1550-1888.**
Katia de Queiros Mattoso.   New Brunswick, New Jersey: Rutgers
University Press, 1986. 250p. bibliog.
An archive-based study of slave life, focusing on Salvador. It deals with the process of
enslavement, slave life and work, rebellions, and adjustment to freedom. The detail is
such that it is primarily of interest to the specialist.

300   **Slave rebellion in Brazil: the Muslim uprising of 1835 in Bahia.**
João José Reis.   Baltimore, Maryland; London: Johns Hopkins
University Press, 1993. 282p. maps. bibliog.
The 1835 revolt of African Muslim slaves in Bahia was the most important urban
slave rebellion in the Americas. This interesting and detailed piece of work portrays
slave conditions, the conspiracy of the Muslim slaves, their revolt, and its suppression.

301   **The black man in slavery and freedom in colonial Brazil.**
Anthony J. R. Russell-Wood.   London: Macmillan, 1982. 296p.
bibliog.
Professor Russell-Wood has compiled a diverse collection of essays on various
aspects of slavery. The volume's coverage includes such topics as the place of
freedmen in society, culture and the economy, lay brotherhoods, family, and kinship,
and the importance of slavery for the mining of gold.

302   **Recent trends in the study of slavery in Brazil.**
       Stuart B. Schwartz.   *Luso-Brazilian Review*, vol. 25, no. 1 (1988),
       p. 1-26.
Provides a useful overview of research on Brazilian slavery a century after
emancipation. A good bibliography of recent work is included, making this a helpful
source paper.

303   **Slaves, peasants and rebels. Reconsidering Brazilian slavery.**
       Stuart B. Schwartz.   Urbana, Illinois; Chicago: University of Illinois
       Press, 1992. 178p.
A collection of essays by Schwartz, not tightly integrated, but covering the nature of
slavery, and the role of slaves in shaping their own lives. The volume includes
discussion of the lifestyle of the slaves, their role in food production, and their
rebellions. A major review essay and a bibliography listing publications up to 1990 is
included.

304   **The abolition of slavery in Brazil.**
       Robert Brent Toplin.   New York: Atheneum, 1975. 300p. bibliog.
This is one of several studies of abolition from the 1970s. It seeks to provide an
explanation of the conditions which led to abolition, especially during the 1880s. The
main themes in the work are the confrontation between planters and abolitionists, and
the consequences of emancipation for planters and freedmen.

Afro-Brazilians

305   **Racism, culture and Black identity in Brazil.**
       Michael Agier.   *Bulletin of Latin American Research*, vol. 14 (1995),
       p. 245-64.
Presents a useful contemporary case-study of persisting racial inequalities and
emerging black identity in Salvador.

306   **Black political protest in São Paulo, 1888-1988.**
       George Reid Andrews.   *Journal of Latin American Studies*, vol. 24
       (1992), p. 147-73.
A helpful account of the articulation of black consciousness during what the author
identifies as four key 'moments' in the history of republican Brazil: the abolition of
slavery; the Vargas era; and the returns to democracy of 1945 and 1985. Each of these
points in time was associated with a wave of black protest, but the paper argues that
although these situations presented opportunities, blacks remain disadvantaged in
Brazilian society. However, it suggests that during the 1980s race became a political
issue to a degree never previously seen in Brazilian politics.

307 **Black and white in São Paulo, Brazil, 1888-1988.**
George Reid Andrews. Madison, Wisconsin; London: University of
Wisconsin Press, 1991. 370p. map. bibliog.

This book contains a good review of debates about the legacy of slavery on race relations in Brazil, but its main concern is the consequence of the post-emancipation migration to the cities and urban employment. It suggests that even there, blacks have tended to remain in low-paid manual jobs.

308 **Up from slavery: Afro-Brazilian activism in São Paulo, 1888-1938.**
Kim D. Butler. *The Americas*, vol. 59 (1992), p. 179-206.

A case-study of the movement of emancipated slaves to the city of São Paulo, their settlement in particular districts, and the creation of organizations and activities to serve their interests.

309 **Neither black nor white. Slavery and race relations in Brazil and the United States.**
Carl N. Degler. Madison, Wisconsin: University of Wisconsin Press, 1986. 302p.

This is an integrated comparative study, which explores the differences between the two countries. It suggests that Brazilian blacks have been able to retain more of their culture, and have been less subject to overt segregation.

310 **The negro in Brazilian society.**
Florestan Fernandes, translated by Jacqueline D. Skiles, A. Brunel,
A. Rothwell. New York; London: Columbia University Press, 1969.
490p.

Fernandes' book is one of the classic studies of race in Brazil. It remains significant as a pioneering work, not least because it is critical of the notion of Brazil as a 'racial democracy'. Using evidence from São Paulo, Fernandes argues that even after emancipation, blacks have remained marginalized in society, politics, and the economy.

311 **The negro in Brazilian society: 25 years on.**
Florestan Fernandes. In: *Brazil: anthropological perspectives*.
Edited by Maxine Margolis, W. E. Carter. New York: Columbia
University Press, 1979, p. 96-113.

This is a pessimistic reflection by Fernandes on his earlier work (item no. 310). He argues that although there has been major economic change in São Paulo, this has had very little impact on the circumstances of the black population.

312 **Africans in the Americas: a history of the black diaspora.**
Michael L. Conniff, Thomas J. Davis. New York: St. Martins Press,
1994. 356p. bibliog.

This is a very up-to-date comparative study of the shared and similar experiences of people of African descent in the Americas. It covers trade and slavery, the end of the slave trade, and abolition. The volume contains some specifically Brazilian sections, and a most useful annotated bibliographical essay.

313 **Race, class and power in Brazil.**
Edited by Pierre-Michel Fontaine. Los Angeles, California: Center
for Afro-American Studies, University of California, 1985. 162p.
Contains a good review of different perceptions of race relations in Brazil. The view
argued by its contributors is that class rather than race perpetuates the marginalization
of the black population, which remains in inferior positions in society, the employment market, and politics.

314 **Orpheus and power. The *Movimento Negro* of Rio de Janeiro and
São Paulo, Brazil, 1945-1988.**
Michael George Hanchard. Princeton, New Jersey: Princeton
University Press, 1994. 204p. bibliog.
Despite its title, this book provides a very good general view of racial issues in Brazil,
in terms of their origins, and of the idea of racial democracy. The study also explores
the emergence of racial consciousness and the limited success of black movements in
Rio de Janeiro and São Paulo in the 1970s and early 1980s.

315 **Beyond all pity.**
Carolina Maria de Jesus, translated by D. St. Clair. London:
Earthscan, 1990. 190p.
When this book first appeared in 1960 as *Quarto de despejo* (Rio de Janeiro, Brazil:
Livraria Francisco Alves) it caused a considerable sensation, since it was the diary of
a black woman shanty-town dweller, chronicling the nature of her impoverished life,
and her aspirations. It remains a graphic account of the hunger, violence and poverty
of *favela* life. See 'The cautionary tale of Carolina Maria de Jesus' (q.v.) for a
commentary.

316 **The cautionary tale of Carolina Maria de Jesus.**
Robert M. Levine. *Latin American Research Review*, vol. 29, no. 1
(1994), p. 55-83.
This is a commentary on *Beyond all pity* (see item no. 315), which also discusses the
reactions caused by its publication in 1960. The book provoked considerable class and
racial hostility towards Carolina Maria de Jesus. Levine argues that this reaction
unmasks the myth of Brazil's racial democracy, since she was initially patronized, but
ultimately her views on poverty, hunger, blacks, and the status of women have been
ignored.

317 **Out of the shadows: black and brown struggles for recognition and
dignity in Brazil, 1964-1985.**
Zelbert L. Moore. *Journal of Black Studies*, vol. 19 (1989),
p. 394-410.
Examines the difficulties faced by Afro-Brazilians during the military régime (1964-
85), when they did not benefit from the 'economic miracle' and remained less
successful than whites in many areas, including the Church, media, education, and
even sport.

318 **Brazil – mixture or massacre? Essays on the genocide of a black people.**
Abdias do Nascimento. Dover, Massachusetts: TM Press, 1989. 216p. bibliog.

A collection of speeches by Nascimento on black issues in Brazil. The volume represents a very critical commentary on the idea of 'racial democracy', claiming that there is marked discrimination against Brazil's black population, which is reflected in employment opportunities and income levels. The work also includes observations on the black contribution to art and religion.

319 **Au Brésil: cent ans de mémoire de l'esclavage.** (To Brazil: a hundred years of remembering slavery.)
Katia de Queiros Mattoso. *Cahiers des Amériques Latines*, vol. 17 (1994), p. 65-84.

A useful assessment of Brazil's attitude to slavery a century after abolition. It suggests that recent black movements have had some success in heightening general awareness of the issue.

320 **Couleur, classe et modernité à travers deux lieux Bahianais.**
(Colour, class and modernity in two places in Bahia.)
Livio Sansone. *Cahiers des Amériques Latines*, vol. 17 (1994), p. 85-106.

This is a comparative survey, made between Salvador and the nearby town of Camaçari, of ethnic identity, black culture, colour, and social position. Bahia probably has the most complex racial mixture in Brazil, and this essay is a useful survey of the nuances of colour designations in the country.

321 **Black into white. Race and nationality in Brazilian thought.**
Thomas E. Skidmore. New York: Oxford University Press, 1974. 300p.

Remains an important study because of its analysis of the intellectual approaches to race which emerged in Brazil with the abolition of slavery. These included 'scientific racism', an idea which emerged in the 1860s and claimed that human races were different species, with Indians and Africans inferior to whites; and 'whitening', an idea current in the late 19th century, which held that the colour mix of Brazil would become progressively whiter through miscegenation, and as blacks became less numerous through lower birth rates and higher mortality. These debates and the encouragement of European immigration were important in shaping Brazilian attitudes to race. The work deals with racial attitudes before and after abolition, and the search for European immigrants. Extensive notes provide a useful guide to Brazilian and English sources.

Immigration

322 The elusive Eden: Frank McMullan's Confederate colony in Brazil.
William Clark Griggs. Austin, Texas: University of Texas Press, 1987. 218p. maps. bibliog.

This is a very detailed and rather specialized history of a colony established in São Paulo by McMullan and other disillusioned Texans, after the defeat of the Confederacy in the US Civil War. The background to the colony and its setting up are carefully chronicled, but the colony met with little success. American settlement in 19th-century Brazil was very limited in comparison with the major streams of Italian and German immigration. In consequence the book has really only a curiosity value.

323 Immigrants on the land. Coffee and society in São Paulo, 1886-1934.
Thomas H. Holloway. Chapel Hill, North Carolina: University of North Carolina Press, 1980. 218p. maps. bibliog.

A detailed study of the recruitment and use of European labour in the São Paulo coffee boom, this work provides important insights into the nature of the coffee economy and society. It contains much detail on the living conditions of the immigrants, and the patterns which emerged between labour and land-holding. Including numerous tables on the sources and destinations of immigrants, on landownership, and on coffee production, the volume represents one of the best portraits of a key element in Brazilian development and society.

324 The social and economic integration of Portuguese immigrants in Brazil in the late nineteenth and twentieth centuries.
Herbert S. Klein. *Journal of Latin American Studies*, vol. 23 (1991), p. 309-37.

Provides a comprehensive review of Portuguese migration circa 1870-1970, which contains a wealth of detail on the source areas of the migrants, and on their demographic structure, economic activity, and social organization.

325 Writing home: immigrants in Brazil and the United States, 1890-91.
Witold Kula, Nina Assorodobraj-Kula, Marcin Kula. Boulder, Colorado: East European Monographs, 1986. 698p. maps.

As its title implies, this is a somewhat specialized volume, but it provides a fascinating insight into migration to Brazil. It consists of letters sent from Brazil (and the United States) by Polish emigrants to relatives and friends in a small part of what was then Russian Poland. The letters were subject to censorship and never delivered. A cache was found just prior to the Second World War and subsequently translated. The rest were destroyed in the war. There are seventy-three letters from southern Brazil, originally in Polish, Yiddish, German, Russian and Lithuanian – reflecting the complex mix of 'Polish' migration at that time. They have considerable poignancy, but also provide original insights into the migrant experience. Useful contextual essays complete this work.

326   **Jews in the tropics. Bahian Jews in the early twentieth century.**
      Esther R. Largman, Robert Levine.   *The Americas*, vol. 43 (1986),
      p. 159-70.
      This is a case-study of a small Jewish community in Salvador in the 1930s and 1940s.

327   **The immigration and integration of Polish Jews in Brazil, 1924-34.**
      Jeffrey Lesser.   *The Americas*, vol. 51 (1994), p. 173-92.
      In the interwar period, in the face of reduced immigrant quotas to North America and
      Argentina, and political disturbances in Poland, there was some Jewish migration to
      Brazil. In the 1920s East Europeans constituted about eight per cent of emigrants to
      Brazil and Jews from Poland were significant among them. This article indicates that,
      in contrast to earlier Polish migration to the Brazilian countryside, these migrants
      tended to settle in the major cities, where they became pedlars and traders.

328   **Immigration and shifting concepts of national identity in Brazil
      during the Vargas era.**
      Jeffrey Lesser.   *Luso-Brazilian Review*, vol. 32, no. 2 (1994),
      p. 23-44.
      Lesser suggests that after the attempts to 'whiten' Brazil's population by European
      immigration, there was some subtle concern about certain immigrant sources in the
      1930s. He describes discrimination against particular groups, including Jews, and
      small groups of non-Aryan German Catholics and Catholics from Iraq.

329   **Germans in Brazil: a comparative history of cultural conflict
      during World War I.**
      Frederick C. Luebke.   Baton Rouge, Louisiana; London: Louisiana
      State University Press, 1987. 248p. map. bibliog.
      This study provides an outline of German settlement in southern Brazil from 1818, but
      its main focus is on friction between the immigrants and Brazilians during the First
      World War. The breaking of diplomatic relations with Germany in 1917 resulted in
      anti-German riots.

330   **Germans in the New World: essays on the history of immigration.**
      Frederick C. Luebke.   Urbana, Illinois; Chicago: University of Illinois
      Press, 1990. 198p.
      Luebke offers a comparative assessment of German immigration to the USA and
      Brazil. Three chapters relate to Brazil, two on a comparative basis, dealing with
      patterns of settlement from 1830-1930 and with immigrant images of the two
      countries, and one on the German experience in Brazil during the First World War.
      The volume contains very useful chapter bibliographies on English and German
      sources.

331 **Pioneers in the tropics: the political organization of Japanese in an immigrant community in Brazil.**
Philip Staniford. London: Athlone Press, 1973. 202p. map. bibliog.
The Japanese were small-scale and relatively late contributors to migration to Brazil. This monograph provides an analysis of the formation and politics of a Japanese community which settled in Pará between 1929 and 1962. It examines the consequences of their need to cooperate, in order to develop their colony and market their produce.

332 **Jews in colonial Brazil.**
Arnold Wiznitzer. New York: Columbia University Press, 1960. 228p. bibliog.
The Jewish population of Portugal was subject to forcible conversion to Christianity in 1497. They became 'New Christians', though many continued to practise their Jewish faith secretly. New Christians arrived in Brazil soon after the discovery, and became active in the sugar industry. This study concentrates on their involvement in the industry during the Dutch occupation of the Northeast, 1630-54.

Emigration

333 **Brazilian immigration to North America.**
Franklin Goza. *International Migration Review*, vol. 28 (1994), p. 136-52.
During the 1970s and 1980s there was out-migration from Brazil, as a response to economic and political pressures. This study examines migration to the USA and Canada during the early 1980s, covering the employment experience and social adaptation of the emigrants.

334 **'To return to the bosom of their fatherland'. Brazilian immigrants in nineteenth century Lagos.**
Lisa A. Lindsay. *Slavery and Abolition*, vol. 15 (1994), p. 22-50.
From the mid-19th century some freed slaves emigrated to Nigeria and survived as a distinct community into the 20th century. This article provides a history of repatriation, and of the life these returnees made in Lagos.

335 **Brazilians and the 1990 US Census: immigrants, ethnicity and the undercount.**
Maxine L. Margolis. *Human Organization*, vol. 54 (1995), p. 52-59.
This paper argues that economic deterioration in Brazil in the 1980s resulted in substantial emigration to the USA, Europe and the Far East. It suggests that there might be 300,000 Brazilians in the US, but they were under-recorded in the 1990 census by choice, or because the census did not ask questions to clearly identify them.

Dicionário de cultos Afro-Brasileiros, com a indicação da origem das palavras. (Dictionary of Afro-Brazilian cults, with an indication of the origin of words.)
See item no. 377.

Sacred leaves of *candomblé.*
See item no. 393.

Why Suyá sing: a musical anthropology of an Amazon people.
See item no. 764.

Cassava and chicha. Bread and beer of the Amazonian Indians.
See item no. 799.

Afro-Braziliana: a working bibliography.
See item no. 900.

Women and Gender Issues

336 **Slave mothers and free children: emancipation and female space in debates on the 'Free Womb' Law, Rio de Janeiro, 1871.**
Martha Abreu. *Journal of Latin American Studies*, vol. 28 (1996), p. 567-80.
The 'Law of the Free Womb' of 1871 declared that children born to slave women would be free, another step on Brazil's slow progress towards emancipation. This paper is an historical study of the impact of this legislation. It argues that although it still placed some constraints on slaves, it did confirm their rights to create families.

337 **'Building politics from personal lives: discussions on sexuality among poor women in Brazil'.**
Carmen Barroso, Cristina Bruschini. In: *Third World women and the politics of feminism*. Edited by C. T. Mohanty, A. Russo, L. Torres. Bloomington, Indiana: Indiana University Press, 1991, p. 153-72.
A prime concern of poor women in Brazilian cities is with birth control and sex education, but the Church and political parties have been opposed to population control policies. This study documents the role of the women's movement on the issue and the activities of a women's group in São Paulo in providing sex education. It includes some cartoon propaganda material.

338 **'Changing images of the Brazilian woman': studies of female sexuality in literature, mass media and criminal trials, 1884-1992.**
Edited by Sueann Caulfield. *Luso-Brazilian Review*, vol. 30, no. 1 (1993), p. 1-118.
This special issue of the Review contains eight papers (four of which are in Portuguese) on a range of issues involving images of women in the media. These include: female stars of film, radio and television; prostitution in São Paulo; and sexual politics in Rio de Janeiro. The paper explores the way in which female images are constructed and disseminated.

339 **Female consciousness or feminist consciousness?: women's consciousness raising in community-based struggles in Brazil.**
Yvonne Corcoran-Nantes. In: *'Viva'. Women and popular protest in Latin America.* Edited by Sarah A. Radcliffe, Sallie Westwood. London: Routledge, 1993, p. 136-55.
A useful discussion of the rise of female consciousness among the urban poor, which suggests a focus on specific gender interests such as health and education. It draws on fieldwork in São Paulo, and the activities of three popular movements, concerned with housing, health and employment.

340 **Gender and industrialization in Brazil.**
Susan Cunningham. In: *Geography of gender in the Third World.* Edited by Janet H. Momsen, Janet Townsend. London; Albany, New York: Hutchinson; State University of New York Press, 1987, p. 294-308.
Provides a useful summary of the growing role of women in the manufacturing industry. The paper examines the rise in female employment since 1940, and demonstrates women's increasing importance in a range of industrial sectors. However, the author suggests that some of this growth is explained by the employers' desire to restrain labour costs, by using lower-paid female labour, rather than men.

341 **Emancipating the female sex: the struggle for women's rights in Brazil, 1850-1940.**
June E. Hahner. Durham, North Carolina: Duke University Press, 1990. 302p. bibliog.
This is a helpful and wide-ranging study of the movement for women's rights in education, employment and suffrage. It concentrates on these issues in the period up to 1930, but sets them into the context of the emerging feminist movement of the 1970s.

342 **Housewives in the field: power, culture and gender in a South-Brazil village.**
Ineke van Halsema. Amsterdam: CEDLA, 1991. 172p. map. bibliog.
The author argues that there has only been limited study of rural women in Brazil, and that such work as there is has tended to focus on their role in the labour force. Her own study seeks to provide a broader view of women's place in the community and the household, as well as in the fields. She suggests, however, that although external influences have widened men's power and opportunities, they have had little impact upon the women. The research was carried out in a community of largely Italian origin in Rio Grande do Sul.

343 **Gender and work in the Third World: sexual divisions in industry in Brazil.**
John Humphrey. London: Tavistock Publishers, 1987. 230p.
This study sets female employment within the context of the domestic labour and family ideologies of Brazil. It outlines the development of manufacturing industry and employment, and the emergence of gender hierarchies in factories and the labour market.

344 **House and street. The domestic world of servants and masters in nineteenth-century Rio de Janeiro.**
Sandra Lauderdale Graham. Cambridge, United Kingdom; New York: Cambridge University Press, 1988. 214p. maps. bibliog.
A detailed historical monograph on the lives and circumstances of slave and free women in Rio in the period 1860-1910. The book polarizes the situation of women by considering the two worlds of the servants and the masters, though the latter section is uneven.

345 **The participation of women in the health movement of Jardim Nordeste, in the eastern zone of São Paulo, Brazil: 1976-1985.**
Leda Machado. *Bulletin of Latin American Research*, vol. 7 (1988), p. 47-63.
This is a detailed study of the mobilization of women in a low-income area of São Paulo to secure a health centre, and to sustain it and to foster community interest in improved health care.

346 **A condição feminina no Rio de Janeiro. Seculo XIX.** (The female condition in Rio de Janeiro in the 19th century.)
Míriam Moreira Leite. São Paulo, Brazil: Editora Hucitec, 1993. 224p. bibliog.
A fascinating exploration of women's lives as recorded by foreign visitors to Rio. It deals with family life, economic activities, and the social round.

347 **Disappearance of the dowry: women, families and social change in São Paulo, Brazil, 1600-1900.**
Murial Nazzari. Stanford, California: Stanford University Press, 1991. 246p. bibliog.
The dowry was part of Luso-Brazilian society, but the custom had disappeared by the early 20th century. The author argues that this was a reflection of social and economic change. As class replaced clan and individualistic society was replaced by the market economy, the notion of a dowry became less relevant.

348 **Brazilian women in exile: the quest for an identity.**
Angela Neves-Xavier de Brito. *Latin American Perspectives*, vol. 13,
no. 2 (1986), p. 58-80.
An interesting study of the experience of women, mainly political activists who were
forced to leave Brazil after the military coup of 1964. They moved initially to other
parts of Latin America, particularly Chile. However, due to changing political circumstances in Chile in the 1970s, they needed to move again, mainly to Europe, and to
adjust to new environmental and cultural circumstances.

349 **Women's history in Brazil: production and perspectives.**
Maria Beatriz Nizza da Silva. In: *Writing women's history.*
International perspectives. Edited by Karen Offen, Ruth Roach
Pearson, Jane Rendall. London: Macmillan, 1991, p. 369-80.
Offers a brief review of domestic and foreign work on Brazilian women, and of the
feminist movement. The work contains useful notes on the literature.

350 **Brazilian women speak: contemporary life stories.**
Daphne Patai. New Brunswick, New Jersey: Rutgers University
Press, 1988. 398p.
A collection of life stories of ordinary women, which will be of particular interest to
feminist readers. The contributions are from women of various ages, classes, marital
status and ethnic origin, and present their views of their lives.

351 **Power and everyday life: the lives of working women in
nineteenth-century Brazil.**
Maria Odila Silva Dias, translated by Ann Frost. Cambridge, United
Kingdom: Polity Press, 1995. 222p. bibliog.
Presents a detailed study of the work opportunities for women on the margins of
society. This is a case-study of São Paulo in the period 1800-88, and of women's work
as street-traders, laundresses and in other menial jobs.

Women of the forest.
See item no. 277.

AIDS and women in Brazil: the emerging problem.
See item no. 425.

Language

General

352 **The urbanization of rural dialect speakers: a socio-linguistic study in Brazil.**
Stella M. Bortoni-Ricardo.   New York; Cambridge, United Kingdom: Cambridge University Press, 1985. 266p.

The author argues that while there has been much study by social scientists of social and economic changes affecting migrants from country to town, there has been little consideration of the impact of such movement on linguistic changes. This is a case-study of modification to the rural *caipira* dialect among migrants to the satellite towns of Brasília.

353 **Locuções tradicionais no Brasil. Coisas que o povo diz.** (Traditional expressions in Brazil. Things that people say.)
Luis da Camara Cascudo.   Belo Horizonte, Brazil: Editora Itatiaia, 1986. 314p.

A rather specialist reference book, which provides a comprehensive exposition of the origin and meaning of popular phrases and expressions.

354 **Dicionário histórico das palavras Portuguesas de origin Tupi.** (A historical dictionary of Portuguese words of Tupi origin.)
Antônio Geraldo da Cunha.   São Paulo, Brazil: Edições Melhoramentos, 1978. 358p.

Tupi was the principal lingua franca used by the Portuguese to communicate with the Indians in the colonial period. This volume provides a comprehensive listing of Tupi words which have passed into Brazilian-Portuguese usage, along with cited sources and examples.

355 **Crônicas brasileiras. A Portuguese reader.**
Alfred Hower, Richard A. Preto-Rodas.   Gainesville, Florida: Center
of Latin American Studies, University of Florida, 1971. 224p.
A collection of articles to aid the development of a reading, speaking and writing
knowledge of Brazilian Portuguese. It draws on diverse topics to give some
introduction to modern urban Brazil.

356 **The Portuguese language.**
J. Mattoso Camara, Jnr., translated by A. J. Naro.   Chicago; London:
University of Chicago Press, 1972. 270p. bibliog.
Provides an introduction to the grammar of Portuguese. As the author was Brazilian,
the book gives some weight to the variants of Brazilian Portuguese.

357 **Brazilian Portuguese grammar.**
Maria de Lourdes Sá Pereira.   Boston, Massachusetts: D. C. Heath
and Co., 1948. 404p.
A basic introduction to the learning of Portuguese as used in Brazil, for beginners.

358 **Readings in Portuguese linguistics.**
J. Schmidt-Radefeldt.   Amsterdam; Oxford; New York: North
Holland Publishing Co., 1976. 480p.
Presents a collection of essays for the specialist, on the major characteristics of
Portuguese linguistics. A number relate specifically to Brazilian Portuguese.

359 **The syntax of spoken Brazilian Portuguese.**
Earl W. Thomas.   Nashville, Tennessee: Vanderbilt University Press,
1969. 364p.
This is intended as a guide to usage of the Portuguese habitually spoken by Brazilians
of moderate/higher education levels.

360 **An essential companion to modern Portuguese.**
Robert Clive Willis.   London: Harrap, 1971. 524p.
A basic teaching grammar, this volume is aimed at first-year university students with
no prior knowledge of the language. Essentially a starter text, it includes some
discussion of the variants of Brazilian Portuguese.

Dictionaries

361 **Dicionário tecnico Inglês-Português.** (English-Portuguese technical dictionary.)
Joaquim Alves Martins. Sintra, Portugal: Publicações Europa-América, [s.d.]. 230p.
A dictionary providing translations from English to Portuguese in the areas of engineering, vehicles, agricultural machinery, and naval construction.

362 **Novo dicionário da lingua Portuguesa.** (New dictionary of the Portuguese language.)
Aurélio Buarque de Holanda Ferreira. Rio de Janeiro, Brazil: Editora Nova Fronteira, [s.d.]. 1,518p.
This is a comprehensive Portuguese dictionary, defining the meanings of words. It is a reference-level source.

363 **Dicionário popular brasileiro.** (Popular Brazilian dictionary.)
J. Fernando. São Paulo, Brazil: Ícone Editora, 1987. 434p.
A basic dictionary of Brazilian Portuguese.

364 **Harraps English-Brazilian Portuguese business dictionary.**
Terence Lewis. London: Harrap, 1982. 282p.
Provides Portuguese translations of commercial English terms, relating to transport, banking and the law.

365 **Dicionário Inglês-Português de termos econômicos e comerciais.**
(English-Portuguese dictionary of economic and commercial terms.)
J. Candido Marques Cavalcante. Petropolis, Brazil: Editora Vozes, 1979. 408p.
A Brazilian-produced dictionary which provides an English-to-Portuguese usage of economic terms.

366 **Noronha's legal dictionary.**
Durval de Noronha Goyos. São Paulo, Brazil: Editora Observador Legal, 1993. 510p.
This English-Portuguese dictionary lists terms used in law, particularly international law as it relates to banking, finance, taxation, trade, and the environment.

367 **Dicionário sobre comércio exterior.** (Dictionary of external trade.)
Y. Silva Pontes. São Paulo, Brazil: Edições Aduaneiras, 1990.
3rd ed. 426p.
A Portuguese-English and English-Portuguese dictionary covering the language of trade matters.

368 **Dicionário contrastivo Luso-Brasileiro.** (Dictionary of
Luso-Brazilian contrasts.)
Mauro Villar. Rio de Janeiro, Brazil: Editora Guanabara, 1989. 318p.
bibliog.
Provides a useful and important guide to variations between the Portuguese and
Brazilian usage of words. It offers examples of variations in both directions.

369 **Collins Portuguese dictionary. English-Portuguese/
Portuguese-English.**
John Whitlam, Vitoria Davies, Mike Harland. London: Harper
Collins, 1991. 368p.
A good, basic two-way dictionary.

370 **Oxford-Duden pictorial Portuguese-English dictionary.**
Oxford: Clarendon Press, 1995. Not conventionally paginated.
This unusual two-way dictionary presents its material not alphabetically, but linked to
detailed illustrations of subjects and activities – for instance art, forestry, railways and
hotels. It would be of particular use to the business person and traveller seeking to
communicate on specific topics. The volume provides an alphabetical word listing in
both languages, and it covers some 28,000 items.

Religion

371 Opting for the poor: Brazilian Catholicism in transition.
Madeleine Adriance.   Kansas City, Kansas: Sheed & Ward, 1986.
200p.
This is a study of religion and social change in Brazil, which explores church involvement in: liberation theology, political activism and human rights, and the rise of *Comunidades ecclesial de base* (CEBs – Christian Base Communities). CEBs are small groups of lay Christians who meet on a parish basis to read the Bible and decide upon areas of community action. They operate democratically, with their leaders often carrying out religious duties. CEBs have been especially significant in incorporating the rural and urban poor into church activities.

372 Promised land: Base Christian Communities and the struggle for the Amazon.
Madeleine Adriance.   Albany, New York: State University of
New York Press, 1995. 202p. map. bibliog.
A further study of the CEBs and their involvement in movements for land reform and human rights. It argues that they form a political movement motivated by religious beliefs, which is often at odds not only with large landowners and the government, but with the church hierarchy. The work is based on six case-studies from eastern Amazonia, and includes some discussion of the role of women in the land struggle.

373 The African religions of Brazil: toward a sociology of the interpenetration of civilizations.
Roger Bastide, translated by Helen Sebba.   Baltimore, Maryland;
London: Johns Hopkins University Press, 1978. 494p.
First published in 1960 as *Les religions Afro-Bresiliennes* (Paris: Presses Universitaires de France), this remains a key text for the understanding of Afro-Brazilian religion in Brazil. It traces the complexity of the dual heritage of the Portuguese and African religious traditions, in which the African element was subjugated by slavery

and Catholicism. The emergence of a black Catholicism is noted, but the book also points to a religious element in racial conflict, particularly where Islam gave slaves an identity and a focus for resistance. The volume also contains a substantial examination of the contemporary circumstances of Afro-Brazilian religion, which explores the geographical variations in its practices, and describes the functioning of the African sects. A glossary and over 1,200 footnotes on sources are included.

374 **Umbanda. Religion and politics in urban Brazil.**
Diana DeGroat Brown.   Ann Arbor, Michigan: University Microfilms, 1986. 256p. bibliog.

Provides a very comprehensive review of *umbanda*, a spirit-possession religion which emerged in the 1920s and 1930s, and which incorporates elements of Catholicism, and Afro-Brazilian and Indian beliefs. The book examines its origins, rituals, organization and the social background of its practitioners. It suggests that the religion has been de-Africanized from its roots by the urban middle classes.

375 **The church in Brazil: the politics of religion.**
Thomas C. Bruneau.   Austin, Texas: University of Texas Press, 1982. 238p. map. bibliog.

Explores the influence of the Roman Catholic Church on the beliefs and practices of its members as it has become involved in socio-political activities. The volume concentrates on the diocesan level, and activism over human rights, land issues, and Indian issues. Such a dynamic and socially-committed role has been an important facet of the Church in recent years, and is at odds with its traditionally conservative stance.

376 **Looking for God in Brazil: the progressive Catholic Church in urban Brazil's religious arena.**
John Burdick.   Berkeley, California; London: University of California Press, 1993. 280p. bibliog.

A study of Christian Base Communities and their involvement in struggles for social justice. The work also appraises links between the CEBs and pentecostal and *umbanda* movements.

377 **Dicionário de cultos Afro-Brasileiros, com a indicação da origem das palavras.** (Dictionary of Afro-Brazilian cults, with an indication of the origin of words.)
Olga Gudolle Cacciatore.   Rio de Janeiro, Brazil: Forense Universitaria, 1988. 3rd ed. 264p.

Provides an introduction to the African origins of Brazil's black population, and the rise of *umbanda* and *candomblé* movements. The latter is an Afro-Brazilian religion, brought by slaves from Nigeria, which draws together people and the forces of nature. The prime importance of the book is in its detailed dictionary of the terminology of these cults, for such things as ceremonies, names of deities, and of rituals, plants, and musical instruments.

378 **The Mormon Church and German immigrants in southern Brazil: religion and language.**
Mark L. Grove. *Jahrbuch für Geschichte von Staat, Wirtschaft und Gesellschaft Lateinamerikas*, vol. 26 (1989), p. 295-308.
This is a study as much of politics as religion in Brazil in the 1930s, as it explores the links between a church and an immigrant group. The Mormon Church worked with German communities in southern Brazil from 1928, finding common ground in notions of hierarchies of race. German was the language of the church and the communities, until President Vargas imposed compulsory use of Portuguese for all public meetings.

379 **The many rooms of spiritism in Brazil.**
David J. Hess. *Luso-Brazilian Review*, vol. 24, no. 2 (1987), p. 15-34.
A discussion of the European origins of spiritism, which were developed by the French educator, Allan Kardec, in the 1850s. It explores spiritism's role as a religion of the white middle class in Brazil, and its relations with the State and the Roman Catholic Church.

380 **Spirits and scientists: ideology, spiritism and Brazilian culture.**
David J. Hess. University Park, Pennsylvania: Pennsylvania State University, 1991. 260p. bibliog.
This book provides a much fuller account of spiritism in Brazil, which is a mainly middle-class belief in communication with the dead via mediums, and of healing through spiritual therapies. The volume discusses the history and practice of spiritism, and examines a number of its key texts.

381 **Samba in the night: spiritism in Brazil.**
David J. Hess. New York: Columbia University Press, 1994. 214p. map. bibliog.
A further contribution to the analysis of Brazilian spiritism. In this case the perspective is ethnographic, based on a detailed narrative account of spiritist practices.

382 **Base Christian Communities and social change in Brazil.**
Warren E. Hewitt. Lincoln, Nebraska; London: University of Nebraska Press, 1991. 150p. bibliog.
The Base Christian movement is lay, lower class, and politically oriented towards the needs of the poor. This book provides a detailed and critical analysis of the CEBs in the late 1980s – their origins, nature, organization and socio-political impact.

383 **The Roman Catholic Church and environmental politics in Brazil.**
Warren E. Hewitt. *Journal of Developing Areas*, vol. 26 (1992), p. 239-58.
An interesting review of Church responses to environmental issues. It suggests that there is a degree of conservatism, because of a traditional view of a God-given right to utilize resources, and more recent 'people-first' ideas, which put human necessity before environmental protection.

384 The Catholic Church in colonial Brazil.
Eduardo Hoornaert. In: *Cambridge history of Latin America. Vol. I.*
Edited by Leslie Bethell.   Cambridge, United Kingdom; New York:
Cambridge University Press, 1984, p. 541-56. bibliog.

Presents two contrasting views of the early role of the Church in Brazil – as spiritual, in seeking the conversion of the Indians, or as an agent in their enslavement. The chapter provides an account of the activities of the clergy in different parts of the country.

385 Kingdoms come: religion and politics in Brazil.
Rowan Ireland.   Pittsburgh, Pennsylvania: University of Pittsburgh
Press, 1991. 268p. bibliog.

This is an ethnographic study of the diversity of religion in a town in Pernambuco in northeast Brazil, which explores the activities of Roman Catholics, spiritists, pentecostalists, and Afro-Brazilian cults. It sets these various denominations into the context of Brazilian politics, and argues that political issues in the 1980s were strongly debated within these faiths. Though a case-study, it conveys a good sense of the religious diversity of contemporary Brazil.

386 The Catholic Church and politics in Brazil, 1916-1985.
Scott Mainwaring.   Stanford, California: Stanford University Press,
1986. 328p.

The Church has been a major factor in Brazilian society and politics since the colonial period. Traditionally it has been closely associated with the State and the dominant classes. This work portrays this traditional role over the period from 1916 to 1964. However, it then goes on to chart the Church's reaction to the period of military repression (1964-85), during which time it became radicalized and turned into an element of resistance against the abuse of human rights. This changed role reflected the rise of 'liberation theology' in Latin America, and saw close involvement with peasants and urban workers. The author suggests that this radicalism dwindled after 1985, with the return to democracy, and that the Church saw the re-emergence of more conservative traditions. Although no bibliography is included, copious end-notes provide a valuable reference source.

387 Coping with poverty. Pentecostals and Christian Base Communities in Brazil.
Cecília Loreto Mariz.   Philadelphia, Pennsylvania: Temple University
Press, 1994. 196p.

The author emphasizes the importance of religion in Brazilian society and culture, and argues that recent changes in the religious life of the poor, particularly the growth in pentecostalism, has affected their lifestyle and culture. She compares the material, cultural and political strategies of various religious groups which seek to help the poor.

388   **Brazil. Journey in the light of the eucharist.**
John Paul II.   Boston, Massachusetts: Daughters of St. Paul, 1980.
404p.

These are the collected addresses made by Pope John Paul on his visit to Brazil in 1980. Though primarily a series of homilies, there are some reflections on the liberation theology of Latin America, and addresses to particular groups, such as Indians, Polish and German immigrants, and shanty-town dwellers, which are of particular interest.

389   **Messianic movements in Brazil.**
René Ribeiro.   *Luso-Brazilian Review*, vol. 29, no. 1 (1992), p. 71-82.

Provides a useful long view of Messianic movements in Brazil, among the Indians before and after the arrival of the Portuguese, and among the rural mestizo population in the 19th and 20th centuries. The article offers a good summary and assessment of this element in Brazilian society and religion.

390   **Prestige, power and piety in colonial Brazil: the Third Orders of Salvador.**
A. J. R. Russell-Wood.   *Hispanic American Historical Review*,
vol. 69 (1969), p. 61-89.

The Third Orders were lay brotherhoods established to exemplify Christian ideals by thought and deed, performing charitable works. Their members were known as 'tertiaries' and these secular orders were an important element in society and the Church in colonial Brazil. This paper discusses their membership and activities in the colonial capital.

391   **Trail of miracles: stories from a pilgrimage in Northeast Brazil.**
Candace Slater.   Berkeley, California; London: University of
California Press, 1986. 290p.

Padre Cícero (1844-1934) was an important religious and political figure in the Northeast. His parish, Juazeiro, in Ceará, has become an important place of pilgrimage, and this volume provides both a history and an account of tales and miracles associated with him.

392   **Miracle stories and *milagres* in northeast Brazil.**
Candace Slater.   *Journal of Latin American Lore*, vol. 16, no. 1
(1990), p. 109-27.

A study of two key elements in northeastern folk Catholicism – miracle narratives and votive objects. The stories in this paper deal with the miracles of Padre Cícero, and with the ex-votos of wood, clay and other materials which are offered to fulfil spiritual bargains.

393   **Sacred leaves of *candomblé*.**
R. Voeks.   *Geographical Review*, vol. 80 (1990), p. 118-31.

A commentary on the use of plants for spiritual and medicinal purposes in *candomblé*. These include both plants imported from the Old World and substitutes from the New.

Society and Social Conditions

General

394 **Social change in Brazil, 1945-1985: the incomplete transition.**
Edited by Edmar L. Bacha, Herbert S. Klein. Albuquerque, New
Mexico: University of New Mexico Press, 1989. 346p.

This collection of essays provides a very helpful overview of recent trends in most of
the social fields – population, rural issues, urbanization, employment, inequality,
social welfare, education and health. It is a good introduction to the contemporary
social scene.

395 **Social change in contemporary Brazil.**
Edited by Geert Banck, Kees Koonings. Amsterdam: CEDLA, 1988.
218p.

Examines the 'big issues' facing modern Brazil – of economic growth, industrialization, and urbanization – but argues that there are also smaller-scale issues to be
considered in a complex multi-dimensional society. These include the return to
democracy, social change, and relations between culture, politics and religion.

396 **Modern Brazil. Elites and masses in historical perspective.**
Edited by Michael L. Conniff, Frank D. McCann. Lincoln, Nebraska;
London: University of Nebraska Press, 1989. 306p.

A very helpful discussion of the diversity of social groups in Brazil. The work deals
with national, regional, economic and military 'élites', and with rural 'masses' in the
Northeast, South, and the cities. It also discusses religion and mass communications.

397 **The emergence of the Brazilian Gay liberation movement, 1977-1981.**
James N. Green. *Latin American Perspectives*, vol. 21, no. 1 (1994), p. 38-55.
Argues that the emergence of Brazilian gay culture was a reflection of the international gay movement, and the easing political situation within Brazil.

398 **Assault on paradise. Social change in a Brazilian village.**
Conrad P. Kottak. New York: McGraw Hill, 1992. rev. ed. 350p. bibliog.
An interesting study of change brought to a traditional fishing community in Bahia by the arrival of a mineral-processing factory in the 1970s. This revised edition also takes note of the impact of television and the intrusion of images of a wider world on the lives of the people.

399 **Brazil's New Republic: the social-liberal path.**
J. G. Merquior. *Bulletin of Latin American Research*, vol. 6 (1987), p. 269-77.
This is a useful survey of the major issues facing Brazil in the return to democracy – debt, inflation, and inequality. The paper explores the social implications of these problems, and possible approaches to them.

400 **Stability and social policy in Brazil: the way ahead.**
Marcelo de Paiva Abreu. *Bulletin of Latin American Research*, vol. 6 (1987), p. 249-68.
Provides a very useful survey of social circumstance in Brazil, which sets the country in an international context, and then explores regional social indicators such as infant mortality, water provision, and literacy. The paper also takes on a predictive role, by setting some targets to be met in these areas by 2000 AD.

401 **Bodies, pleasures and passions: sexual culture in contemporary Brazil.**
Richard G. Parker. Boston, Massachusetts: Beacon, 1991. 204p.
A study of human sexual behaviour and gender in Brazil. It summarizes interpretations of gender roles and sexual conduct, and explores the significance of carnival and samba in sexual behaviour.

402 **Death by weeping: the violence of everyday life in Brazil.**
N. Scheper-Hughes. Berkeley, California: University of California Press, 1992. 614p. bibliog.
The focus of this sprawling tome is an account of child death in the Northeast, painting a harsh portrait of urban poverty in a shanty area of a plantation town. Although in essence an ethnographic study, it is a complex mix of anecdote, narrative conversation, social medicine, and critical protest. In the pseudonymous shanty of Alto do Cruzeiro in Bom Jesus da Mata the author gives a very detailed account of the elements of hunger, disease, everyday violence, and infant death. She argues that the

prevalent conditions of poverty inure mothers to the loss of their children. Much detail is included on maternal attitudes, the nature of infant mortality, religion, and the ritual of carnival.

403 **Integration and change in Brazil's middle Amazon.**
Rolf Wesche, Thomas Bruneau. Ottawa, London, Paris: University of Ottawa Press, 1990. 82p. bibliog.
An interesting but brief study of the impact of development on a small town in Amazonas. The arrival of a highway introduced developments in agriculture, forestry, fishing and commerce, and brought change to land tenure and resource use.

404 **State and society in Brazil. Continuity and change.**
Edited by John D. Wirth, Edson de Oliveira Nunes, Thomas E. Bogenschild. Boulder, Colorado; London: Westview Press, 1987. 350p.
There is a strong economic element to the nine essays in this collection, which tackle issues of unionism, social movements, employment, and citizenship. The work's concern is with Brazil's need to organize itself to face the end of the authoritarian régimes and return to democracy. It suggests that in the mid-1980s an emergence of grass-roots activity in society was clearly evident, involving not only trade unions, but neighbourhood associations, the Base Christian Movement, and in rural movements to secure titles to land. The editors provide an excellent summary of the new circumstances of Brazil, and the essays address three major themes: the new economic society created by recent industrialization; the new organizational structures of the State, the unions, and voluntary groups; and policy objectives for the State.

Crime

405 **Brazil: authorized violence in rural Brazil.**
Amnesty International. London: Amnesty International Publications, 1988. 80p. map.
Amnesty provides a report on the killing of smallholders in Amazonia in the 1980s, and asserts that there is often official failure to properly investigate such killings.

406 **Torture in Brazil.**
Archdiocese of São Paulo/Joan Dassin, translated by Jaime Wright.
New York: Vintage Books, 1986. 240p.
This is a controversial study by the Catholic Church of the use of torture during the military rule of 1964-85. The work charts the institution of repression from 1964-79, abuses of human rights, and provides detailed testimony of the torture of leftist opponents of the régime. It is an important study of a notorious period in Brazil's recent history.

407 **Brazil: war on children.**
Gilberto Dimenstein. London: Latin American Bureau, 1991. 88p.
map.
In recent years Brazil has experienced considerable notoriety regarding the abuse of
children who live on the streets. This is a graphic account of the maltreatment and
murder of such children by vigilante gangs.

408 **Policing Rio de Janeiro. Repression and resistance in a
nineteenth-century city.**
Thomas H. Holloway. Stanford, California: Stanford University
Press, 1993. 370p. bibliog.
This is a detailed history of policing in Rio de Janeiro from 1808-89, based on police
and judicial sources. It presents the police as agents of repression and, in consequence,
a force to be resisted by the populace.

409 **From slavery to vagrancy in Brazil: crime and social control in the
Third World.**
Martha K. Huggins. New Brunswick, New Jersey: Rutgers University
Press, 1985. 184p. maps. bibliog.
A study of Pernambuco in the 19th century, where arrest was used as a means to
secure field labour at times of shortage. With the ending of the slave trade, workers
were increasingly difficult to find, especially in the case of the seasonal demands of
sugar production. This study details the way in which the law was manipulated to
provide convict field labour.

410 **Dangerous encounters: meanings of violence in a Brazilian city.**
Daniel T. Linger. Stanford, California: Stanford University Press,
1992. 290p. maps. bibliog.
Presents an interesting analysis of urban violence. It is a portrait of modern urban
Brazil, but also a case-study of more general interest. It explores the perils of face-to-
face encounters with street violence in the bacchanal of carnival and in street brawls.
The fieldwork is from São Luis, in northeast Brazil.

411 **Brazil: the fight for childhood in the city.**
Anthony Swift. Florence, Italy: Innocenti Studies, UNICEF, 1991.
42p.
This brief policy document explores street children and their culture in Brazil. It also
presents a report on an urban programme in Goiás designed to assist them.

Health

412 **Brazil's contribution to tropical medicine and malaria: personalities and institutions.**
Renato C. Bacellar.   Rio de Janeiro, Brazil: Editora Olímpica, 1963.
380p. bibliog.
Presents a long perspective on medicine in Brazil since the colonial period, but focuses on tropical diseases from the 18th century onwards. The volume devotes particular attention to research centres such as the Instituto Butantã, the Instituto Oswaldo Cruz, and the schools of tropical medicine at the universities of São Paulo and Rio de Janeiro.

413 **Brazil: the new challenge of adult health.**
John Briscoe.   Washington, DC: World Bank, 1990. 114p. map.
bibliog.
This is a useful examination of current causes of mortality in Brazil, which comments on the increasing significance of cardiovascular diseases, strokes and cancer. It outlines the way in which Brazil's health system operates and the challenges it faces.

414 **Lead poisoning among children from Santo Amaro, Brazil.**
Fernando M. Carvalho, Annibal M. Silvany Neto, Tania M. Tavares,
Maria E. C. Lima, Harry A. Waldron.   *Bulletin of the Pan-American
Health Organization*, vol. 19 (1985), p. 165-75.
A clinical study of the impact of the installation of a lead smelter in 1960 in a town in Bahia. Evidence of lead poisoning resulted in the introduction of pollution control measures. This paper offers a useful insight into the impact of exporting hazardous factories from the developed to the Third World, where labour is cheap and environmental protection laws are weak.

415   The politics of disease control: yellow fever and race in nineteenth
       century Rio de Janeiro.
       Sidney Chalhoub.   *Journal of Latin American Studies*, vol. 25 (1993),
       p. 441-63.

An interesting piece of medical history, which reveals late-19th-century interpretations of the causes of yellow fever, which were entwined with ideas about race. There
was disagreement among doctors as to whether the disease was caused by contagion,
and transmitted from person to person, or by infection, from noxious emanations in
the atmosphere. The paper discusses this debate, and also suggests that the outbreak of
the 1850s may have contributed to the ending of the slave trade, since there were
claims that the disease was generated in the slave ships. A second major outbreak, in
the 1870s, saw the city's slums as a hotbed of infection, resulting in slum clearance
and urban renewal programmes.

416   Human settlements, demographic patterns and epidemiology in
       lowland Amazonia: the case of Chagas' disease.
       C. Coimbra.   *American Anthropologist*, vol. 90 (1988), p. 82-97.

Chagas' disease is a major health hazard in parts of Brazil. It is transmitted by beetles,
and affects the heart and kidneys. This paper studies its impact on Indians, and the
risks associated with housing materials and domesticated animals in the transmission
of the disease.

417   Water-contact patterns and socioeconomic variables in the
       epidemiology of schistosomiasis mansoni in an endemic area in
       Brazil.
       M. F. F. L. Costa, M. H. A. Magalhães, R. S. Rocha, C. M. F. Antunes,
       N. Katz.   *Bulletin of the World Health Organization*, vol. 65, no. 1
       (1987), p. 57-66.

Schistosomiasis, also known as bilharzia, is a parasitic disease caused by flukes called
schistomes and acquired by contact with infested lakes, streams and irrigation
systems. This paper is a study of an area of endemic schistosomiasis in southeast
Brazil. Risks were found to be greatest where the head-of-household was in manual
work, and dwellings were of poor construction and lacked piped water. Infection
arises from contact with stream water used in laundry, for swimming, bathing and
drinking.

418   Migration and the dissemination of malaria in Brazil.
       Agostinho Cruz Marques.   *Memórias do Instituto Oswaldo Cruz*,
       vol. 81, Special issue, Supplement II (1986), p. 17-30.

A valuable study of the increases in malaria fostered by migration to Amazonia, where
forest clearance, poor housing, ignorance of preventative measures, and deficient
health care all contribute to rising incidence of the disease.

419 **Sexuality, politics and AIDS in Brazil: in another world?**
Herbert Daniel, Richard G. Parker. London: Falmer Press, 1993.
168p. bibliog.
Argues that 'Western' models are inadequate for an understanding of HIV and AIDS
in Brazilian culture, particularly as regards sexual identity. The study charts the course
and social effects of AIDS in Brazil, and considers issues of sexual identity, blood
supplies, and drug abuse. Some of the essays have a strong personal poignancy, as one
of the authors died of AIDS in 1992.

420 **Malaria vectors in Brazil.**
L. M. Deane. *Memórias do Instituto Oswaldo Cruz*, vol. 81, Special
issue, Supplement II (1986), p. 5-14.
An excellent review of malaria in Brazil, and of its transmission vectors. The first
probable case of malaria was recorded in 1587, but major epidemics became
significant only from the 1870s, in Amazonia. In 1985 there were 400,000 recorded
cases, mainly in Amazonia.

421 **Malaria studies and control in Brazil.**
L. M. Deane. *American Journal of Tropical Medicine and Health*,
vol. 38, no. 2 (1988), p. 223-30.
Provides a very good historical review of experiments and control in Brazil since
1900. Malaria was in decline in Brazil from 1900 to the 1970s, but its occurrence is
now rising again, mainly in Amazonia. In 1986 ninety-nine per cent of all cases
occurred there, a result of the in-migration from other parts of Brazil of people
without immunity.

422 **Social inequality in mortality in São Paulo state, Brazil.**
B. B. Duncan, D. Rumel, A. Zelmanowicz, S. Serrate Mengue, S. dos
Santos, A. Dalmaz. *International Journal of Epidemiology*, vol. 24,
no. 2 (1995), p. 359-65.
This paper claims that there has been little research in the Third World on the
significance of social inequality in levels of illness and mortality. It investigates
differentials in mortality among adult males in São Paulo, and reports a threefold
variation between the least, and most, socially favoured groups.

423 **Malaria rates and fate: a socioeconomic study of malaria in Brazil.**
Rogelio E. Fernandez Castilla, Diane Oya Sawyer. *Social Science
and Medicine*, vol. 37 (1993), p. 1,137-45.
A study of risk factors related to malaria. The study shows that risk falls with higher
economic status, knowledge of the vector, and DDT spraying. The poor and landless
are at highest risk, and there is most need for control programmes to work on their
behalf.

424   **Chagas' disease: control and surveillance through use of insecticides and community participation in Mambaí, Goias, Brazil.**
M. T. A. García-Zapata, P. D. Marsden. *Bulletin of the Pan-American Health Organization*, vol. 27, no. 3 (1993), p. 265-79.

A major spray campaign against the insect vector in 1980 effectively reduced the incidence of Chagas' disease in this community in the Centre-West. Control is maintained by a community programme of minimal surveillance and the spraying of infested houses.

425   **AIDS and women in Brazil: the emerging problem.**
Donna M. Goldstein. *Social Science and Medicine*, vol. 39 (1994), p. 919-29.

According to the World Health Organization, Brazil has the third largest number of people with AIDS. This paper explores the contrast between public discourse on AIDS and the experience of women on low incomes in Rio de Janeiro and São Paulo. It argues that while male sexual freedom is protected in the name of freedom for all, women's sexuality is constrained by Brazilian cultural norms regarding virginity, fidelity and sexual practices. In consequence, women may be placed at particular risk.

426   **Pharmaceuticals in two Brazilian villages: lay practice and perception.**
Hilbrand Haak. *Social Science and Medicine*, vol. 27 (1988), p. 1,415-27.

This paper contains a useful summary of Brazil's pharmaceutical industry. However, its main concern is that although modern medicines are appreciated even in rural areas, poverty and ignorance frequently mean that they are used in self-medication in ways which are inappropriate and incomplete.

427   **The nutritional links with slave infant and child mortality in Brazil.**
Kenneth F. Kiple. *Hispanic American Historical Review*, vol. 69 (1989), p. 677-90.

An interesting study in medical history, exploring the existence of endemic beriberi in Brazil's slave population. It suggests that this thiamine-deficiency disease was caused by undue dependence on manioc and dried meat in the slave diet.

428   **Chagas's disease in the Amazon basin.** *Trypanosoma cruzi* **infections in silvatic mammals, triatomine bugs, and man in the State of Pará, Brazil.**
R. Lainson, J. J. Shaw, H. Fraiha, M. A. Miles, C. C. Draper. *Transactions of the Royal Society of Tropical Medicine and Hygiene*, vol. 73 (1979), p. 193-204.

There is concern about the possible endemic development of Chagas' disease in Amazonia with the opening up of the region by highways. This study examines the occurrence of the disease in various animals, insects, and man. It suggests that without proper control measures the disease could spread.

429 **Malnutrition among children of adolescent mothers in a squatter community of Recife, Brazil.**
M. Lima, F. Figueira, G. J. Ebrahim. *Journal of Tropical Pediatrics*, vol. 36, no. 1 (1990), p. 14-19.

A study of the health problems of children of adolescent mothers in a Recife shanty town, where ten per cent of mothers are under fifteen and sixty per cent under twenty years of age at the time of their first child. Many are poor, single parents, who have had limited education and live in poor housing. Their children are malnourished and in poor health.

430 **Yellow Fever in Rio de Janeiro and the Pasteur Institute Mission, 1901-1905. The transfer of science to the periphery.**
Ilana Löwy. *Medical History*, vol. 34 (1990), p. 144-63.

The context of this paper is the diffusion of European science to 'peripheral' countries at the turn of the 19th century. The Pasteur Institute Mission transferred high European standards in bacteriology and tropical medicine to Brazil, and stimulated high-quality research in tropical diseases. The paper traces work on yellow fever in Brazil from 1880, and describes local resistance to the control methods introduced in Rio by Oswaldo Cruz during the 1903 epidemic.

431 **Prospective studies of the illness burden in a rural community in northeast Brazil.**
J. F. McAuliffe, M. Auxiladora de Sousa, Marilyn K. Nations, David S. Shields, Isabel L. Tavares, Joanne Leslie, J. Galba Araujo, Richard L. Guerrant. *Bulletin of the Pan-American Health Organization*, vol. 19 (1985), p. 139-46.

A most interesting report on the impact of common illnesses on the poor. This study examines the frequency and nature of febrile, respiratory and diarrhoeal illnesses among the poor of Ceará.

432 **Muscosal leishmaniasis ("espundia" Escmel, 1911).**
P. D. Marsden. *Transactions of the Royal Society of Tropical Medicine and Hygiene*, vol. 80, no. 6 (1986), p. 859-76.

Leishmaniasis is a parasitic disease transmitted by sandfly bites, which can affect the skin, causing ulcers, or the internal organs, when it may be fatal. Although this paper is concerned with a very specific form of leishmaniasis, it also provides a wide-ranging review of the occurrence of the disease in Brazil, and its treatment.

433 **The Brazilian Leishmaniasis control program.**
Mariza Mendes Lacerda. *Memórias do Instituto Oswaldo Cruz*, vol. 89 (1994), p. 489-501.

Leishmaniasis occurs in seventeen of Brazil's states, and is generally associated with poor socio-economic conditions – poor education, nutrition and sanitation. The control programme began in the 1950s, but lapsed and was re-started in the 1980s, following a significant rise in cases from 1984, especially in Amazonia and the Northeast. The programme involves control of the sandfly vector and treatment of the disease.

434 **Mystification of a simple solution: oral rehydration therapy in northeast Brazil.**
Marilyn K. Nations, L. A. Rebhun. *Social Science and Medicine*, vol. 27, no. 1 (1988), p. 25-38.
Diarrhoeal dehydration is a major cause of child death in Brazil. Treatment by ORT (oral rehydration therapy) is a simple process, but in the Northeast its use is complicated by a range of social, economic and political factors, in which the medical establishment is hostile to domestic use of ORT. This case-study from Ceará suggests ways in which it could be made more accessible.

435 **Pluralistic etiological systems in their social context: a Brazilian case study.**
Ndolamb Ngokevey. *Social Science and Medicine*, vol. 26, no. 8 (1988), p. 793-802.
An interesting study of perceptions of illness-causation in a Northeastern town. It demonstrates that people may attribute their illnesses to natural phenomena, socio-economic conditions, or supernatural influences.

436 **Cancer mortality in Rio de Janeiro.**
C. B. Pinto, M. P. Coleman. *International Journal of Cancer*, vol. 46, no. 2 (1990), p. 173-77.
Eleven per cent of deaths from 1979-81 in the State of Rio de Janeiro were attributed to cancer. Levels of lung and liver cancer are particularly high in the state, and the study suggests that there are considerable regional differences in cancer mortality in Brazil.

437 **What is happening to hospital utilization in Brazil?**
José Rodrigues. *Health Policy and Planning*, vol. 4, no. 4 (1989), p. 354-56.
A brief survey of hospital utilization in Brazil, discussing the various types of hospital provision. Although seventy per cent of hospitals are private, a high proportion of the use of private beds comes from the national insurance scheme.

438 **Economic and social consequences of malaria in new colonization projects in Brazil.**
Donald Sawyer. *Social Science and Medicine*, vol. 37, no. 9 (1993), p. 1,131-36.
Based on a study in Rondônia, this paper suggests that endemic malaria is a significant problem for the transient workers in agriculture, mining, and commerce. Its occurrence affects the possible location of settlements, and their long-term viability, imposing economic and social costs upon the migrants, beyond those of treatment and disease control.

439 **An outbreak of dengue virus at Rio de Janeiro, 1986.**
H. G. Schatzmayr, R. M. R. Nogueira, A. P. Travassos da Rosa. *Memórias do Instituto Oswaldo Cruz*, vol. 81 (1986), p. 245-46.
Dengue fever is transmitted by the mosquito and causes severe headaches, joint and muscle pain, giving it the popular name of 'breakbone fever'. This is a report on an

outbreak of dengue in a suburb of Rio in March 1986, the first outbreak in the city since 1923. By May over 100,000 cases were reported, though no fatalities.

440 Trends in health, nutrition, and socio-economic status in Nigeria, India and Brazil (1960-1990).
V. P. Shah. *Journal of Tropical Pediatrics*, vol. 39 (1993), p. 118-27.

An interesting comparative study of links between economic development and general health. It considers variables such as calorie intake, sanitation, water supply, immunization, life expectancy, and mortality. Brazil comes out relatively well from the analysis, with improvements in life expectancy, water supply and immunization levels over the period, and with falling death rates and declining infant mortality.

441 Primary health workers in north-east Brazil.
Christel Stock-Iwamoto, Rolfe Korte. *Social Science and Medicine*, vol. 36 (1993), p. 775-82.

Assesses the use of minimally-trained primary health care workers in São Luis, Maranhão. The paper suggests that they have been successful in improving health care delivery, and health conditions among the rural and urban poor.

442 Trust in a rent-seeking world: health and government transformed in northeast Brazil.
Judith Tendler, Sara Fredheim. *World Development*, vol. 22 (1994), p. 1,771-91.

Examines the success of a state government health programme in Ceará, in which basic health services and advice, and vaccination programmes are provided on a decentralized basis.

443 Health and education: university, NGOs, and public policies in Brazil.
Victor V. Valla. *Latin American Perspectives*, vol. 21, no. 3 (1994), p. 104-16.

A report of a study of health issues in a poor district of Rio de Janeiro. It describes *favela* conditions, the lack of education, and poor health care, and the resulting problems of dengue fever, leprosy, and cholera.

444 Malaria among gold miners in south Pará, Brazil: estimates of determinants and individual costs.
Stephen A. Vosti. *Social Science and Medicine*, vol. 30, no. 10 (1990), p. 1,097-105.

Malaria has become more prevalent in frontier areas of Brazil, which has called into question existing control strategies. This paper studies the costs of infection to individual miners.

445 **Social movements and the State: health reform in Brazil.**
Kurt Weyland. *World Development*, vol. 23 (1995), p. 1,699-712.
This paper describes the failure of Brazil's recent efforts to introduce equity-enhancing health reforms. Difficulties include bureaucratic policies and entrenched practices of patronage, both of which inhibit necessary changes.

446 **Primitive religion and healing: a study of folk medicine in northeast Brazil.**
Paul V. A. Williams. Cambridge, United Kingdom: D. S. Brewer for the Folklore Society, 1979. 212p. map. bibliog.
A detailed study of the role of *caboclo* folk medicine, derived mainly from African traditions, which includes prayer and other rituals, and the use of herbs. The paper contains an interesting list of herbs, accompanied by their Portuguese names, and various uses.

Urban Development

447 **L'emprise urbaine. Famille, familialisme et modernité à Bahia (Brésil).** (The urban world. Family, family systems and modern life in Bahia, Brazil.)
Michel Agier. *Cahiers des Sciences Humaines*, vol. 28/3 (1992), p. 413-37. map. bibliog.
Presents a detailed study of changing family structures in Salvador, northeast Brazil.

448 **Itinéraires urbains autour de Brasília: entre le localif et l'invasion.** (Urban itineraries around Brasília: between renting and invasion.)
Catherine Aubertin, Florence Pinton. *Cahiers des Ameriques Latines*, vol. 8 (1989), p. 91-112.
This is a valuable discussion of the occupation of satellite towns in the Federal District around Brasília, through the occupation of lots and land invasions.

449 **Popular movements in Brazil: a case study of the Movement for the Defence of *Favelados* in São Paulo.**
Anne Boran. *Bulletin of Latin American Research*, vol. 8 (1989), p. 83-109.
A study of the evolution of popular movements in Brazil, and the activities of the MDF (Movement for the Defence of *Favelados*) in the 1980s to secure improved urban services in the shanty towns. The paper provides a very detailed account of the meetings, marches, and other protests organized by the *favelados* (shanty-town residents). It points to the particular problems faced by such groups, in securing their goals and sustaining their impetus. The detail contained is such that the paper will be primarily of interest to the urban political scientist.

450   **Building up walls: the new pattern of spatial segregation in São Paulo.**
Teresa P. R. Caldeira.   *International Social Science Journal*, vol. 147 (1990), p. 55-66.
This paper argues that social and spatial segregation has intensified in São Paulo, out of fear of the poor by the rich. The affluent increasingly live in closed enclaves of walled communities with private security guards.

451   **The future of the past in the Latin American city: the case of Brazil.**
John Dickenson.   *Bulletin of Latin American Research*, vol. 13 (1994), p. 13-25.
An outline of the conservation of Brazilian cities, and the problems of reconciling the preservation of the past with rapid urban growth. The paper provides a detailed analysis of the nature and distribution of the sites protected by Brazil's conservation agency, and indicates the conflicts which exist between a diverse cultural heritage and the pressure for economic development.

452   **Two Brazilian capitals. Architecture and urbanism in Rio de Janeiro and Brasília.**
Norma Evenson.   New Haven, Connecticut; London: Yale University Press, 1973. 328p. maps. bibliog.
This book remains the essential and standard reference on the planning of Brasília, and on planning strategies in Rio de Janeiro, its precursor as capital. It is a very detailed study of two capital cities, tracing the urban improvement of Rio from the late-19th century, and then the emergence of the idea of a new capital. The work includes a comprehensive outline of the major entries from the design competition for Brasília, and a thorough discussion of the winning design of Lúcio Costa. As well as being an essential source on the design of the new capital, the volume contains much discussion of Brazilian architectural traditions, and is richly illustrated by drawings and photographs.

453   **Labor-force reproduction and urban movements. Illegal subdivision of land in São Paulo.**
Tilman Evers.   *Latin American Perspectives*, vol. 14 (1987), p. 187-203.
An examination of the issue of illegal subdivision of land in the rapidly growing metropolis of São Paulo. It describes the responses of residents, real-estate firms and municipal authorities to the situation.

454   **Metropolitan São Paulo: problems and perspectives.**
V. Faría.   In: *Cities in crisis: the urban challenge in the Americas.* Edited by M. Edel, R. Hellman.   New York: Bilner Center, 1989, p. 19-36.
This essay explores the development of Brazil's largest city, and its problems of rapid growth, poverty and pollution.

455 Law and urban change in Brazil.
Edesio Fernandes. Avebury, United Kingdom: Brookfield, 1995. 182p. bibliog.

Provides an interesting introduction to Brazil's urban policies from 1930-88. The volume's main value, however, lies in its excellent overview of urban law, and of the ways in which it affects land division, the regularization of *favelas*, and environmental matters.

456 Boom towns of the Amazon.
Brian J. Godfrey. *Geographical Review*, vol. 80 (1990), p. 103-17.

In spite of its role as a frontier, Amazonia is becoming an increasingly urban society. By 1980 over half the population lived in towns and cities. This paper examines the rapid growth of boom towns created by migration to work in mines, lumbering, and agro-pastoralism. The focus is on southeastern Pará with a case-study of the road-junction town of Xinguara.

457 Modernising the Brazilian city.
Brian J. Godfrey. *Geographical Review*, vol. 81 (1991), p. 18-35.

An exploration of the evolution of the city form in Brazil, from its colonial roots. The paper provides a good summary, which focuses on Rio de Janeiro and São Paulo. It describes the emergence of the modern metropolis, and the contemporary trends towards urban dispersal and social segregation.

458 The development of the under-developed city: public sanitation in São Paulo, Brazil, 1885-1913.
G. M. Greenfield. *Luso-Brazilian Review*, vol. 17 (1980), p. 107-18.

This is an interesting survey of key elements in the improvement of the urban infrastructure of a booming late-19th-century city. It describes the need for, and process of, providing street cleaning and garbage disposal.

459 The modernist city. An anthropological critique of Brasília.
James Holston. Chicago; London: University of Chicago Press, 1989. 370p. maps. bibliog.

A fascinating analysis of the progress of the city of Brasília, which explores the successes and failures of the utopian notions of architects and government. It draws upon perspectives from anthropology, architecture, social history, and urban studies. Providing a penetrating critique of the city three decades after its creation, the book assesses the limitations of the original design and the adjustments made to it by its inhabitants. An important element of the text is its discussion of the unplanned components, the squatter settlements, and the planned and unplanned satellite cities. The volume provides an important companion to Evenson's earlier work (see item no. 452) for an understanding of the city.

460 **The transformation of São Paulo.**
G. Leite de Barros. In: *I saw the city invincible: urban portraits of Latin America.* Edited by G. M. Joseph, M. D. Szuchman. Wilmington, Delaware: Scholarly Resources Imprint, 1996, p. 149-64.
Provides a summary history of the growth of the city to circa 1940.

461 **The singular city of Salvador.**
Robert M. Levine. *Luso-Brazilian Review*, vol. 30 (1993), p. 59-70.
This paper offers a very nice portrait of the growth of the city and of its townscape. It also deals with the people, Afro-Brazilian traditions, and conditions of work and life. The main focus of the study is on the 19th century.

462 **State retreat, governance and metropolitan restructuring in Brazil.**
Marcus C. Melo. *International Journal of Urban and Regional Research*, vol. 19 (1995), p. 342-57.
1982 marked the end of a period in which the military government had intervened in urban issues. This paper describes its housing policies, the role of the National Housing Bank, and the construction boom. It also notes that in the subsequent period of economic difficulty, there has been a stagnation in urban and housing policy.

463 **The myth of marginality. Urban poverty and politics in Rio de Janeiro.**
Janice E. Perlman. Berkeley, California; London: University of California Press, 1976. 342p. maps. bibliog.
This remains the best and most detailed study of *favela* life in Brazil. It provides an extensive analysis of Rio's shanty towns and their inhabitants. There is discussion of the place of the shanty town within the city structure, and of the characteristics of the migrant to the urban slum. A thorough review of the literature on notions of the marginality of the urban poor is followed by the evidence of Dr. Perlman's research as to the features of the social, cultural, economic and political marginalization of the *favelados*.The work also sets efforts to remove the shanties into a political context.

464 **Dark mirror of modernization. The favelas of Rio de Janeiro in the boom years, 1948-1960.**
Julio César Pino. *Journal of Urban History*, vol. 22 (1996), p. 419-53.
An excellent study of the rapid expansion of *favelas* in Rio in parallel with the economic expansion of the city. Important detail is provided on their location and function, and the race and occupations of their residents.

465 **Habitat ouvrier de Volta Redonda: du symbole populiste à la logique capitaliste.** (Workers' housing in Volta Redonda: from populist symbol to capitalist logic.)
Rosélia Piquet. *Cahiers des Amériques Latines*, vol. 5 (1985), p. 42-53.

Volta Redonda was Brazil's first modern steelworks, which opened in 1946 along with an associated company town. This study examines the development of the latter, and its transformation from a planned company town to a municipality with private dwellings.

466 **Restructuring in large Brazilian cities: the centre/periphery model.**
Luiz César de Queiroz Ribeiro, Luciana Correa do Lago.
International Journal of Urban and Regional Research, vol. 19 (1995), p. 369-82.

This is a useful comparative paper, which suggests that Brazil shares a common experience of economic crisis and urban restructuring with other parts of Latin America. It provides evidence of declining population densities in metropolitan areas, and new forms of socio-spatial segregation. The paper also deals with the emergence of a separation of the middle class, and the spread of poverty in the urban landscape.

467 **Squatters and urban growth in Amazonia.**
J. Timmons Roberts. *Geographical Review*, vol. 82 (1992), p. 441-57.

The development of the Carajás iron mine in Amazonia required the construction of a planned town for its workers. However, the project also attracted large numbers of migrants. This paper describes the growth of the spontaneous boom town of Parauapebas adjacent to the company town of Carajás.

468 **Social policy in a non-democratic régime: the case of public housing in Brazil.**
Gil Shidlo. Boulder, Colorado; Oxford: Westview Press, 1990. 164p. bibliog.

Though focused largely on a single housing project in São Paulo, this is a study of the use of patron-client links to secure urban political support. It provides an outline of housing finance systems from 1880, and of the activities of the National Housing Bank from 1964-86.

469 **The capital of hope: Brasília and its people.**
Alex Shoumatoff. Albuquerque, New Mexico: University of New Mexico Press, 1980. 212p.

A journalistic view of the origins of Brasília and how it evolved. It is an anecdotal account, which looks at the project, its frontier role, and the lives of its people. It also contains some description of the area's natural history.

470 **Structural sources of socio-economic segregation in Brazilian metropolitan areas.**
Edward E. Telles. *American Journal of Sociology*, vol. 100 (1995), p. 1,199-223.

Examines the impact of industrialization and urbanization on residential segregation, as measured by income. The paper uses data from the 1980 census to test several hypotheses using statistical methods. It suggests that more-industrialized cities have lower segregation because inequalities of income are less marked. In some cities, therefore, segregation is by class; in others, especially in the Northeast, there is segregation by poverty and race.

471 **Housing in Brazil: an introduction to recent literature.**
L. Valladares, A. Figueredo. *Bulletin of Latin American Research*, vol. 2, no. 2 (1983), p. 69-91.

Although essentially a review article, this paper provides a very good introduction to housing issues from 1950-80. Its coverage includes *favelas*, self-help housing, government housing policy, and social movements related to housing.

472 **Manchester and São Paulo: problems of rapid urban growth.**
Edited by John D. Wirth, Robert L. Jones. Stanford, California: Stanford University Press, 1978. 224p.

These two cities form a somewhat improbable pairing, but in this study they are argued as being paradigm sites which exemplify rapid urban change brought about by industrialization. Some of the essays contained are comparative, while others focus on only one of the cities. Thus religion, soccer, intellectual ideas and legal institutions are compared, while industry and modernist poets are considered for São Paulo alone.

Politics and Government

General

473 **To get out of the mud. Neighbourhood associativism in Recife, 1964-88.**
Willem Assies. Amsterdam: CEDLA, 1991. 332p. maps. bibliog.
This is a detailed study of municipal politics, which explores the formation of neighbourhood associations under changing political circumstances at the national level. It discusses the growth of Recife, the populist politics of the period 1945-64, the impact of the military régime, and the activities of a left-wing council after 1985.

474 **Electoral participation in Brazil (1945-1978): the legislation, the party system, and electoral turnouts.**
Olavi Brasil de Lima. *Luso-Brazilian Review*, vol. 20, no. 1 (1983), p. 65-92.
A useful introduction to post-1945 politics in Brazil, which had two major periods: pluralism from 1945-64, and authoritarianism from 1964-78. The paper examines the participation rates of the electorate at federal and state elections, and offers reflections on the party system.

475 **Urban politics in Brazil: the rise of populism 1925-1945.**
Michael L. Conniff. Pittsburgh, Pennsylvania: University of Pittsburgh Press, 1981. 230p. map. bibliog.
Populism has been a key element in Brazilian politics in the 20th century. This study concentrates on Rio de Janeiro, and provides a good portrait of the city in the 1920s and 1930s. It explores the emergence of a mass urban electorate and the rise of charismatic leaders in the 1920s, and Rio's links with the populist régime of Getúlio Vargas from 1930-45.

476 **Brazil: a political analysis.**
Peter Flynn. London: Ernest Benn; Boulder, Colorado: Westview Press, 1978. 564p. map. bibliog.
This remains the best overview of the politics of Republican Brazil. It covers the period 1889-1977, concentrating on: the coffee oligarchy and the Old Republic; the Vargas era; post-1945 democracy; the instability of the early 1960s; and the authoritarian years. It is an essential reference source for any student of the politics of Brazil in the 20th century.

477 **Amazonia and the politics of geopolitics.**
R. Foresta. *Geographical Review*, vol. 82 (1992), p. 128-42.
A useful short appraisal of the role of geopolitics in shaping the policy of Brazil's military régime towards Amazonia. An awareness of the military attitudes to the occupation of the national territory and the defence of political borders is essential to an understanding of Brazil's advance into Amazonia in the 1970s.

478 **Popular organization and democracy in Rio de Janeiro: a tale of two favelas.**
Robert Gay. Philadelphia, Pennsylvania: Temple University Press, 1994. 192p. maps. bibliog.
Offers two case-studies of different approaches made by the urban poor of Rio de Janeiro to obtain improvements. In one case the strategy to secure water, education and electricity, etc., is via delivering block votes to political candidates; in the other, these services are secured by community action.

479 **Latin American laws and institutions.**
Albert S. Golbert, Yenny Nun. New York: Praeger, 1982. 574p. map.
This is a guide to legal concepts and institutions, on a continental basis. It covers: legal traditions; constitutions; external relations; and international and labour law. Use of the index will yield material on Brazilian constitutions, the law relating to economic and social matters, and foreign relations. Though it is a general reference, it does provide Brazilian material and some grounds for comparison between legal systems across the continent.

480 **Civil Service reform in Brazil: principles versus practice.**
Lawrence S. Graham. Austin, Texas; London: University of Texas Press, 1968. 234p.
Essentially an historical study of unsuccessful attempts to introduce a US-style civil service into Brazil in the period 1930-64. Although it is a specialized piece of work, it does provide useful insights into the nature of the Brazilian bureaucracy.

481 **Patronage and politics in nineteenth century Brazil.**
Richard Graham. Stanford, California: Stanford University Press, 1990. 382p. map. bibliog.
Patronage has been a significant element in Brazilian politics since independence. This study deals with the period 1840-89, and explores the way in which local and national élites used the patronage of protection and jobs to secure their interests.

482   **The politics of Amazonian deforestation.**
      Andrew Hurrell. *Journal of Latin American Studies*, vol. 23 (1991),
      p. 197-215.

A very useful contribution to the debate about Amazonia, arguing that concerns
relating to the region's complex and fragile environment are compounded by domestic,
transnational and international pressures. The paper provides a good, wide-ranging
assessment of the subject.

483   **The Workers' Party and democratization in Brazil.**
      Margaret E. Keck.   New Haven, Connecticut; London: Yale
      University Press, 1992. 316p. bibliog.

The PT (Partido dos Trabalhadores – Workers' Party) emerged in the 1970s from an
upsurge of labour activity and debates on the Left about the kind of political parties
which should develop with Brazil's return to democracy. The PT differed profoundly
from traditional parties, by being socialist and democratic. This book concentrates on
its development from the 1970s to the early 1980s, but makes reference to the strong
support for the PT candidate (Luís Inácio da Silva – generally known as 'Lula') in the
presidential elections of 1989.

484   **Legal opposition politics under authoritarian rule in Brazil.**
      The case of the MDB, 1966-79.
      Maria D'Alva Kinzo.   Basingstoke, United Kingdom: Macmillan,
      1988. 284p. bibliog.

In 1966 the military régime dissolved existing political parties to create a two-party
system of 'government' and 'opposition'. This book explores the problems of creating
and sustaining a party in opposition within an authoritarian system. The MDB
(Movimento Democrático Brasileiro – Brazilian Democratic Movement) defined itself
essentially by opposition to the régime and pressure for a return to democracy.

485   **The 1989 presidential election: electoral behaviour in a Brazilian**
      city.
      Maria D'Alva Kinzo.   *Journal of Latin American Studies*, vol. 25
      (1993), p. 313-30.

A case-study of voting behaviour in Brazil's first direct presidential election for
twenty-nine years, based on research in Presidente Prudente in western São Paulo.

486   **A new type of party. The Brazilian PT.**
      Michael Lowy.   *Latin American Perspectives*, vol. 14 (1987),
      p. 453-64.

The Partido dos Trabalhadores (PT), founded in 1979, was distinct in Brazil in that it
was a mass party for working people, which was democratic and anti-capitalist. It has
secured some notable success in post-1984 elections. This paper traces the party's
origins and early history.

487 **'Governing for everyone': the Workers' Party administration in São Paulo, 1989-1992.**
Fiona Macauley. *Bulletin of Latin American Research*, vol. 15 (1996), p. 211-29.
Rather to its own surprise, the Workers' Party won control of Brazil's largest city in the elections of 1989. This paper explores the party's organization of the municipal government, its approach to specific problems, such as urban transport, and the conflicts which arose within the party, and between the party and the administration.

488 **The transition to democracy in Brazil.**
Scott Mainwaring. *Journal of Interamerican Studies*, vol. 28, no. 1 (1986), p. 149-79.
A very useful near-contemporary study of the return to democracy and the crucial activities of 1983-85 in Brazilian politics. It explores the circumstances and key elements in this crucial phase of Brazil's recent political history.

489 **Democracy in Brazil and the Southern Cone: achievements and problems.**
Scott Mainwaring. *Journal of Interamerican Studies*, vol. 37, no. 1 (1995), p. 113-79.
Presents an extensive study of the achievements and failures of the countries which returned to democracy after 1983. Argentina, Uruguay, Brazil and Chile are examined on the basis of their economic performance, ability to deal with poverty and inequity, democratic practices, and degree of popular support. In the case of Brazil there are reservations, because despite economic growth there were inflationary problems, inequalities persisted, early democracy was weak, and popular support was modest.

490 **La géographie électorale du Brésil après l'élection présidentielle du 1989.** (The electoral geography of Brazil after the 1989 presidential election.)
Odile Marchal, Hervé Théry, Philippe Waniez. *Cahiers des Sciences Humaines*, vol. 28 (1992), p. 535-54.
An interesting analysis of voting patterns in the two rounds of the presidential election of 1989. The paper is a detailed piece of political geography and contains some fascinating maps.

491 **For the liberation of Brazil.**
Carlos Marighela, translated by John Butt, Rosemary Sheed.
Harmondsworth, United Kingdom: Penguin Books, 1971. 190p.
Carlos Marighela was an orthodox and leading Communist in Brazil until 1967, when he became an urban guerrilla involved in opposition to the military régime of the late 1960s. These collected letters and other writings articulate the thinking and strategy of Marighela's Action for National Liberation movement, which became active in the cities, rather than the countryside. Marighela was shot dead by the police in 1969.

492 **Electoral behaviour in Brazil: the 1994 presidential election.**
R. Meneguello. *International Social Science Journal*, vol. 146
(1995), p. 627-41.

1994 was the year of Brazil's second post-military election. This article argues that President Cardoso's success was a reflection of popular support for his economic policies, but also of the continuing weakness of party politics.

493 **The Brazilian voter: mass politics in democratic transition, 1974-1986.**
Kurt von Mettenheim. Pittsburgh, Pennsylvania: University of
Pittsburgh Press, 1995. 296p. bibliog.

This is an exploration of voting practices in the volatile period of Brazil's return from authoritarian rule to democracy. Despite its title, it takes a long view and includes a useful history of the party system from 1822-1989.

494 **Democracy, citizenship and representation: rural social movements in southern Brazil, 1978-1990.**
Zander Navarro. *Bulletin of Latin American Research*, vol. 13
(1994), p. 129-54.

A portrait of the re-emergence of rural social protest movements in southern Brazil in the 1980s, after the return to democracy. The paper deals with the protests of a number of groups: small farmers displaced by dams; rural workers; the landless (*sem terra*); and, since 1989, women rural workers. It discusses the dilemmas faced by these movements in attempting to secure their objectives in the 1990s.

495 **Dictatorship and armed struggle in Brazil.**
João Quartim, translated by David Fernbach. London: New Left
Books, 1971. 222p. map.

This is an insider's account of revolutionary opposition to the military régime of the 1960s. It examines the evolution of Brazilian politics from 1930-69, the breakup of the traditional Left, and the adoption of guerrilla resistance in the cities rather than in the countryside.

496 **Bureaucrats and politicians in current Brazilian politics.**
Eliza P. Reis. *International Social Science Journal*, vol. 123 (1990),
p. 19-30.

An exploration of the problems faced by Brazil in the return to democracy after twenty years of bureaucratic authoritarian rule.

497 **Brazil: politics in a patrimonial society.**
Riordan Roett. New York; London: Praeger Publishers, 1992. 4th ed.
190p. map. bibliog.

A helpful exploration of the role of institutions and socio-economic groups in what is essentially an élitist political system. It outlines the evolution of the system, and of the political parties of the period 1945-64. It devotes major attention to the role of the military before 1964, and to the Military Republic, but also considers other players such as the Church, labour, students, business, and the state bureaucracy.

498 **Without fear of being happy: Lula, the Workers Party and Brazil.**
Emir Sader, Ken Silverstein. Cambridge, United Kingdom;
New York: Verso, 1991. 178p.

A study of the rise of the PT (Workers' Party) and the success of its leader, 'Lula' (Luís Inácio da Silva), in coming a close second in the presidential election of 1989. The PT is the largest explicitly socialist party in Latin America, with a platform which includes land reform, 'democratization' of the state sector, and a domestically-oriented economic policy.

499 **"Order and Progress": a political history of Brazil.**
Ronald M. Schneider. Boulder, Colorado: Westview Press, 1991.
486p. map. chapter notes.

Uses the national motto to explore the tension between progress and order, particularly the role of the military, the Church, landowners and industrialists. It spans the period from colonial rule to the Collor government of 1990. The volume contains helpful chapter notes.

500 **Politics in Brazil, 1930-1964. An experiment in democracy.**
Thomas E. Skidmore. London; New York: Oxford University Press,
1967. 446p. bibliog.

An essential and highly readable review of a crucial period in Brazil's political and economic history. It explores the major elements of this era – the Vargas dictatorship, the economic boom of the Kubitschek years, the uncertainty of the early 1960s, and the military coup of 1964 – in great detail. Skidmore provides a meticulous portrait of the political and economic circumstances of the time, and his discussion of the prelude to the military takeover is of particular importance. This is a key reference work on the period.

501 **Urbanization, race and class in Brazil.**
Glaucio Ary Dillon Soares, Nelson do Valle Silva. *Latin American
Research Review*, vol. 22, no. 2 (1987), p. 155-76.

This paper provides a detailed analysis of the 1982 state and municipal elections – the first free elections in Brazil for twenty years. It concentrates on the elections in Rio de Janeiro, and the influence of social class and race on voting patterns.

502 **Brazil in transition.**
Robert G. Wesson, David V. Fleischer. New York: Praeger, 1983.
198p. maps. bibliog.

A useful overview of the Brazilian political scene, this volume covers political history, Brazil as a political society, political institutions, and the history of political parties from 1945-82.

The military

503 Brazil.
Adrian J. English. In: *Regional defence profile number 1. Latin America.* London: Jane's Publishing Co. Ltd., 1988, p. 52-76. maps.

Provides a summary of the structure of Brazil's armed forces, with details of each branch in terms of units, weapons and deployment. The essay's focus is on the military as an armed force, rather than a political one.

504 Civilian-military relations in Brazil, 1889-1898.
June E. Hahner. Columbia, South Carolina: University of South Carolina Press, 1969. 232p. bibliog.

This is an historical study, which provides a broad view of the military involvement in the first decade of the Old Republic. The military had helped to establish republican government, and saw themselves as its guardian. In addition to its inherent interest, this book is of relevance with regard to the continuing influence of the military in Brazilian politics.

505. The armed nation: the Brazilian corporate mystique.
Robert A. Hayes. Tempe, Arizona: Center For Latin American Studies, Arizona State University, 1989. 282p. bibliog.

Examines the historic role of the military, and the mystique that there is a distinct role reserved for the armed forces in Brazilian politics. They are perceived to have a constitutional mission as a permanent national institution, securing organization, structure and integration to public life.

506 Perspectives on armed politics in Brazil.
Henry H. Keith, Robert A. Hayes. Tempe, Arizona: Center for Latin American Studies, Arizona State University, 1976. 258p. maps.

A very important long view of the military from the colonial period. This book is a major reference work on the role of the military in Brazilian politics. It explores military intervention in national and state politics, and in foreign policy, as well as its participation in foreign military campaigns.

507 The politics of military rule in Brazil, 1964-85.
Thomas E. Skidmore. New York; Oxford: Oxford University Press, 1988. 420p. map.

This substantial volume is a sequel to item no. 500, written with the same readable thoroughness. It charts the changing nature of twenty years of military rule in Brazil, from the 1964 coup to the deep repression of 1969-77, and the gradual relaxing of military control. In addition to this political analysis, there is appraisal of the 'economic miracle' of the period, and the role of the Church and the unions. Also included is an early assessment of the prospects for Brazil's return to democracy. This is a key text for the understanding of recent Brazilian politics. There is no bibliography, but copious notes provide an important source for further reading.

Amazonia and Siberia. Legal aspects of the preservation of the environment and development in the last open spaces.
See item no. 100.

Law and urban change in Brazil.
See item no. 455.

Foreign Relations

508 United States penetration of Brazil.
Jan Knippers Black. Manchester, United Kingdom: Manchester
University Press, 1977. 314p. bibliog.
A detailed study of US involvement in the coup of 1964, and its activities in
influencing the military, big business, the media, and labour in the years of the
military régime. It is a critical commentary, which suggests collusion between US
government and private interests in support of what were seen as the best interests of
the United States in the hemisphere, and to counter popular movements hostile to
foreign investments. The book examines American involvement in the manipulation of
the media, containment of rural and urban protest, and the 'special relationship'
between the United States and Brazilian military élites. The author makes use of a
wide range of American and Brazilian government sources.

509 The rich neighbour policy: Rockefeller and Kaiser in Brazil.
Elizabeth Anne Cobbs. New Haven, Connecticut; London: Yale
University Press, 1992. 274p. bibliog.
Represents a rather unusual, supportive view of foreign interest in Brazil. It explores
the transfer of technology and capital from the United States in the period after 1945,
with Nelson Rockefeller and Henry Kaiser encouraging American assistance in
Brazil's agricultural and vehicle industries.

**510 The Americanization of Brazil. A study of U.S. Cold War
diplomacy in the Third World, 1945-54.**
Gerald K. Haines. Wilmington, Delaware: Scholarly Resources Inc.,
1989. 228p. bibliog.
An extensive review of US policy regarding world peace, democracy and open trade
as it affected Brazil. Brazil was seen as a market for goods and capital, a source of raw
materials, and as a country to be protected from international Communism. This
volume provides an interesting portrait of the United States' self-perception of its role
in the Americas.

120

511 **Requiem for revolution: the United States and Brazil, 1961-1969.**
Ruth Leacock. Kent, Ohio; London: Kent State University Press,
1990. 318p. map. bibliog.

This is a highly-critical study of US involvement in the overthrow of the Goulart
government in 1964, and of its continuing support for the military régime, despite its
increasingly repressive policies during the 1960s.

512 **Averting a Latin American nuclear arms race: new prospects and
challenges for Argentinian-Brazilian nuclear co-operation.**
Edited by Paul L. Leventhal, Sharon Tanzer. Basingstoke, United
Kingdom: Macmillan, 1992. 258p.

Following an accord in 1990 between Brazil and Argentina over nuclear weapons,
these papers explore related issues of cooperation, economic benefits, and surveillance
of nuclear activities. They provide an interesting insight into the politics of nuclear
arms control, but also of positive relations between two countries which have been
traditional rivals.

513 **The Brazilian-American alliance, 1937-1945.**
Frank D. McCann, Jnr. Princeton, New Jersey: Princeton University
Press, 1973. 528p. map. bibliog.

A detailed study of the complex relations between Brazil and the United States during
the Second World War, which involved attitudes towards Germany and Brazil's
German immigrant community, Brazil's economic development, and the participation
of Brazilian troops in the Allied forces in Italy.

514 **International politics and the sea: the case of Brazil.**
Michael A. Morris. Boulder, Colorado: Westview Press, 1979. 292p.

The particular interest of this work is that it examines the place of the oceans in
Brazil's domestic and foreign politics. It also considers the topics of the navy,
shipping, and offshore resources.

515 **Brazil and the quiet intervention, 1964.**
Phyllis R. Parker. Austin, Texas; London: University of Texas Press,
1979. 148p. bibliog.

A rather journalistic account of US involvement in the overthrow of the Goulart
régime and the installation of the military régime. It argues that the United States,
hostile to leftist governments in Latin America, believed that this intervention of the
military in Brazilian politics was also in the best interests of America.

516 **Contemporary Brazilian foreign policy: the international strategy
of an emerging power.**
William Perry. Beverley Hills, California; London: Sage, 1976. 90p.
bibliog.

Brazil is viewed in this work as a potential great power. Its foreign policy is reviewed
in the context of economic, political and strategic considerations. There is also
discussion of policy as it relates to the United States, Latin American neighbours,

European countries, the then Communist bloc, and other Third-World countries. Although rather dated and brief, the volume provides a useful introduction.

517 **The challenge of cooperation: Argentina and Brazil, 1939-1955.**
Gabriel Porcile. *Journal of Latin American Studies*, vol. 27 (1995), p. 129-59.

Brazil and Argentina are traditional rivals in South America. This study analyses economic cooperation between them in the light of external factors, and the influences of their domestic political and economic circumstances.

518 **Absent-minded imperialism: Britain and the expansion of empire in nineteenth-century Brazil.**
Peter Rivière. London; New York: Tauris Academic Studies, 1995. 194p. map. bibliog.

This is a rather peripheral work, but it is an interesting portrait of foreign relations over territorial boundaries. It provides a detailed study of a small boundary dispute between Britain and Brazil along the border of British Guiana, which began in 1838 and was only resolved by arbitration sixty years later.

519 **Brazil: foreign policy of a future world power.**
Ronald M. Schneider. Boulder, Colorado: Westview Press, 1976. 236p. map. bibliog.

The focus of this book is on the foreign policy of the Geisel administration (1974-79), but it also explores the factors shaping Brazil's foreign policies in general, and provides a useful insight into the motivation of the various players: the president; the military; the foreign and economic ministries; and non-governmental agencies such as business, the Church, and the press. It thus offers a general introduction to Brazil's foreign affairs, as well as a specific case-study.

520 **Brazil's foreign policy under Collor.**
Ademar Seabra de Cruz Jnr., Antonio Ricardo F. Cavalcante, Luiz Perone. *Journal of Interamerican Studies*, vol. 35, no. 1 (1993), p. 119-44.

Following a general introduction to Brazilian foreign policy, this paper explores global issues of debt, technology, drugs and the environment, and then regional-level links with, for example, the United States, Europe and Latin America.

521 **The Brazilian monarchy and the South American republics, 1822-1831.**
Ron Seckinger. Baton Rouge, Louisiana: Louisiana State University Press, 1984. 188p. maps. bibliog.

This is a study of Brazil's early foreign relations. It explores the shaping of dealings between Brazil and the newly-independent republics of former Spanish America. The book suggests that the latter were suspicious of Brazil's monarchical system, and over issues of territory, boundaries and trade.

522 **Brazil's multilateral relations. Between First and Third Worlds.**
Wayne A. Selcher. Boulder, Colorado: Westview, 1978. 302p.
Provides a very broad view of Brazil's external relations in a number of spheres.
These include: dealings with the United Nations and other inter-governmental
organizations; involvement in international commodity agreements such as those for
coffee, sugar, cocoa and iron ore; participation in inter-American agencies; and links
with Africa.

523 **Brazil's relations with Latin America: a pattern of bilateral
cooperation.**
Wayne A. Selcher. *Journal of Interamerican Studies*, vol. 28, no. 2
(1986), p. 67-99.
In a sense, this is a more detailed and specific extension of item no. 522. It provides a
useful summary of intra-continental links over the period 1970-86, dealing with
political, economic and security issues.

524 **Cold warriors and coups d'etat.**
W. Michael Weis. Albuquerque, New Mexico: University of New
Mexico Press, 1993. 264p.
This volume examines the deterioration of US-Brazil relations between 1945 and
1964, following their close collaboration during the Second World War. The decline is
ascribed to American attitudes during the Cold War, and suspicion of anyone 'soft on
Communism'.

525 **The United States and Brazil: limits of influence.**
Robert Wesson. New York: Praeger, 1981. 180p. bibliog.
A study of the evolving relationship between the United States and Brazil since the
1930s. Opening with the Vargas period, the book's main concern is with the years
1960-80, detailing America's involvement in the military coup and support for the
régime. It then refers to Brazilian 'independence' from American influence in the
1970s, and later friction over nuclear power and human rights. Also discussed are
issues of trade, aid and investment.

Economy

General

526 The Brazilian economy. Growth and development.
Werner Baer. New York; London: Praeger, 1989. 3rd ed. 402p. map.
bibliog.

This is the definitive introduction to the economy of Brazil, giving a good historical perspective and contemporary breadth. The volume provides a comprehensive economic history from colonial times to 1987, with considerable detail on post-1945 advances and setbacks. It then deals with a range of contemporary issues, which include inflation, foreign investment, the public sector, regional imbalances, and trends in agriculture and manufacturing.

527 Brazil and Mexico: patterns in late development.
Edited by S. A. Hewlett, R. S. Weinart. Philadelphia, Pennsylvania: Institute for the Study of Human Issues, 1984. 350p.

Consists of a set of comparative essays, which explore development patterns, foreign investment, the role of the State, and trade unionism in the two countries.

528 Underdevelopment and development in Brazil.
Nathaniel H. Leff. London; Boston, Massachusetts: George Allen & Unwin, 1982. 2 vols.

This study of Brazil's economic development is an attempt to explore the reasons for the varying growth rate of the Brazilian economy since independence. The first volume, *Economic structure and change, 1822-1947*, explores the growth process in the 19th century and from 1900-47. The second volume, *Reassessing the obstacles to economic development*, provides a more critical appraisal of the factors inhibiting rapid progress in the 19th century.

529 **The political economy of poverty, equity and growth: Brazil and Mexico.**
Angus Maddison and associates.   Washington, DC: World Bank/
Oxford University Press, 1992. 248p. bibliog.

A critical evaluation of the economic experience of Brazil and Mexico from 1950-85, examining the processes which resulted in growth, and their impacts on poverty and equity. In both cases capital accumulation and rapid growth of the labour force are seen as key factors, but there is a suggestion that a fuller play of market forces, as favoured by the World Bank, would have been even more stimulating. Brazil is discussed on pages 17-110.

530 **The roots of state intervention in the Brazilian economy.**
Gustavo Maia Gomes.   London; New York: Praeger, 1986. 378p.
bibliog.

This book provides a political critique of Brazil's development strategies, arguing that the country is characterized by blatant class exploitation, and that the dominant class has used the State to maintain and expand its dominance. It concentrates on the period 1930-64, when the State became involved in industrialization, and the period of military rule from 1964-85. It argues that economic policy is a product of a social process in which the working class is controlled by wage policy and corporate unionization.

531 **The Brazilian economy in the eighties.**
Jorge Salazar-Carillo, Roberto Fendt, Jnr.   New York; Oxford:
Pergamon Press, 1985. 192p.

Discusses a number of key issues for the Brazilian economy in the early 1980s. It provides a useful introduction to the topics of debt, inflation, trade and foreign investment.

532 **Explaining bureaucratic independence in Brazil: the experience of the National Economic Development Bank.**
Eliza J. Willis.   *Journal of Latin American Studies*, vol. 27 (1995),
p. 625-61.

The BNDE (National Economic Development Bank) has had a crucial role in the economic development of Brazil since the 1950s. This study explores the ways in which it secured a degree of autonomy from presidential interference and was able to foster economic progress.

Fishing, forestry and mining

533 **Alternatives to deforestation. Steps toward sustainable use of the Amazon rain forest.**
Anthony B. Anderson. New York: Columbia University Press, 1990. 282p. maps.

This study deals with the Amazon rainforest in Brazil and neighbouring countries, and explores alternative uses to deforestation, including those practised by the inhabitants. It deals with natural forest management, agro-forestry, and landscape recovery. Useful bibliographies are included at the ends of chapters.

534 **The subsidy from nature. Palm forests, peasantry and development on an Amazon frontier.**
Anthony B. Anderson, Peter H. May, Michael J. Balick. New York: Columbia University Press, 1991. 234p. maps. bibliog.

A detailed study of the future potential of the babassu palm as a resource. The work outlines the environment and natural history of the tree, and its present use in the household and market economies.

535 **Brazil's export promotion policy (1980-1984): impacts on the Amazon's industrial wood sector.**
John Browder. *Journal of Developing Areas*, vol. 27 (1987), p. 285-304.

The exploitation of the rainforest has been controversial, particularly in the extraction of mahogany. This paper explores the consequences of government export incentives in stimulating a timber boom, and the specific consequences for mahogany.

536 **Anatomy of the Amazon gold rush.**
David Cleary. Basingstoke, United Kingdom: Macmillan, 1990. 246p. maps. bibliog.

A very good assessment of small-scale gold-mines (*garimpos*) in Maranhão, discussing the social and economic issues prompted by the spontaneous 'rushes' to gold discoveries. It also comments on the Serra Pelada gold-mine, and the conflicts between the gold-prospectors (*garimpeiros*), formal mining companies, and the State.

537 **Sons of the sea goddess. Economic practice and discursive conflict in Brazil.**
Antonius C. G. M. Robben. New York: Columbia University Press, 1989. 310p. map. bibliog.

A detailed monograph on the economy of a northeastern fishing community. It deals with ecology and fishing practices, and with the settlement, life and society of the fishermen.

538 **Tropical hardwood from the Brazilian Amazon. A study of the timber industry in western Pará.**
M. A. F. Ros-Tonen. Saarbrücken, Germany; Fort Lauderdale, Florida: Verlag breitenbach Publishers, 1993. 280p. maps. bibliog.
This study is distinct in that it provides a thorough and straightforward account of forestry as an economic activity in Amazonia.

539 **Man, fishes and the Amazon.**
Nigel J. H. Smith. New York: Columbia University Press, 1981. 180p. maps. bibliog.
Essentially this is an account of peasant fishing in Amazonia, which considers fishing methods, yields and folklore. It is a detailed study, but gives a useful portrait of an important element in the subsistence economy of Amazonia.

Energy

540 **Hydroelectric dams on Brazil's Xingú river and indigenous peoples.**
Leinad Ayer do O. Santos, Lúcia M. M. de Andrade, translated by Robin Wright. Cambridge, Massachusetts: Cultural Survival Inc; São Paulo, Brazil: Pro-Indian Commission of São Paulo, 1990. 192p. maps.
This volume was part of a campaign to promote discussion of the impact of a seven-dam project on the Xingú upon native peoples. The work is wide-ranging, covering energy policy and technology, environmental impacts, and native groups. It makes highly effective use of advertisements and press cuttings, and provides a very good insight into the conflict between energy policy and the environment.

541 **The politicized market: alcohol in Brazil's energy strategy.**
Michael Barzelay. Berkeley, California; London: University of California Press, 1986. 290p. bibliog.
Brazil's response to the world oil crisis of the early 1970s was to develop the production of fuel alcohol from sugar cane. This resulted in an increase in cane production, the construction of distilleries, and the installation of new car production lines. Barzelay's study of political economy examines the relations between the key players – the State, cane growers, and the State oil monopoly.

542 **Brazil's National Alcohol Program. Technology and development in an authoritarian regime.**
F. Joseph Demetrius. New York: Praeger, 1990. 186p. bibliog.
The National Alcohol Program was a bold scheme, involving government, agriculture, and industry at the time of the oil crisis of the 1970s. This study looks at the agro-industrial base, the market, and the political programme. It contains an appendix on

the technology involved in using cane-alcohol as fuel. The work provides a good review of an important economic episode, which embraced the State, technology, large-scale agriculture, and industrial production.

543 **Industrialization and energy in Brazil. Third World case study 6.**
John Humphrey, David Wield. Milton Keynes, United Kingdom:
Open University Press, 1983. 52p. maps. bibliog.

This is a brief summary of recent trends in Brazilian industrialization, concentrating on the car industry, and the consequences of the 1973 oil crisis for fuel provision.

544 **Alcohol fuels revisited: the costs and benefits of energy dependence in Brazil.**
Marc Levinson. *Journal of Developing Areas*, vol. 21 (1987), p. 243-58.

Outlines Brazil's alcohol fuel policy since 1975, and examines debates over its continued use.

545 **The Light: Brazilian Traction, Light and Power Co. Ltd., 1899-1945.**
Duncan McDowall. Toronto; Buffalo, New York; London:
University of Toronto Press, 1988. 460p. maps.

The 'Light' was a crucial element in the early modernization of Rio de Janeiro and São Paulo. This is a detailed study of a key Canadian-based company, which was responsible for pioneering the provision of electricity and urban services in the two cities.

546 **The political economy of Brazilian oil.**
Laura Randall. Westport, Connecticut; London: Praeger, 1993. 316p.
maps. bibliog.

An excellent survey of Brazil's petroleum industry, outlining its history and reporting in detail on the State oil monopoly, Petrobrás. The company was established in 1953, as an element of economic nationalism, to control oil production and distribution. It became one of Brazil's major companies, with a wide range of activities. The book deals with the organization and development of the industry, and issues of employment, research and environmental impacts.

547 **Large scale hydroelectric projects and Brazilian politics.**
Rolf Sternberg. *Revista Geografica*, vol. 101 (1985), p. 29-44.

A useful summary of the development of large-scale hydroelectric plants in Brazil. It contains a good review of the process since 1964, and the recent development of schemes in excess of 200-megawatt capacity, such as Itaipu and Tucuruí. The role of the State power company, Eletrobrás, is also discussed.

548   **Brazil.**
   In: *Energy in Latin America. Production, consumption, and future growth.*   Kang Wu, Cynthia Obadia.   Westport, Connecticut; London: Praeger, 1995, p. 69-90.

This chapter provides a brief but up-to-date summary of the industry, covering energy sources and consumption. The data used cover the period up to 1992.

Agriculture

549 Sowing the whirlwind: soya expansion and social change in southern Brazil.
Edited by Geert A. Banck, Kees den Boer. Amsterdam: CEDLA, 1991. 196p. map. bibliog.

The soyabean has become a significant crop in Brazil only since the 1970s, and the country now ranks as a major exporter. Its introduction has had a marked effect on the rural economy of the South, with a shift from small-scale polyculture to agribusiness production for the world market. This study traces the soyabean's rise in output in Brazil and the consequences for rural communities in the South.

550 Just one foot in the market: internal strategies of small horticultural farmers in northeast Brazil.
Henrique de Barros. *Bulletin of Latin American Research*, vol. 12 (1993), p. 273-92.

A case-study of agrarian change in Pernambuco, which explores the adjustments made by small farmers to survive in the market.

551 Propriedade da terra: oppressão e miséria. O meio rural na história social do Brasil. (Land ownership: oppression and misery. The rural environment in the social history of Brazil.)
João Bosco Feres. Amsterdam: CEDLA, 1990. 660p. maps. bibliog.

This is a major study of the formation of the agrarian structure of Brazil, and of its impact on contemporary agriculture. It provides an extensive survey of the evolution of the control of land from the colonial period, with its adverse effects on Indians, African slaves, immigrants, and rural labourers. The work describes the regional pattern of society and economy in the 19th century. In considering the Old Republic, it gives weight to the major commercial products of coffee, cocoa, and rubber, and of rural unrest in the form of the Canudos revolt and Messianic movements. In the 20th century, it examines the place of agriculture in the development strategies of Vargas,

Kubitschek and the military. This is followed by a long case-study of the recent frontier in Paraná, where it describes conflict over land, and the friction between the peasant and modernizing agriculture.

552 Fruticulture and uneven development in northeast Brazil.
C. Caviedes, K. D. Muller. *Geographical Review*, vol. 84 (1994), p. 380-93.

Examines the differential impact of a large irrigation project in Rio Grande do Norte. The paper concludes that although large enterprises producing melons, grapes and other fruit for export have benefitted, there has been little impact on small farmers.

553 Human carrying capacity of the Brazilian rain forest.
Philip M. Fearnside. New York: Columbia University Press, 1986. 294p. maps. bibliog.

Though the author has become a prolific critic of Brazil's advance into the rainforest, this study offers models to estimate the carrying capacity of Amazonia for agriculture. It outlines the ecology of the forest, describes the colonization process, and examines various potential agricultural systems which might be used in the region.

554 30 years of agricultural growth in Brazil – crop performance, regional profiles and recent policy review.
Douglas Graham, Howard Gauthier, José Roberto Mendonça de Barros. *Economic Development and Cultural Change*, vol. 36 (1987), p. 1-34.

This is an important study of the agricultural sector at a time of rapid economic growth in Brazil. Advance in agriculture is attributed here to modernization, the frontier and new crops.

555 An outline of agrarian policy and sustainable development for strengthening household agriculture in Brazil.
C. E. Guanziroli. *Land Reform* (1995), p. 31-51.

This is a formal statement of technical cooperation between the UN Food and Agriculture Organization and INCRA, Brazil's agrarian reform agency, in 1994, which was to formulate new rural development strategies for Brazil. It seeks to identify the potential for the development of family-scale agriculture, which might include agrarian reform. In 1985 more than two-thirds of Brazil's farms were classed as 'family farms', but they accounted for only one-fifth of the farm area.

556 Adaptive responses of native Amazonians.
Edited by Raymond B. Hames, William T. Vickers. New York; London: Academic Press, 1983. 518p. maps. bibliog.

In this collection, most of the papers relate to Brazil, and explore cultivation, hunting, fishing and nutrition in the subsistence economies of the Indians. It provides an interesting commentary on subsistence agriculture in the rainforest.

557 **Peasant Brazil: agrarian history, struggle and change in the Paraguaçu Valley, Bahia.**
Colin Henfrey. *Bulletin of Latin American Research*, vol. 8 (1989), p. 1-24.

An important study of the existence and experience of the peasant sector of agriculture in the Northeast, particularly in the face of the expansion of large-scale, capitalist agriculture. There is some theoretical discussion of the nature of the peasant economy, and considerable detail on the development of peasant movements.

558 **Tropical forests, people and food. Biocultural interactions and applications to development. Man and the biosphere series Vol 13.**
Edited by C. M. Hladik, A. Hladik, O. F. Linares, H. Pagezy, A. Semple, M. Hadley. Paris: UNESCO, 1993. 852p.

This is a wide-ranging report of a UNESCO symposium. It contains numerous papers on forest products in Amazonia – fruits, nuts and palms – and their uses.

559 **Ecological impact of agricultural development in the Brazilian *cerrados*.**
C. A. Klink, A. G. Moreira, O. T. Solbrig. In: *The world's savannas: Man and the biosphere series, vol. 12.* Edited by D. Young, O. T. Solbrig. Paris: UNESCO, 1993, p. 259-82. maps. bibliog.

Brazil has sought to develop its savanna grasslands of the central and southern uplands since the 1960s. This essay assesses the social and environmental costs of such development. It suggests that there has been extension of the frontier rather than intensification of land use, and that commercial crops rather than staple foodstuffs have been favoured. There have been problems of erosion, water pollution and habitat loss. It is a useful review of development in an area which has been suggested as an alternative to Amazonia for Brazil's agricultural advance.

560 **The agricultural economy of northeast Brazil.**
Gary P. Kutcher, Pasquale L. Scandizzo. Baltimore, Maryland; London: Johns Hopkins Press, 1981. 272p. bibliog.

Based on a World Bank survey of landholding in the Northeast, this book provides a good survey of agricultural production and costs, and of landholding patterns in the region.

561 **Government policies toward drought and development in the Brazilian *sertão*.**
Ian Livingstone, Marcio Assunção. *Development and Change*, vol. 20 (1989), p. 461-500.

Episodic drought has always been a problem in the interior of the Northeast. This study examines two broad strategies: the building of reservoirs before 1970, and later efforts to foster irrigation. It argues that both failed to understand the nature of the *sertão* (interior) rural economy, and were therefore of limited impact.

562 **The cashew industry of Ceará, Brazil: case study of a regional development option.**
Anne Meaney-Leckie. *Bulletin of Latin American Research*, vol. 10 (1991), p. 315-24.
The cashew nut is a traditional crop of the Northeast, grown on land too poor to sustain subsistence agriculture. In the 1960s it became part of a regional development plan to increase employment and income in the region. This paper charts its history, and the progress of the programme.

563 **Amazon caboclo society: an essay on invisibility and peasant economy.**
Stephen Nugent. Providence, Rhode Island; London: Berg, 1993. 278p. maps. bibliog.
It is argued that the peasant society and economy of the *caboclo* has been neglected. This study examines *caboclo* patterns of kinship and production of commodities in the region of Santarém, on the lower River Amazon. It is a useful survey of traditional agriculture in Amazonia.

564 **Structural change and State policy: the politics of sugar in Brazil since 1964.**
Barbara Nunberg. *Latin American Research Review*, vol. 21, no. 2 (1986), p. 53-92.
This is an exploration of the relations between the development policies of the military government, and the producer class. There was strong desire to increase sugar production and modernize the industry, which saw the rise of large-scale, capital-intensive producers and cooperatives, and a clear shift in production towards the Southeast from the once-dominant Northeast.

565 **Essays on coffee and economic development.**
Carlos Manuel Paláez, Mauro M. Matta. Rio de Janeiro, Brazil: Instituto Brasileiro do Café, 1973. 550p.
Although rather old, this is an excellent review of the Brazilian coffee industry and its development. It is particularly useful on issues of labour, internal coffee support programmes, and international coffee agreements. The volume also includes essays on other economic themes.

566 **Contesting the household estate: southern Brazilian peasants and modern agriculture.**
Frans Papma. Amsterdam: CEDLA, 1992. 268p. map. bibliog.
A detailed study of the dynamics of peasant property ownership through inheritance. Intra-generational issues are set into the wider context of rural changes consequent upon the introduction of soyabeans and market activities, and of the rise of peasant movements to defend their agricultural traditions.

567 **Agrarian reform and the rural workers' unions of the Pernambuco sugar zone, Brazil 1985-1988.**
Anthony W. Pereira. *Journal of Developing Areas*, vol. 26 (1992), p. 169-92.

Though an agrarian reform was announced in 1985, it received little support from rural trade-union leaders, who were sceptical of the government's will to implement reform, and fearful of hostility from landlords. This paper explores the reasons for this attitude.

568 **Fences in the jungle: cattle raising and the economic and social integration of the Amazon region in Brazil.**
Fabio G. M. N. Poelhekke. *Revista Geografica*, vol. 104 (1986), p. 33-47.

A useful study of the original phase of beef cattle development in Amazonia, 1972-82. It discusses the economic groups involved, the role of the State, and the impact on Indians and squatters.

569 **Brazil: one hundred years of the agrarian question.**
Elisa P. Reis. *International Social Science Journal*, vol. 124 (1990), p. 153-68.

Provides a good overview of the experience of rural labour since 1889. The paper also discusses Brazil's failure to implement any agrarian reform during this period.

570 **Agrarian structure and politics in present-day Brazil.**
Bernardo Sorj. *Latin American Perspectives*, vol. 7 (1980), p. 23-34.

This article offers a helpful brief commentary on the structure of agriculture in Brazil, which discusses the rural population, patterns of landholding, and regional levels of modernization.

571 **Les "assentamentos", manifestations de la lutte pour la terre au Brésil.** (The "assentamentos" – manifestations of the struggle for land.)
Rosa Maria Viera Meideros. *Les Cahiers d'Outre-Mer*, no. 193 (1996), p. 95-108.

An important issue in rural Brazil in the 1990s has been the campaign for land by the MST (Movement of rural workers without land). Their crusade for land reform has included occupation of large holdings. This paper discusses the issues and explores the activities of the MST in Rio Grande do Sul.

The 'Frontier'

572 **Indian lands, environmental policy, and military geopolitics in the development of Brazilian Amazonia: the case of the Yanomami.**
Bruce Albert. *Development and Change*, vol. 23 (1992), p. 35-70.
A very useful appraisal of military policy towards Amazonia, the environment and native peoples in the late 1980s. It is a well-argued overview of the consequences of the advance of the frontier. The study uses the case of the Yanomami Indians, on the border between Brazil and Venezuela, to reveal the way in which the military régimes modified laws relating to Indian lands in order to protect what they saw as national sovereignty.

573 **Calha Norte: military development in Brazilian Amazonia.**
Elizabeth Allen. *Development and Change*, vol. 23 (1992), p. 71-100.
This paper outlines a major military project along Brazil's northern borders. It was intended to integrate the region into the national economy, and secure the frontier against guerrillas, drug smugglers, and perceived threats from neighbouring states.

574 **The colonization of the Amazon.**
Anna Ozorio de Almeida. Austin, Texas: University of Texas Press, 1992. 372p. maps. bibliog.
A very useful and welcome study of recent developments in Amazonia. In contrast to the plethora of generally hostile and external books on the topic, this is written by a Brazilian who makes a measured attempt to explore the aims, achievements and limitations of Brazil's deliberate, large-scaled planned colonization scheme of the 1970s. It considers the colonization process, the role of the State, the impact of the market, and the experience of the settlers. This is a rare, balanced assessment. While recognizing the failure of the scheme, it explores its attractions, the mobility of settlers, its implications for rural income distribution as well as the environment, and the alternatives to such a strategy.

575 **Smokestacks in the rainforest: industrial development and deforestation in Amazonian Brazil.**
Anthony B. Anderson. *World Development*, vol. 18 (1990), p. 1,191-205.

One of the controversial consequences of the development of the Greater Carajás project in Pará has been the emergence of unplanned activities, and their impact on the environment and native peoples. This paper is a critical study of the negative impact of charcoal-based industries which have sprung up along the Carajás railway.

576 **Frontières: mythes et pratiques (Brésil, Nicaragua, Malaysia).**
(Frontiers: myths and practices.)
Edited by Catherine Aubertin, Philippe Léna. *Cahiers des Sciences Humaines*, (special issue) vol. 22, nos. 3/4 (1986), p. 261-443.

All but one of the twelve articles in this volume relate to Brazil. Although their main concern is with agricultural frontiers in Amazonia, they offer comparative insights into other areas, and on industrialization, dam-building, and the impact of Brasília.

577 **After the Frontier: problems with political economy in the modern Brazilian Amazon.**
David Cleary. *Journal of Latin American Studies*, vol. 25 (1993), p. 331-49.

A useful discussion of the relevance of ideas about 'the frontier' to the Brazilian experience. A particular virtue is that it draws upon Brazilian sources, rather than merely recycling British 'green' ideas.

578 **The struggle for land: a political economy of the pioneer frontier in Brazil from 1930 to the present day.**
Joe Foweraker. Cambridge, United Kingdom; New York: Cambridge University Press, 1981. 260p. maps. bibliog.

This much-cited work is an important study of the issue of land 'ownership' on the recent frontier in Brazil, exploring issues of the law, the bureaucracy, and rural violence. Most of its evidence comes from the recent frontier in Paraná.

579 **The forest frontier. Settlement and change in Brazilian Roraima.**
Edited by Peter A. Furley. London; New York: Routledge, 1994. 236p. maps. bibliog.

An excellent all-round survey of contemporary frontier processes in northern Amazonia. Roraima is an area which has only recently begun to be developed. The contributions to the volume deal with the history of settlement, the processes of forest clearance and agricultural development, and their environmental consequences. It is a very good study of the modern frontier in Amazonia.

580 **The future of Amazonia: destruction or sustainable development?**
Edited by David Goodman, Anthony Hall. Basingstoke, United
Kingdom: Macmillan, 1990. 420p. maps.
This is a first-rate and comprehensive multi-disciplinary survey of the processes and
consequences of development in Amazonia since 1970. It deals with three major
themes: the various development strategies; their environmental and social consequences; and the potential of techniques of sustainable development. The book has a
distinguished range of contributors and offers a range of insights into the impact of
different frontiers.

581 **The ecopolitics of development in the Third World: politics and
environment in Brazil.**
Roberto P. Guimarães. Boulder, Colorado; London: Lynne Rienner
Publisher, 1991. 272p.
A useful study of the way in which the political system of Brazil addresses environ-
mental issues, especially since the UN Conference on the Human Environment held in
Stockholm in 1972. The volume considers political, institutional, and planning issues.
It is a good examination of the formal aspects of the frontier.

582 **Developing Amazonia. Deforestation and social conflict in Brazil's
Carajás programme.**
Anthony L. Hall. Manchester, United Kingdom; New York:
Manchester University Press, 1989. 296p. map. bibliog.
The Greater Carajás scheme in Pará has been among the most notorious of Brazil's
development projects in Amazonia. This is a critical review of its impact on
deforestation and conflicts over land.

583 **Expansion de la frontière économique, accès au marché et
transformation de l'espace rural en Amazonie brésilienne.**
(Expansion of the economic frontier, access to the market, and
transformation of rural space in the Brazilian Amazon.)
Philippe Léna. *Cahiers de Sciences Humaines*, vol. 28 (1992),
p. 579-601. map.
A very useful concise summary of the impact of the frontier on various economic
groups. These include the Indians, the *caboclos*, the rubber-tappers, and Brazil-nut
gatherers.

584 **Frontier development policy in Brazil: a study of Amazonia.**
Dennis J. Mahar. London; New York: Praeger Publishers, 1979.
184p. bibliog.
This is the essential reference source on the formal strategies of Brazil's development
of Amazonia. It is by far the best and most comprehensive summary of the various
development policies applied to the region between 1945 and 1979.

585 **The moving frontier: social and economic change in a southern Brazilian community.**
Maxine L. Margolis. Gainesville, Florida: University of Florida Press, 1973. 276p. maps. bibliog.

Although recent attention has focused upon Amazonia, Brazil has had other active frontiers elsewhere in the period since 1930. This volume is a detailed study of a community in a major colonization scheme in northern Paraná. The colony is on the margin of the southward advance and retreat of Brazil's coffee frontier, and the book chronicles the economic and social patterns of its development from 1952-66.

586 **Developing the Amazon.**
Emilio F. Moran. Bloomington, Indiana: Indiana University Press, 1981. 292p. maps. bibliog.

A key element in Brazil's Amazon development strategy was agricultural colonization along the Transamazonica highway. Though the strategy was largely abandoned by 1974, this study is a valuable analysis of the colonization experience, which details the nature of the environment, its traditional uses, the nature of the migrant colonists, and their economic activities and lifestyle.

587 **The dilemma of Amazonian development.**
Edited by Emilio F. Moran. Boulder, Colorado: Westview Press, 1983. 350p. maps.

In spite of its title, this collection is more an extensive record of processes of Amazon development than a critique of the dilemmas they pose. Its utility is twofold. Firstly it provides wide coverage of the ways in which Amazonia is utilized, for agriculture, pastoralism, and fishing, and considers the activities of Indians, peasants, ranchers and urban dwellers. Secondly, it includes some non-Brazilian material, thus demonstrating that Brazil and 'the rainforest' are not coterminous, and the problems of forest use not uniquely Brazilian.

588 **Big business in the Amazon.**
Marianne Schmink. In: *People of the tropical rain forest.* Edited by Julie S. Denslow, Christine Padoch. Berkeley, California; London: University of California Press, 1988, p. 163-74.

The role of big business, particularly foreign companies, operating in Amazonia has been controversial both in Brazil and abroad. This is a useful summary of major projects such as the Fordlandia rubber plantation and the Jari afforestation scheme, and of more general logging, ranching and mining activities.

589 **Contested frontiers in Amazonia.**
Marianne Schmink, Charles H. Wood. New York; Oxford: Columbia University Press, 1992. 388p. maps. bibliog.

A case-study of the frontier in southern Pará. The book provides the background to the frontier process, including what it calls the 'militarizing' of Amazonia from 1964-85, and then details the conflicts which have arisen between Indians, settlers, loggers, and gold prospectors. It offers an excellent portrait of a frontier society.

590 **Rainforest corridors. The Transamazon colonization scheme.**
Nigel J. H. Smith. Berkeley, California; London: University of
California Press, 1982. 248p. maps. bibliog.

This is a critical assessment of the colonization project, which argues that in addition
to the environmental damage it caused, planners failed to anticipate the constraints
imposed by the physical and biotic conditions. There is a significant section on
disease, health care and folk medicine.

591 **Where cultures meet. Frontiers in Latin American history.**
Edited by David J. Weber, Jane M. Rausch. Wilmington, Delaware:
Scholarly Resources Inc., 1994. 234p. bibliog.

This is an essential reader for anyone interested in the broad field of frontier studies. It
brings together classic papers on the frontier in general and in Latin America. Seven
of the twenty papers are concerned directly with Brazil. The volume also contains a
list of relevant films, several of which relate to Brazil.

Industry

592 Industrial policy, sectoral maturation, and postwar economic growth in Brazil: the resource curse thesis.
R. Auty. *Economic Geography*, vol. 71 (1995), p. 257-72.

Argues that resource-rich countries such as Brazil under-perform economically, because their self-sufficient development policies are unsustainable. The paper includes a useful outline of Brazil's autarkic policies, especially the 'Big Pushes' of 1956-60 and 1974-79.

593 The development of the Brazilian steel industry.
Werner Baer. Nashville, Tennessee: Vanderbilt University Press, 1969. 202p. map. bibliog.

A comprehensive study of the rise of iron and steel production in Brazil, from its colonial beginnings to major expansion after 1945. It examines the impact of the industry on the national economy, and the quality of its internal and external performance. The author concludes that, although there have been widespread doubts about the logic of establishing heavy industries in developing countries, the Brazilian case demonstrates that a successful steel industry is viable, given the necessary raw materials, a large market, and established technical skills.

594 The food industry in Brazil: towards a restructuring?
Walter Belik. London: University of London, Institute of Latin American Studies Research Paper 35, 1994. 42p. bibliog.

A brief study of the development of agro-industries, especially since the 1950s, and the role of foreign capital.

595 **Brazilian privatization in the 1990s.**
A. Castelar Pinheiro, F. Giambiaji. *World Development*, vol. 22 (1994), p. 737-53.
In the 1990s Brazil set out to privatize numerous sectors of the economy, in line with World Bank ideas about market forces. The privatization involved firms dealing in steel, petrochemicals, fertilizers, chemicals and transport. This paper suggests that the impact has been limited in terms of either reducing debt or increasing efficiency.

596 **Creating a growth pole: the industrialization of Belo Horizonte, Brazil, 1897-1987.**
Marshall C. Eakin. *The Americas*, vol. 47 (1991), p. 383-410.
The city of Belo Horizonte was inaugurated in 1897, as a new capital for the state of Minas Gerais. This paper examines the role of the state government in fostering an industrial centre in a traditionally agrarian state. It describes the use of industrial estates, and the initiative of Juscelino Kubitschek as prefect of the city and governor of the state, especially the impact of his 'binomial' of energy and transport, which provided essential infrastructure.

597 **Dependent development. The alliance of multinational, state and local capital in Brazil.**
Peter Evans. Princeton, New Jersey: Princeton University Press, 1979. 362p. bibliog.
The 'triple alliance' of state, domestic and foreign capital was a crucial factor in Brazil's industrial growth in the 1970s. Though this work offers a longer perspective, it provides a detailed analysis of the interaction of these sources of capital, especially in key sectors such as petrochemicals and pharmaceuticals.

598 **Development, technology and flexibility: Brazil faces the industrial divide.**
João C. Ferraz, Howard Rush, Ian Miles. London; New York: Routledge, 1992. 274p. bibliog.
A consideration of the role of innovation in helping developing countries to advance their manufacturing sectors. The work examines the impact of innovation in a range of industries, and the implications for competitiveness, quality, and employment generation.

599 **Capital-intensive industries in Newly Industrializing Countries. The case of the Brazilian automobile and steel industries.**
Bernhard Fischer. Boulder, Colorado: Westview Press, 1988. 326p. bibliog.
This is a study of Brazil's place in the international division of labour, and the role of two major industries in export growth from 1967-86. It suggests that export incentives were significant in the growth of the vehicle industry, and factor endowments in the case of steel.

600 **Quality and productivity in the competitive strategies of Brazilian industrial enterprises.**
Afonso Fleury. *World Development*, vol. 23 (1995), p. 73-85.
After a long period of protection, Brazilian firms are facing new competition. This paper considers a range of industries, and suggests there is a need for new technology and investment strategies.

601 **'Public-private partnership'. Lessons from the Brazilian armaments industry.**
Patrice Franko-Jones. *Journal of Interamerican Studies*, vol. 29, no. 4 (1987), p. 41-68.
Brazil ranks among the world's top ten arms exporters. This paper suggests that this is the product of the effective role of the State as a technical and trade agent, and the manufacturing firms as innovators. Brazil fills a niche for conventional weapons just below the superpowers, supplying aircraft, armoured vehicles and missiles.

602 **Foreign direct investment in Brazil: its impact on industrial restructuring.**
Winston Fritsch, Gustavo Franco. Paris: OECD, 1991. 156p. bibliog.
Brazil has been a major recipient of foreign investment, and this study examines its contribution in important areas such as electronics, vehicles and capital goods. There is a policy element to the document, examining investment issues for Brazil in the 1990s.

603 **The spatial strategies of the state in the political-economic development of Brazil.**
Pedro P. Geiger, Fany R. Davidovich. In: *Production, work, territory: the geographical anatomy of industrial capitalism.* Edited by Allen J. Scott, Michael Storper. London; Boston, Massachusetts: Allen & Unwin, 1986, p. 281-98.
This is an interesting overview of the spatial consequences of state involvement in Brazilian industrialization since the 1930s. Government intervention has been an important force in determining the location of industry.

604 **Poverty and distorted industrialization in the Brazilian Northeast.**
William W. Goldsmith, Robert Wilson. *World Development*, vol. 19 (1991), p. 435-55.
The authors claim that despite regional development programmes for the Northeast, especially since 1960, the regional economy is weak, industrial development is too closely tied to other parts of the country, and social inequality persists. The paper includes a good history of development strategies since 1930.

605   **The role of transnational companies in the Brazilian defence tripod.**
Raul de Gouvea Neto.   *Journal of Latin American Studies*, vol. 23 (1991), p. 573-99.
Brazil is a major armaments producer and exporter. This study argues that success was achieved by state involvement and the encouragement of domestic and multinational capital and technology.

606   **Telecommunications in developing countries: the challenge from Brazil.**
Michael Hobday.   London; New York: Routledge, 1990. 222p. bibliog.
Explores the impact of strategies for new technology in the development policies of developing countries. The book examines Brazil's desire to move into micro high technology in the telecommunications sector via Research and Development, and involvement with multinational companies.

607   **Japan's economic strategy for Brazil. Challenge for the United States.**
Leon Hollerman.   Lexington, Massachusetts: Lexington Books, 1988. 284p.
This study argues that Japan, in contrast to the United States, has a clear economic and political strategy towards Brazil, in which it seeks to diversify and multiply its global interests. In recent years it has developed a series of joint ventures and subsidiaries in Brazil, in industry, finance and trade.

608   **The Brazilian capital goods industry, 1929-64.**
Nathaniel H. Leff.   Cambridge, Massachusetts: Harvard University Press, 1968. 186p.
Focuses particularly on the heavy engineering industry, which grew more rapidly than the overall economy in the 1950s, reducing Brazil's dependence on imports. The study explores the themes of labour, know-how, demand and the market.

609   **Industrialization, trade and market failures: the role of government intervention in Brazil and South Korea.**
Mauricio Moreira.   Basingstoke, United Kingdom: Macmillan, 1995. 228p. bibliog.
This comparative study examines attempts by governments to intervene in the economy, specifically to foster industrialization by various means. In the case of Brazil it concludes that the strategy to secure export growth was badly designed.

610 **L'espace et l'industrie dans l'état de São Paulo (Brésil).** (Space and industry in São Paulo State, Brazil.)
Silvana Maria Pintaudi, Ana Fani Allessandri Carlos. *Les Cahiers d'Outre-Mer*, no. 1,193 (1996), p. 31-51.

A useful analysis of the industrialization of São Paulo, which argues that after its initial concentration in São Paulo city, industry has migrated to other cities within 200 km of the capital, along the highways, and towards the interior of the state. However, tertiary activities tend to remain concentrated in the capital.

611 **State-owned enterprise in high-technology industries: studies in India and Brazil.**
Ravi Ramamurti. New York; London: Praeger, 1987. 308p. bibliog.

It is argued that state-owned enterprises have an important role in developing countries in successfully mastering complex technologies and fostering commercial success. This study explains the broad context, and provides case-studies of Brazil's aviation and computer industries.

612 **Shaping Brazil's petrochemical industry. The importance of foreign firm origin in tripartite joint ventures.**
Wilma Roos. Amsterdam: CEDLA, 1991. 254p. bibliog.

An alliance of state, domestic and foreign capital was important in Brazilian economic development in the 1970s and 1980s. This study considers joint ventures with Japan, Europe and the United States, focusing on the petrochemical complex of Camaçari. It provides a useful history of the chemical industry and of Brazil's petrochemical complexes.

613 **High-tech for industrial development: lessons from the Brazilian experience in electronics and automation.**
Edited by Hubert Schmitz, José Cassiolato. London; New York: Routledge, 1992. 322p. bibliog.

Examines the role of government in fostering electronics-based industries. It considers Brazil's protection of its computer industry, and the use of automation in banking, petrochemicals, electronics and the service sector.

614 **Engines of growth: the State and transnational auto companies in Brazil.**
Helen Shapiro. Cambridge, United Kingdom: Cambridge University Press, 1994. 268p.

This book explores the development of the car industry, which was a crucial part of Brazilian economic development from 1956. In spite of difficulties, the country attracted investment from a range of transnational car firms, and by 1975 was the world's ninth largest car producer.

615   **The Newly Industrial Countries and the information technology revolution: the Brazilian experience.**
Arlindo Villaschi.   Aldershot, United Kingdom: Avebury, 1994. 204p. bibliog.

A study of perceived opportunities for Brazil in the IT field, and the role of the State in fostering national systems of innovation. It provides a good outline of economic circumstances, the institutional framework, human resources, Research and Development, and science parks.

Commerce and Trade

General

616 **Changing patterns of financing investment in Brazil.**
Luiz Bresser Pereira. *Bulletin of Latin American Research*, vol. 6 (1987), p. 233-48.
This article explores the changing pattern of investment in Brazil from the 1970s, identifying a shift from a dependence on state and external financing, to a greater role for private capital. It includes an assessment of likely financing patterns in the late-1980s.

617 **Foreign trade strategies and their impact on employment: the case of Brazil.**
Benedict J. Clements. *Bulletin of Latin American Research*, vol. 6 (1987), p. 183-95.
An analytical paper exploring alternative ways by which Brazil might deal with the major economic problems of the debt burden, the need for high rates of economic growth, and the necessity of creating at least 1.5 million jobs a year, simply to keep unemployment from increasing. The study explores the possibilities offered by production for export, import substitution, and the production of non-tradeables in dealing with these concerns. Its conclusion is that export production is the most successful in generating blue-collar employment.

618 **The Collor Plan: shooting the tiger?**
John Crabtree. *Bulletin of Latin American Research*, vol. 10 (1991), p. 119-32.
The Collor Plan of 1990 set out to tackle Brazil's ongoing high levels of inflation, with a series of drastic measures. This paper was written soon after its initiation, and outlines its objectives and methods, the implications of stabilization policies for

different social groups, and the consequences of the elections for governors and federal and state congresses held in late-1990.

619 **The Brazilian borrowing experience: from miracle to debacle and back.**
Jeffrey A. Frieden. *Latin American Research Review*, vol. 22, no. 1 (1987), p. 95-131.
A thorough study of the debt crisis of the 1980s and its impact on Brazil's economic and political development. It indicates the dependence on foreign loans by public and private companies, and banks.

620 **Inflation and stabilization: recent Brazilian experience in perspective.**
Nader Nazmi. *Journal of Developing Areas*, vol. 29 (1995), p. 491-506.
The period 1984-94 was one of persistently high inflation, but despite a series of plans (1986, 1987, 1988 and 1990), the government was unable to bring it under control. This paper details the plans and explores the underlying problems of the economy.

621 **Performance and perspectives of Brazilian macro-economic performance during the Transition.**
João do Carmo Oliveira. *Bulletin of Latin American Research*, vol. 6 (1987), p. 217-32.
A study of the formulation and failure of the 1986 Cruzado Plan, intended to counter Brazil's high inflation of the mid-1980s. It is a detailed account of events during the period 1985-87. The author argues that the plan failed because its diagnosis of the causes of inflation were in error, and that the policies implemented were too late and inappropriate.

622 **Heterodox shock in Brazil: técnicos, politicians, and democracy.**
Lourdes Sola. *Journal of Latin American Studies* vol. 23 (1991), p. 163-95.
An extensive study of the Cruzado Plan, Brazil's first attempt after the return to democracy to control inflation. The plan was not a success and the paper explores the gap between the strategy proposed and the results achieved. It sets the plan into the distinct context of the return to democracy.

623 **Brazilian inflation from 1980 to 1993: causes, consequences and dynamics.**
G. Tullio, M. Ronci. *Journal of Latin American Studies*, vol. 28 (1996), p. 635-66.
This paper is an economic analysis of Brazil's recent experience of inflation. It suggests that high inflation was due to a number of factors – excessive growth of the money supply and high budget deficits, compounded by the 'shocks' derived from oil prices and exchange rates. The authors argue that the Central Bank needs greater autonomy from the government. This is a detailed paper, of interest primarily to the economist.

624 **Learning from failed stabilization: high inflation and the *Cruzado* plan in Brazil.**
Carlos D. Winograd.   London: University of London, Institute of Latin American Studies Research Paper 38, 1995. 60p.
A brief case-study of one of Brazil's many attempts to control inflation, 1986-87.

Business and banking

625 **Brazil: a guide to the structure, development and regulation of financial services.**
Edited by Anthony Edwards.   London: Economist Publications, 1988. 152p.
An indispensable guide for business people. It provides a thorough introduction to Brazil's financial sector, outlining government controls, sectoral structure, and recent developments. The work lists: commercial, development, savings and investment banks; stock and commodity exchanges; and insurance companies. It also provides practical advice on setting up in Brazil, with regard to taxation and exchange controls, etc.

626 **Doing business in Brazil.**
Price Waterhouse.   São Paulo, Brazil: Price Waterhouse, 1994. 218p.
This may be seen as an essential guide for business people. It provides a useful introduction to the people and economy, and information for visitors. The volume's main value, however, is its comprehensive discussion of the business environment, which covers such topics as: investment opportunities, incentives and restrictions; banking and trade; taxation; and labour relations.

627 **The formation of modern Brazilian banking, 1906-1930: opportunities and constraints presented by the public and private sectors.**
Gail D. Triner.   *Journal of Latin American Studies*, vol. 28 (1996), p. 49-74.
A very thorough review of the establishment of Brazil's banking system, within the limits posed by government economic policies and concepts of property rights.

628 **Capital markets in the development process: the case of Brazil.**
John H. Welch.   Pittsburgh, Pennsylvania: University of Pittsburgh Press; London: Macmillan, 1993. 232p.
It is argued that financial and capital markets have a crucial role in economic development. This study suggests that the creation of agencies such as the Central Bank, National Housing Bank and National Development Bank were important in Brazilian development from 1965-85.

Overseas trade

629 **Foreign trade strategies, employment, and income distribution in Brazil.**
Benedict J. Clements. New York; London: Praeger, 1988. 168p. map.
An examination of the role of differing trade strategies in generating employment and reducing income inequities. The study suggests that Brazil's Import Substitution Industrialization programme of 1945-64 was less successful in these areas than the Export Promotion of 1964-79.

630 **The EEC and Brazil: trade, capital investment and the debt problem.**
Edited by Peter Coffey, Luiz Corrêa do Lago. London; New York: Pinter Publishers, 1988. 194p.
A very useful set of essays on Brazil's historical links with the EEC, and on trade patterns and investment flows. Also considered is the entry of Portugal and Spain into the EEC in 1986, and the debt issue, since European banks are Brazil's largest creditors.

Brazil: the giant of Latin America.
See item no. 7.

Transport

631 **The highways of Brazil.**
Adonais Filho, translated by Richard Spock. Rio de Janeiro, Brazil: Agência Jornalística Image, 1973. 96p. maps.
This is a government-sponsored account of Brazil's highway developments of the early 1970s. Its coverage includes the Transamazonica, Northern Perimetral, and several coastal highways, together with discussion of road maintenance and safety.

632 **Railroads in nineteenth century Minas Gerais.**
P. L. Blasenheim. *Journal of Latin American Studies*, vol. 26 (1994), p. 347-74.
An interesting study of the development of the railway system in the coffee area of southern Minas Gerais, which explores the role and influence of planters and planter-politicians in securing the development of particular routes. The paper devotes particular attention to the Leopoldina railway, described as 'a coffee railroad par excellence'.

633 **South Atlantic seaway. An illustrated history of the passenger lines and liners from Europe to Brazil, Uruguay and Argentina.**
N. R. P. Bonsor. St. Brelade, Jersey: Brookside Publications, 1983. 526p.
Very much a transport history, this is a standardized survey of over seventy shipping lines dealing with South Atlantic ports from circa 1850. A brief history of each company is included, but the volume consists mainly of details of individual liners.

634 **Streetcars and politics in Rio de Janeiro: private enterprise versus municipal government in the provision of mass transit, 1903-1920.**
Christopher Boone. *Journal of Latin American Studies*, vol. 27 (1995), p. 343-65.
An interesting study of the development of Rio's urban transport system, which explores the way in which the local authorities successfully negotiated an extensive tramway network from a Canadian utilities company.

635 **Airlines of Latin America since 1918.**
R. E. G. Davies. London: Putnam & Co., 1984. 712p.
Essentially a broad history of the development of aviation in Latin America, the volume deals with Brazil on pages 333-506. The coverage of the country's various airlines is detailed, and the material spans the period 1918-80.

636 **Autos over rails: how US business supplanted the British in Brazil, 1910-28.**
Richard Downes. *Journal of Latin American Studies*, vol. 24 (1992), p. 551-83.
The British had a large role in the construction of Brazil's railways. However, this paper charts the usurpation of British railway interests by the emergence of the American motor industry. It details the activities of US lobbyists, officials and entrepreneurs.

637 **Public and private operation of railways in Brazil.**
Julian S. Duncan. New York: AMS Press, 1968. 244p.
First published in 1932 (New York: Columbia University Press), this work provides a history of railway policy and the development of the railroad system from 1835 to 1930, with studies of six major railway companies. It assesses the experience of government- and privately-owned lines, and includes extensive data appendices. Despite its age, it remains a good review of Brazilian railway history.

638 **Brazil.**
In: *Jane's world railways, 1987-88*. Edited by Geoffrey F. Allen. London; New York: Jane's Transport Press, 1987, p. 576-83.
This chapter provides a brief commentary on the main railway systems and recent developments. It covers the federal system, the Paulista railways, the suburban networks of Rio and São Paulo, and the main mineral lines.

639 **Public policy and private initiative: railway building in São Paulo, 1860-1889.**
Colin M. Lewis. London: University of London, Institute of Latin American Studies Research Paper 26, 1991. 84p. map.
A study which provides some background to the national railway strategy, and the evolution of the São Paulo system. In the latter case, it examines the varied interests of the State, the province of São Paulo, coffee producers, and foreign investors.

640 **Business interest groups and communications: the Brazilian experience in the nineteenth century.**
Eugene W. Ridings. *Luso-Brazilian Review*, vol. 20 (1983), p. 241-57.

Provision of internal communications was necessary for Brazilian development, but the high cost of their installation encouraged links between the business élite and foreign capitalists. This paper discusses the provision of railways, river and coastal navigation, and the telegraph system.

641 **A history of Brazilian railways. Part I: The first railways.**
Pedro C. da Silva Telles. Bromley, United Kingdom: P. E. Waters & Associates, 1987. 70p. map. bibliog.

This is a brief study of the early history of Brazilian railways, which examines the early need for them and the first legislation. It describes the development of pioneer railways around Rio, São Paulo, Salvador and Recife.

Labour

642 Recent strikes in Brazil. The main tendencies of the strike movement of the 1980s.
Ricardo Antunes. *Latin American Perspectives*, vol. 21, no. 1 (1994), p. 24-37.

As the military régime began to ease its control and moved towards the *abertura* (opening up) in the late 1970s, there was considerable strike activity, with the expansion of middle-class and rural unions. The paper discusses the nature of these strikes, which included both general strikes and strikes within companies.

643 The state and trade unions in Brazil.
Armando Boito, Jnr. *Latin American Perspectives*, vol. 21, no. 1 (1994), p. 7-23.

Labour history in Brazil was shaped by the creation of state-linked trade unions by President Vargas, as the means by which government dealt with workers. The Ministry of Labour established trade unions in a decree of 1931. Strikes were forbidden, but there was wage-bargaining, labour courts to defend workers' rights, and a range of social provisions. This article describes the radicalization of labour in the 1980s, and the persistence of the corporatist trade unions created by Vargas.

644 The manipulation of consent: the State and working-class consciousness in Brazil.
Youssef Cohen. Pittsburgh, Pennsylvania: University of Pittsburgh Press, 1989. 190p. bibliog.

This book suggests that from the 1930s the State and élite exercised ideological control over the working classes, particularly via a corporative labour system. It is argued that this led them to accept the values and beliefs of an authoritarian ideology, and acquiesce to the coup of 1964.

645 **The Brazilian workers' ABC: class conflict and alliance in modern São Paulo.**
John David French. Chapel Hill, North Carolina: University of North Carolina Press, 1992. 378p. map. bibliog.
'ABC' is the main industrial region of Greater São Paulo, and this is a study of emerging urban politics and labour relations, from 1900-53. It examines the role of workers in Brazilian politics via the state-linked trade unions created by President Vargas in 1931.

646 **Poverty and politics: the urban poor in Brazil, 1870-1920.**
J. E. Hahner. Albuquerque, New Mexico: University of New Mexico Press, 1986. 416p. maps. bibliog.
This is an archival study of labour history, focusing on Rio de Janeiro. The work examines workers' lives and their poverty, the abuses they suffered, and their demonstrations of distress. It includes discussion of diet, disease, slum housing, and urban disturbances.

647 **Japanese production management and labour relations in Brazil.**
John Humphrey. *Journal of Development Studies*, vol. 30, no. 1 (1993), p. 92-114.
A commentary on the introduction of Japanese management techniques into Brazilian industry. These required new working practices, in return for improved conditions of employment and work, and higher worker skills and responsibilities.

648 **Economic crisis and tertiarization in Brazil's metropolitan labour market.**
Lena Lavinas, Maria Regina Nabuco. *International Journal of Urban and Regional Research*, vol. 19 (1995), p. 358-68.
Examines economic restructuring in the labour markets of São Paulo, Rio de Janeiro, Belo Horizonte and Recife. In these cities the informal sector has been dynamic in providing productive services for the industrial sector (in outworking and sales, for example), and as a basic survival strategy in street trading and domestic services.

649 **Metropolitan poverty in Brazil: economic cycles, labour markets, and demographic trends.**
Sonia Rocha. *International Journal of Urban and Regional Research*, vol. 19 (1995), p. 383-94.
This is a methodological study which seeks to relate short-term economic cycles and poverty. Its prime value is in the data on poverty in metropolitan areas, and on the nature of the labouring poor, whether as juveniles, in the informal sector, or in under-employment.

650 **Social change and labour unrest in Brazil since 1945.**
Salvador M. Sandoval.   Boulder, Colorado; Oxford: Westview Press,
1993. 246p. bibliog.

Provides an important examination of the relationship between the State and labour
during a period of rapid economic change, but where there were varying political
circumstances. The volume points to the paradox that while the military was trying to
constrain union action in older industries, within the established corporatist union
structure, State encouragement of new, capital-intensive industries created new groups
of workers which became important units of opposition to the military in the late
1970s. It explores the history of strikes under populism and repression.

651 **Manufacturing militance: workers' movements in Brazil and
South Africa, 1970-1985.**
Gay W. Seidman.   Berkeley, California; London: University of
California Press, 1994. 362p. bibliog.

A comparative study of broad labour movements in the two countries, in which the
working class challenged authoritarian rule. In the Brazilian case it explores the
emergence of militant labour movements against the existing corporatist labour
structures, with the development of 'new unionism' rooted in the factory. The result
was the rise of militant labour groups linked to the workplace and community, rather
than to the corporate union.

652 **Coffee planters, workers, and wives: class conflict and gender
relations on the São Paulo plantations, 1850-1980.**
Verena Stolcke.   Basingstoke, United Kingdom: Macmillan; New
York: St. Martin's Press, 1988. 344p. bibliog.

Provides an account of rural workers in the periods of transition from slavery to share-
cropping to wage labour. It is a good general portrait of labour on the coffee
plantations but, notwithstanding its title, the discussion of the particular experience of
women is modest.

653 **The industrialist, the State, and the issue of worker training and
social services in Brazil, 1930-50.**
Barbara Weinstein.   *Hispanic American Historical Review*, vol. 70
(1990), p. 379-404.

A useful guide to the establishment of basic industrial training in the Vargas period by
the National Industrial Training Service (SENAI), and the provision of cheap food and
basic education in health, home economics and labour relations, by the Industrial
Social Service (SESI).

654 **Working women, working men: São Paulo and the rise of Brazil's
industrial working class 1900-1955.**
Joel Wolfe.   Durham, North Carolina; London: Duke University
Press, 1993. 312p. bibliog.

This is a study of the development of a working class in São Paulo, as a consequence
of the process of industrialization. It chronicles the search for status by workers in an

authoritarian political system, and the increasing political importance of the working class in the period up to 1950. There is discussion of leaders and the Left, but also of grass-roots movements and gender roles. It draws mainly on the experience of the metallurgical and textile industries.

655 **The Faustian bargain not made: Getúlio Vargas and Brazil's industrial workers, 1930-45.**
Joel Wolfe. *Luso-Brazilian Review*, vol. 31, no. 2 (1994), p. 77-96.
Vargas was a key figure in Brazil's labour relations, creating a state-centred industrial relations system to institutionalize the class struggle and to provide him with political support. Trade unions were established to negotiate, via state institutions, on matters of wages, work, and social conditions. The paper outlines this innovative scheme, but indicates that it did not incorporate all of the labour force.

Education

656 The diversification of secondary education in Latin America: the case of Brazil.
Nigel Brooke. In: *Education in Latin America.* Edited by Colin Brock, Hugh Lawlor. London; Dover, New Hampshire: Croom Helm, 1985, p. 146-62.
This is an appraisal of the impact of Brazil's educational reforms of 1971, which created a single type of diversified secondary school.

657 What is happening in Brazilian education?
Cláudio de Maura Castro. In: *Social change in Brazil, 1945-1985: the incomplete transition.* Edited by Edmar L. Bacha, Herbert S. Klein. Albuquerque, New Mexico: University of New Mexico Press, 1989, p. 263-310.
A very good review of what was a crucial period of change in Brazilian education. It covers the primary, secondary and tertiary sectors, and also scientific education.

658 Brazil.
Burton R. Clark, Guy Neave. In: *Encyclopedia of higher education*, vol. 1. Oxford: Pergamon Press, 1992, p. 89-92. bibliog.
Provides a good historical outline of the development of the university sector. There is a most useful discussion of the legislative frame and university reforms of 1988. It also provides some basic facts on staffing, and on academic careers.

659 Cultural action for freedom.
Paulo Freire. Harmondsworth, United Kingdom; Baltimore, Maryland: Penguin, 1972. 96p. bibliog.
In the early 1960s Freire was a pioneer in his attempts to improve adult literacy among the poor. He saw traditional education as an instrument of oppression, and set

out to make it a means of liberation for the poor. This volume presents an outline of his methods, in which learning is not merely a matter of memorizing language, but of reflecting upon the process of reading and writing, and on the significance of language. He describes the adult literacy process as 'cultural action for freedom'.

660 **Des écoles pour les favelas: les Centres Intégrés d'Education Publiques (CIEPS) à Rio de Janeiro 1983 à 1987.** (Schools for the favelas: the Integrated Centres of Public Education in Rio de Janeiro, 1983-87.)
Camille Goirand. *Cahiers des Amériques Latines*, vol. 16 (1993), p. 47-62.

An interesting study of a new type of school introduced in the State of Rio de Janeiro by Governor Brizola, to provide a basic education of literacy and arithmetic, but also offering three meals a day and health support. The paper discusses the aims and implementation of the plan, and opposition to it.

661 **Education performance for the poor: lessons from rural northeast Brazil.**
Ralph W. Harbison, Eric A. Hanushek. Washington, DC; Oxford: Oxford University Press for World Bank, 1992. 362p.

Presents a detailed report on the achievement of a Brazilian Government/World Bank project for rural education. The aim was to expand access to schooling, reduce drop-out rates, and improve achievement levels. The nature of the project and its progress are described, and there is a substantial collection of data on education in the region.

662 **Society and education in Brazil.**
Robert J. Havighurst, J. Roberto Moreira. Pittsburgh, Pennsylvania: University of Pittsburgh Press, 1965. 264p. maps.

A considerable part of this book is given over to a general introduction to Brazil, but its value is in a discussion of the role of education in a developing society and economy. It deals with Brazil's education system over the period 1945-65, examining the primary, secondary, and tertiary sectors of education in some detail. The volume also offers important perspectives on the major agencies involved in education – the State, the Church, teachers and the family. Although dated, it is a major background source on the subject.

663 **Education and national development in Brazil.**
Hugh Lawlor. In: *Education in Latin America.* Edited by Colin Brock, Hugh Lawlor. London; Dover, New Hampshire: Croom Helm, 1985, p. 130-45.

This paper provides a brief summary of the history of Brazil's education system, before describing the changes made to create an eight-year pattern of compulsory primary and secondary education. It is a useful introduction to recent developments in Brazil's education system.

664 **Perspectives on Brazilian education: papers on an Anglo-Brazilian seminar.**
London: Institute of Education, University of London, 1987. 92p.
Contains a series of reports by Brazilian educationalists on the tertiary sector, dealing with the transfer of technology and the training of research workers.

665 **The expansion of education: a Brazilian case study.**
D. N. Plank. *Comparative Education Review*, vol. 31 (1987), p. 361-76.
An interesting exploration of the diffusion of education in Brazil from 1940-80, which it relates to wider social, economic and political change.

666 **Knowledge as a constraint on growth.**
S. Schwartzman. In: *Growth and development in Brazil: Cardoso's Real challenge.* Edited by Maria D'Alva Kinzo, Victor Bulmer-Thomas. London: Institute of Latin American Studies, University of London, 1994, p. 109-29.
This essay offers a very good summary of constraints on development posed by deficiencies in general education, professional training, and in science and technology. It covers the situation and policies in all sectors of education.

667 **Paulo Freire as Secretary of Education in the Municipality of São Paulo.**
Carlos Alberto Torres. *Comparative Education Review*, vol. 38 (1994), p. 181-214.
Freire was a distinguished and innovative educationalist. When the Partido dos Trabalhadores (Workers' Party) won the municipal elections for the metropolis of São Paulo, Freire was appointed to direct its education system (1989-92). This is an exploration of the introduction of popular education ('education for liberation') to the city.

Science, Technology and the History of Ideas

Science and technology

668   **Generation of scientists and engineers. Origins of the computer industry in Brazil.**
Erick D. Langer.   *Latin American Research Review*, vol. 24, no. 2 (1989), p. 95-111.

A study of nationalistic protection of the computer market, and the training of the necessary technical expertise in universities and research institutions from the 1950s onwards.

669   **Brazil.**
In: *Science and technology in Latin America.*   Christopher Roper, Jorg Silva.   London: Longman, 1983, p. 32-57.

This is an invaluable resource for researchers seeking points of reference and contacts in Brazil. The paper outlines the organization, financing, and policy-making of science and technology. It lists universities and their fields of interest, and research agencies in the fields of agriculture, industry, meteorology, medicine and nuclear studies, etc.

670   **A space for science. The development of the scientific community in Brazil.**
Simon Schwartzman.   University Park, Pennsylvania: Pennsylvania State University, 1991. 286p. bibliog.

An excellent history of science in Brazil, covering the natural sciences in the 18th century, the Empire, and the 1930s. As a revision of a 1979 book, discussion of post-war university expansion and the 'great leap forward' in science in Brazil has been added. The book also devotes considerable attention to the role of science in development.

671 **Beginnings of Brazilian science. Oswaldo Cruz, medical research and policy, 1890-1920.**
Nancy Stepan.   New York: Science History Publications, 1976. 226p. bibliog.

In spite of its precise title, this book offers a useful study of the history of science in Brazil in the colonial and Empire periods. Its main focus, however, is upon the rise of urban health problems and the contribution of the Brazilian scientist Oswaldo Cruz (1872-1917) to their solution. Cruz is credited with eradicating yellow fever, smallpox and malaria from the city of Rio de Janeiro. The work also raises issues relating to policy on matters of science in the developing world.

The history of ideas

672 **The green wave of coffee. Beginnings of tropical agricultural research in Brazil, 1885-1900.**
Warren Dean.   *Hispanic American Historical Review*, vol. 69 (1989), p. 91-115.

An interesting study of early agricultural research, particularly to improve coffee production. It chronicles the efforts to establish an Agricultural Research Institute at Campinas, in the state of São Paulo.

673 **The beginnings of professionalism in the Brazilian military: the eighteenth century Corps of Engineers.**
Roberta M. Delson.   *The Americas*, vol. 51 (1995), p. 555-74.

This paper argues that military engineers were among the first educated group in Brazil, as the Portuguese permitted training in the construction of forts and other military installations.

674 **Race and identity: Sílvio Romero, science, and social thought in late nineteenth century Brazil.**
Marshall C. Eakin.   *Luso-Brazilian Review*, vol. 22, no. 2 (1985), p. 151-74.

An exploration of the role of Romero, a leading literary critic and social commentator, who sought to apply European social theories to Brazil, and to reconcile contemporary scientific ideas to Brazilian circumstances in the late-19th century. Important issues which attracted his interest included social evolutionism and miscegenation.

675 **Sur l'influence scientifique Française au Brésil aux XIXe et XXe siècles.** (The scientific influence of France in Brazil in the 19th and 20th centuries.)
Michel Paty, Patrick Petitjean. *Cahiers des Amériques Latines*, vol. 4 (1985), p. 31-47.

There were strong cultural and scientific ties between Brazil and France in the 19th century. This paper looks at the influence of French individuals and institutions in stimulating intellectual advance in Brazil, such as the Brazilian Academy of Sciences in Rio de Janeiro, and the Ouro Prêto School of Mines in Minas Gerais.

Literature

General

676 **Historical source and biographical context in the interpretation of Euclides da Cunha's *Os Sertões*.**
Frederic Amory. *Journal of Latin American Studies*, vol. 28 (1996), p. 667-85.

Os sertões, first published in 1902, and translated as *Rebellion in the backlands* in 1944, is one of the most important works in Brazilian literature. It is based on events in interior Bahia in the late-19th century, and is rooted in the author's deterministic views about people and their environment, which are set out in a preamble to the novel. This paper provides a useful summary of scholarship on the book, and explores some of the sources for da Cunha's ideas. In particular, it looks at European and Brazilian sources for his views on race.

677 **Race and colour in Brazilian literature.**
David Brookshaw. Metuchen, New Jersey; London: Scarecrow Press Inc., 1986. 348p. bibliog.

This is a study of racial stereotypes, which explores the way that blacks have been seen by white and black writers. It examines the changing nature of the image held by whites since abolition, and Afro-Brazilians' view of their experiences of, and reaction to, white stereotyping.

678 **Paradise betrayed. Brazilian literature of the Indian.**
David Brookshaw. Amsterdam: CEDLA, 1988. 250p. bibliog.

An examination of the portrayal and role of the Indian in Brazilian literature from the colonial period. It argues that the Indian in literature is often a symbol removed from his natural context, derived from the cultural values of the writer and historical circumstances.

679 The problematic heroines in the novels of Rachel de Queiroz.

Joanna Courteau. *Luso-Brazilian Review*, vol. 22, no. 2 (1985), p. 124-50.

This is an exploration of themes of the life, character, and social role of women in the Northeast in the novels of Rachel de Queiroz (1910-). It looks at the social inequality of women and their self-fulfilment, as described in a number of her novels.

680 Introduction to literature in Brazil.

Afranio Coutinho, translated by Gregory Rabassa. New York; London: Columbia University Press, 1969. 326p. bibliog.

Although dated, this is a standard reference source on Brazilian literature and the methods employed to study it. The volume contains a wide-ranging bibliography of works relating to literary methods, folklore, the history of Brazilian culture, and a range of genres. Its text discusses a number of major themes from the baroque and romanticism to regionalism and modernism.

681 Life in the textile factory. Two 1933 perspectives.

Mary L. Daniel. *Luso-Brazilian Review*, vol. 31, no. 2 (1994), p. 97-113.

A discussion of two pioneering proletarian novels of urban factory life in the 1920s which concern female garment workers – Amando Fontes' *Os corumbas* (Forgotten places) and Patricia Galvão's *Parque industrial*.

682 Brazilian fiction. Aspects and evolution of the contemporary novel.

Robert E. DiAntonio. Fayetteville, Arkansas; London: University of Arkansas Press, 1989. 222p. bibliog.

Offers a useful review of recent trends in Brazilian literature, drawing upon case-study novels. The work explores themes of myth, absurdist visions, and socio-political narratives.

683 Clarice Lispector.

Earl E. Fitz. Boston, Massachusetts: Twayne Publishers, 1985. 160p.

Lispector is a major figure in modern Brazilian writing. This study provides a biography, an assessment of her place in Brazilian literature and reviews of her novels, stories and non-fiction. It includes a bibliography of her work and criticisms of it.

684 Machado de Assis.

Earl E. Fitz. Boston, Massachusetts: Twayne Publishers, 1989. 150p. bibliog.

This study seeks to demonstrate Machado's importance as a novelist of the late-19th/ early 20th centuries, and to set his work in the context of that of his European contemporaries. It includes critical commentary on the full range of his activities: novels, poetry, drama, essays and literary criticism.

685 **The deceptive realism of Machado de Assis. A dissenting interpretation of *Dom Casmurro*.**
John Gledson.   Liverpool, United Kingdom: Francis Cairns, 1984.
216p. bibliog.

This scholarly monograph presents an original interpretation of one of Machado's key novels, which instead of offering the standard literary approach, argues that it provides a portrait of the Rio de Janeiro society to which the author belonged. The book provides a detailed analysis of key elements, such as the political context of the novel, drawn from other work by Machado and contemporary views of 19th-century Brazil.

686 **Brazilian fiction: Machado de Assis to the present.**
John Gledson.   In: *Modern Latin American fiction: a survey*.   Edited by John King.   London; Boston, Massachusetts: Faber & Faber, 1987, p. 18-40.

A useful, concise summary of 20th-century trends, including modernism and the regional novel of the Northeast. Among the writers discussed are Machado de Assis, Euclides da Cunha, Mário de Andrade, Oswaldo de Andrade, Graciliano Ramos, Clarice Lispector, João Guimarães Rosa, and Autran Dourado. The essay includes commentary on many of the novels included in this bibliography.

687 **A history lesson: Machado de Assis's 'Conto de escola'.**
John Gledson.   In: *Portuguese, Brazilian and African Studies presented to Clive Willis on his retirement*.   Edited by T. F. Earle, N. Griffin, R. C. Willis.   Warminster, United Kingdom: Aris & Phillips, 1995, p. 217-26.

'Conto de escola' (School story) is one of Machado's most famous and anthologized short stories, dealing with adult-child relations. This essay provides an analysis of the story.

688 **Three sad races: racial identity and national consciousness in Brazilian literature.**
David T. Haberly.   Cambridge, United Kingdom; New York: Cambridge University Press, 1983. 198p. bibliog.

An exploration of the notion that Brazilian literature has its roots in the interaction of Indians, Africans and Portuguese, and the sadness of suffering, exile and loss. The book suggests that the multiracial character of Brazilian literature is in part a search for a viable racial identity. It draws upon the work of several novelists, including Machado de Assis, José de Alencar and Mário de Andrade.

689 **Tropical paths: essays on modern Brazilian literature.**
Edited by Randal Johnson.   New York; London: Garland Publishing Inc., 1993. 234p.

This study provides coverage of the diversity of Brazilian literature from 1800 to the 1980s, dealing with key issues such as nationhood, identity, modernity, sexuality, and politics. Its concluding essay discusses issues facing writers in the 1990s, from the publishing industry, the public, and literary criticism.

690 **The dynamics of the Brazilian literary field, 1930-1945.**
Randal Johnson. *Luso-Brazilian Review*, vol. 31, no. 2 (1994),
p. 5-22.
An interesting contextual exploration of the relationship between literature and
political authority, which assesses President Vargas' involvement of intellectuals and
writers in nation-building during a period of profound change in Brazil.

691 **The city in Brazilian literature.**
Elizabeth A. S. Lowe. London; East Brunswick, New Jersey:
Associated University Press, 1982. 230p. bibliog.
This book is an examination of the literature produced in a period of rapid
urbanization. It suggests that both historical and contemporary writings are urban in
nature, with the city as both setting and symbol. There is a useful appendix on
eighteen contemporary writers.

692 **Black characters in the Brazilian novel.**
Giorgio Marotti, translated by Maria O. Marotti, Harry Lawton. Los
Angeles, California: Center for Afro-American Studies, University of
California, 1987. 450p. bibliog.
Assesses the direct and indirect impact of slavery on Brazilian literature, and explores
how blacks were, and are, represented in the novel.

693 **Myth and ideology in contemporary Brazilian fiction.**
Daphne Patai. Cranbury, New Jersey; London: Associated University
Press, 1983. 260p.
A study of the place of myth in Brazilian literature. It draws upon specific novels by
six contemporary writers: Clarice Lispector, Jorge Amado, Carlos Heitor Cony,
Adonais Filho, Autran Dourado, and Maria Alice Barroso.

694 **Ambiguity and gender in the new novel of Brazil and Spanish
America. A comparative assessment.**
Judith A. Payne, Earl E. Fitz. Iowa City, Iowa: University of Iowa
Press, 1993. 226p. bibliog.
It is claimed that Brazil has one of the world's most neglected literatures. This
comparative study explores attitudes to gender in Latin America, arguing that Brazil
has a greater acceptance of women writers and is more open to less-conventional
approaches in writing than Spanish America.

695 **Exploring women's destinies: *As três Marias* by Rachel de Queiroz.**
Cláudia Pazos Alonso. In: *Portuguese, Brazilian and African studies
presented to Clive Willis on his retirement.* Edited by T. F. Earle,
N. Griffin, R. C. Willis. Warminster, United Kingdom: Aris &
Phillips, 1995, p. 285-95.
De Queiroz is one of Brazil's most successful contemporary women writers. *As três
Marias* (The three Marias), published in 1939, is a reflection on the roles open to

convent-educated women. The story is a commentary on a patriarchal society where women are forced to fit into the pre-existing mould of family.

696 João Guimarães Rosa: an endless passage.
Charles A. Perrone. In: *Modern Latin American fiction: a survey.* Edited by John King. London; Boston, Massachusetts: Faber & Faber, 1987, p. 117-35.

João Guimarães Rosa (1908-67) set much of his work in the backland *sertão* of Minas Gerais, revealing a detailed familiarity with the area's dialect, geography and life. This paper provides a useful analysis of six of his seven major works of fiction. Each of the works is discussed in some detail, and the author points to the challenge posed by Rosa's style and use of language.

697 The female voice in contemporary Brazilian narrative.
Susan C. Quinlan. New York; London: Peter Lang, 1991. 206p. bibliog.

This study draws on three novels of the 1980s to explore recent feminist literature in Brazil, and set them in contemporary context. The novels relate to the Germanic South (Lya Luft: *As parceiras,* 1980), the contemporary urban scene (Márcia Denser: *O animal dos motéis: novela em episódios,* 1981), and the Afro-Brazilian traditions of the Northeast (Sonia Coutinho: *O jogo de Ifá,* 1980).

698 Childhood.
Graciliano Ramos, translated by Celso de Oliveira. London: Peter Owen, 1979. 174p.

Graciliano Ramos (1892-1953) is one of Brazil's greatest writers. This is the story of his childhood in the rural Northeast. Its translator describes it as the best account we have of the region in the 1890s.

699 One hundred years after tomorrow: Brazilian women's fiction in the twentieth century.
Edited by Darlene J. Sadlier. Bloomington, Indiana: Indiana University Press, 1992. 242p.

This is a useful compendium of women's writing from Brazil. It consists of work, previously unpublished in English, from twenty authors, presented in chronological order of publication from 1907-85. The volume also contains a further list of selected writings.

700 Stories on a string: the Brazilian *literatura de cordel.*
Candace Slater. Berkeley, California; London: University of California Press, 1982. 312p. map. bibliog.

The *literatura de cordel* (string literature) is a pamphlet literature for the poor of the Northeast of Brazil. This book examines its origins in traditional stories and ballads, approaches to it, and the poets' visions of their stories. Several tales are analysed, and there are notes on authors and on buyers of the tales.

701 **Dictionary of Brazilian literature.**
Edited by Irwin Stern. New York; London: Greenwood Press, 1988.
402p. map.
This is probably the best introduction to Brazilian literature, with over 300 entries on writers, schools, and cultural movements, mainly from the 20th century. A brief general introduction is followed by entries on literary movements and major authors. The latter include listings of work and bibliographies. The book is particularly valuable for its substantive entries on a range of important themes in Brazilian literature. These include the Indian, immigrants, modernism, feminism, the regional novel, theatre, popular culture, travel literature, and views of Brazil in the work of foreign writers. There is also a useful chronology, which sets important literary events in Brazil against those elsewhere.

702 **João Guimarães Rosa.**
Jon S. Vincent. Boston, Massachusetts: Twayne Publishers, 1978. 182p.
This is a critical study of Rosa's seven volumes of fiction. As they have not all been translated into English, it provides a good introduction to his work.

703 **An anthology of modern Portuguese and Brazilian prose.**
I. R. Warner, A. G. Sousa. London: Harrap, 1978. 172p.
In part this is a collection of prose passages for students of Portuguese, but it also aims to serve as an introduction to the Portuguese fiction of Europe, Africa and Brazil. The volume contains a brief introduction, and the selection includes work by Graciliano Ramos, Lins de Rego and Guimarães Rosa.

704 **Brazil.**
Jason Wilson. In: *Traveller's literary companion to South and Central America.* London: In Print Publishing Co. Ltd., 1993, p. 287-335.
A very useful introduction to Brazilian literature. The paper contains an introductory essay on Brazil, a list of English-language books, including translations, followed by extracts from thirty-two works, and biographical notes on authors. (A few of these, from English writers, are of marginal interest and quality.)

Literature in translation

705 **Mulatto.**
Aluísio de Azevedo, translated by Murray Graeme MacNicoll.
Cranbury, New Jersey; London: Associated University Press, 1990.
298p.
This story is set in the northeastern city of São Luis in the 1870s, the period of abolitionism and republicanism. It provides a melodramatic commentary on racial prejudice, within a detailed portrait of the city, its society, dwellings and people.

706 **The violent land.**
Jorge Amado, translated by Samuel Putnam. New York: Avon
Books, 1979. 278p.
An exciting portrait of the 'cocoa boom' in southern Bahia of the early 20th century,
involving clearance of the forest, and conflicts over land.

707 **Gabriela, clove and cinnamon.**
Jorge Amado, translated by James L. Taylor, William L. Grossman.
London: Chatto and Windus, 1963. 426p.
This story is also set in the cocoa region, but in its 'capital', Ilheus, in the 1920s. It is
a portrayal of local politics, and of the impact of the beautiful Gabriela, a migrant
from the interior, on local society.

708 **Dona Flor and her two husbands.**
Jorge Amado, translated by Harriet de Onis. New York: Avon Books,
1969. 524p.
The later work of Jorge Amado (1912-) tends to be more urban and risqué, often
involving elements of Bahia's Afro-Brazilian heritage. These elements are contained
in this novel, as Dona Flor enjoys the continued attentions of her dead and living
husbands, with some assistance from the gods.

709 **The celebration.**
Ivan Ângelo, translated by Thomas Colchie. New York: Avon Books,
1982. 224p.
A complex story, set in Minas Gerais, involving migrants from the Northeast and a
wealthy urban family, and culminating in the repressive period of the military régime.

710 **Rebellion in the backlands.**
Euclides da Cunha, translated by Samuel Putnam. London: Picador,
1995. 752p. maps.
Described as 'Brazil's greatest book', this epic novel is the story of the brutal
suppression of a rebellion in northern Bahia in 1896-97, in which the followers of a
Messianic leader resisted the Brazilian army.

711 **The voices of the dead.**
Autran Dourado, translated by John M. Parker. Feltham, United
Kingdom: Zenith Books, 1983. 250p.
A story of isolation and passion in a small town in interior Minas Gerais.

712 **The long haul.**
Oswaldo França Jnr., translated by Thomas Colchie. New York:
E. P. Dutton, 1980. 184p.
This might be described as a 'road' novel, as it chronicles the adventures of a lorry
driver travelling across interior Brazil in adverse conditions.

713 **The devil to pay in the backlands.**
João Guimarães Rosa, translated by James L. Taylor, Harriet de Onis.
New York: Alfred A. Knopf, 1971. 498p.

Guimarães Rosa is a major figure in Brazilian literature, and this is one of his key works. It is a story of feuding outlaws, set in interior Brazil, with considerable detail on the environment, and with themes of man against nature, against other men, and against evil.

714 **The hour of the star.**
Clarice Lispector, translated by Giovanni Pontiero. Manchester, United Kingdom: Carcanet Press, 1986. 96p.

A portrait of the life of a poor, unattractive girl from the Northeast working in Rio de Janeiro.

715 **Dom Casmurro.**
Machado de Assis, translated by Helen Caldwell. Berkeley, California: University of California Press, 1966. 270p.

Machado de Assis is a major figure in Brazilian literature, and *Dom Casmurro*, with its strange, original plot, has been described as one of the finest pieces of fiction ever written.

716 **The water house.**
Antônio Olinto, translated by Dorothy Heapy. Walton-on-Thames, United Kingdom: Nelson, 1982. 410p.

This is an account of an Afro-Brazilian family who return to Africa after emancipation from slavery. The early part of the work is set in Brazil, but the bulk of the story takes place in West Africa, and provides interesting links to Afro-Brazilian traditions.

717 **Barren lives.**
Graciliano Ramos, translated by Ralph Edward Dimmick. Austin, Texas: University of Texas Press, 1965. 132p.

'Barren lives' is one of the classic 'regional novels' of Northeast Brazil. It graphically tells the story of a family fleeing from drought across the arid interior towards the city.

718 **São Bernardo.**
Graciliano Ramos, translated by R. L. Scott-Buccleuch. London: Peter Owen, 1975. 156p.

Set in the coastal region of the Northeast in the 1920s and 1930s, at a time of the break-up of large estates, this work chronicles the tragic relationship between a self-made man and his socially-superior wife.

719 **Maíra.**
Darcy Ribeiro, translated by E. H. Goodland, Thomas Colchie.
London: Picador, 1985. 360p.
Ribeiro is a distinguished anthropologist, and this novel is a portrayal of the clash of Indian culture with Brazil's frontier economy. It offers a first-hand literary portrait of a disappearing Indian society.

720 **Sergeant Getúlio.**
João Ubaldo Ribeiro. London: André Deutsch, 1980. 146p.
A complex story of a gunman hired to capture a political enemy for his boss, and his journey of self-discovery. It is set in the harsh interior of the Northeast.

721 **An anthology of Brazilian prose from the beginning to the present.**
R. L. Scott-Buccleuch, Mario Teles de Oliveira. São Paulo, Brazil: Editora Atica, 1971. 534p.
The aim of this study is to introduce a representative selection of Brazilian writing from the colonial period to 1970, using the best work of leading authors, and illustrating Brazilian life and character. It is divided into three periods: Formation, before 1822; Transformation, from 1822-1922; and Modern, from 1922 onwards. Each section has a brief introduction and author biography in English, but the texts are in Portuguese.

722 **The emperor of the Amazon.**
Márcio Souza, translated by Thomas Colchie. London: Abacus, 1982. 192p.
An episodic comic story, describing the misadventures of a journalist in Amazonia. It spans the period 1897-99, and ranges across the region in a multiplicity of brief paragraphs.

723 **The land.**
Antônio Torres, translated by Margaret E. Neves. London: Readers International Inc., 1987. 138p.
A story from the dry interior *sertão* of the Northeast, contrasting the urban dreams of a community experiencing crop failure with the nostalgia of urban shanty-town dwellers for their rural homeland.

Short stories

724 **Modern Brazilian short stories.**
William L. Grossman. Berkeley, California; London: University of California Press, 1974. 168p.
A collection of seventeen stories from Brazil's Modernist tradition, which portray the regional diversity of the country and its literature. It includes contributions from three

key figures in the movement: Mário de Andrade, Antônio de Alcântara Machado, and Ribeiro Couto.

725 Family ties.
Clarice Lispector, translated by Giovanni Pontiero.   Manchester, United Kingdom: Carcanet Press, 1985. 140p.

Comprises seventeen tales about the lives of a range of characters including old ladies, housewives, young girls and others.

726 Looking for some dignity.
Clarice Lispector.   In: *Short stories by Latin American women: the magic and the real.*   Edited by Celia Correas de Zapata.   Houston, Texas: Arte Público Press, p. 121-28.

A tale of a lost and lonely woman in Rio.

727 The psychiatrist and other stories.
Machado de Assis, translated by William L. Grossman, Helen Caldwell.   Berkeley, California: University of California Press; London: Peter Owen Press, 1963. 148p.

This was the first collection of short stories by Machado to be published in English. They were selected by the translators to illustrate the diversity of his methods and ideas. The volume contains twelve stories, from the period 1881-1905.

728 Big-bellied cow.
Nélida Piñón.   In: *Short stories by Latin American women: the magic and the real.*   Edited by Celia Correas de Zapata.   Houston, Texas: Arte Público Press, 1990, p. 156-62.

A rustic tale of the burial of a family pet cow.

Poetry

729 This earth, that sky.
Manuel Bandeira, translated by Candace Slater.   Berkeley, California; London: University of California Press, 1989. 248p.

Manuel Bandeira (1886-1968) was a prolific writer in a variety of poetic forms. This volume contains over 100 poems and a critical review. The translator suggests that the poetic themes include nature, male-female relationships, religious imagery, art, and time. The poems are presented in parallel Portuguese and English text.

730 **An anthology of twentieth-century Brazilian poetry.**
Elizabeth Bishop, Emanuel Brasil. Middletown, Connecticut:
Wesleyan University Press, 1972. 182p.

A collection of the work of fourteen modern poets, provided in English and Portuguese. Among those included are Drummond de Andrade, Cecília Meireles, Oswaldo de Andrade, and Mário de Andrade. The volume also contains a useful discussion of the nature and rules of Brazilian poetry, and of the difficulties of rendering good translations of the poems into English.

731 **Brazilian poetry, 1950-1980,**
Emanuel Brasil, William J. Smith. Middletown, Connecticut:
Wesleyan University Press, 1983. 188p.

This is a collection of work from six poets from the period since 1950, which is seen as an important phase in Brazilian poetic development. Progress in printing technology made it possible to produce visual poetry, so that the layout as well as the text of these examples is significant. The text is provided in parallel English and Portuguese. The poets whose work is featured are Ferreira Gullan, Haroldo de Campos, Augusto de Campos, Décio Pignatari, Mário Faustino, and Lindolf Bell.

732 **Brazil.**
In: *The Penguin book of Latin American verse.* Edited by
E. Caracciolo-Trejo. Harmondsworth, United Kingdom: Penguin,
1971, p. 53-97.

A selection from the work of thirteen Brazilian poets of the 19th and 20th centuries. They include Bilac, Meireles, Drummond de Andrade, and Vinicius de Moraes. The poems are given in both English and Portuguese.

733 **The minus sign: a selection from the poetic anthology.**
Carlos Drummond de Andrade, translated by Virginia de Araujo.
Manchester, United Kingdom: Carcanet Press, 1986. 168p.

A brief biography of Carlos Drummond de Andrade (1902-87) and a portrait of his birthplace, Itabira in Minas Gerais, is followed by fifty-four of his poems which are identified as dealing with the individual, Minas Gerais, and 'being-in-the-world'.

734 **Margins and marginals: new Brazilian poetry of the 1970s.**
Charles A. Perrone. *Luso-Brazilian Review*, vol. 31, no. 1 (1994),
p. 17-37.

A summary of key trends in the 1970s, particularly in the work of young poets, during a period of repression.

735 **An anthology of Brazilian modernist poetry.**
Giovanni Pontiero. Oxford; New York: Pergamon Press, 1969. 246p.
bibliog.

A collection of work from twenty-one poets in the Modernist tradition, which emerged from the São Paulo Week of Modern Art of 1922. A helpful introduction to the Modernist movement and its phases is included. The poems are given in Portuguese, but there is a brief biography of each poet in English, together with a listing of works and criticism.

The Arts

General

736 **Profile of the new Brazilian art.**
P. M. Bardi. Rio de Janeiro, Brazil: Livraria Kosmos Editora, 1970.
160p.

The prime concern of this profusely illustrated book is with the arts in Brazil since the emergence of Modernism in the 1920s, but it does refer to Indian and popular art. After exploring trends in the arts from 1922-45, it provides a wide-ranging survey of architecture, sculpture, painting, advertising, photography, fashion, furniture, theatre, cinema and music. Although it is now dated, the volume affords a valuable portrait of a dynamic half-century of Brazilian artistic activity.

737 **The baroque presence in Brazilian art.**
Leopoldo Castedo. New York: Charles Frank Publishers Inc., 1964.
152p.

Analyses the distinct form of the Brazilian baroque, focusing mainly on the religious architecture and sculpture of Minas Gerais.

738 **The Brazilian puzzle: culture on the borderlands of western culture.**
Edited by David J. Hess, Roberto DaMatta. New York; Chichester, United Kingdom: Columbia University Press, 1995. 306p. map.

A useful collection of essays on Brazilian cultural themes, mainly as seen by Brazilian authors. Its topics include cultural traditions, the elements of national identity, and popular music. Also discussed are wider societal issues such as social relations, religion, and crime.

739   **A hidden view. Images of Bahia, Brazil.**
Edited by Amanda Hopkinson.   London: Frontline/Brazilian
Contemporary Arts, 1994. 112p.
Consists of images and words taken from the work of six artists and photographers of
Bahia. The collection includes photos of rural landscapes and Salvador, and paintings
and photos of Afro-Brazilian subjects.

740   **Brasil. Arte do Nordeste/Art of the Northeast.**
Paulo Lyra.   Rio de Janeiro, Brazil: Spala Editora, 1986. 436p. map.
This bilingual study is a detailed introduction to the arts in the Northeast. The art of
each northeastern state is discussed, and there is systematic coverage of work in wood,
stone, ceramics, tapestry, weaving, and painting. About one-third of the book is text,
with the remainder consisting of excellent colour photographs.

741   **A tropical belle époque: elite culture and society in
turn-of-the-century Rio de Janeiro.**
Jeffrey D. Needell.   Cambridge, United Kingdom; New York:
Cambridge University Press, 1987. 352p. maps. bibliog.
After Brazil gained independence from Portugal in 1822 the country experienced neo-
colonial influence not only in the economy but in culture as well, with a heavy
dependence on France and Britain. This volume explores the place of such culture in
Rio de Janeiro from 1898-1914. It discusses élite institutions such as the clubs and
theatre, the *salon*, fashion, domestic architecture, and literature. It is a good portrait of
the ambience of *fin de siècle* culture in Rio.

742   **Misplaced ideas: essays on Brazilian culture.**
Roberto Schwartz.   London; New York: Verso, 1992. 204p.
This book contains an important series of essays on culture and identity in Brazil,
covering literature, music, theatre and film. It includes four essays on the novelist,
Machado de Assis, and a commentary on the reaction of the cultural scene in Brazil to
the early years (1964-69) of military repression.

Architecture

743   **Roberto Burle Marx. The unnatural art of the garden.**
William Howard Adams.   New York: Museum of Modern Art, 1991.
80p. bibliog.
Burle Marx (1909-94) is a key figure in the creation of the modern Brazilian built
environment, as a landscape architect. This richly illustrated book, produced to
accompany an exhibition of his work at MOMA, describes his career and provides
examples of his work, from private gardens to major public projects in Rio de Janeiro.

744 **The architecture and art of colonial Brazil.**
J. B. Bury. In: *Cambridge history of Latin America. Vol. II.* Edited
by Leslie Bethell. Cambridge, United Kingdom; New York:
Cambridge University Press, 1984, p. 747-69. bibliog.

Essentially a detailed discussion of baroque churches in the Northeast, Minas Gerais
and Rio de Janeiro. It is a very scholarly commentary on religious masterpieces in
Salvador, Ouro Preto, Mariana, Congonhas, and Rio, with some observations on
domestic architecture in addition.

745 **Modern architecture in Brazil.**
Henrique E. Mindlin. London: The Architectural Press, 1956. 256p.
bibliog.

The startling 'modern' architecture of Brazil emerged in the 1930s. This study
documents the progress of the Brazilian style in the period prior to the construction of
Brasília, which began in 1956. It includes the work of more than seventy architects,
and is illustrated by over 700 photographs and drawings.

746 **Oscar Niemeyer.**
Rupert Spade. London: Thames and Hudson, 1971. 136p. bibliog.

Niemeyer (1907-) is among Latin America's leading architects, and a key figure in
the modern architecture of Brazil. This profusely illustrated book traces his work from
the Rio Ministry of Education of 1937 to Brasília, for which he was chief architect.

747 **Brasilia.**
Willy Stäubli. London: Leonard Hill Books, 1966. 200p.

A detailed and illustrated commentary on the site and layout of the city, which was
inaugurated as Brazil's new capital in 1960, with plans and photographs of the
principal buildings. It is a good record of the early development of the city's form.

Painting

748 **Art in Latin America.**
Dawn Ades. New Haven, Connecticut; London: Yale University
Press, 1989. 362p. bibliog.

Published to accompany a major exhibition of art in Latin America since the 1820s,
this beautifully illustrated volume does not contain specific chapters on Brazil.
However, it is an essential contextual reference source, covering the major themes and
movements in art since Independence. It contains a biographical section which
includes not only Brazilian artists such as Portinari and Burle Marx, but important
overseas painters such as Debret and Rugendas. An appendix on artistic 'manifestos'
includes some important Brazilian statements on art, especially relating to the
Modernist movement.

749 **Brazil through its artists/O Brasil por seus artistas.**
Walter Ayala.   Rio de Janeiro, Brazil: Editorial Nórdica Ltda., [s.d.].
212p.

This copiously illustrated bilingual volume explores the way Brazil has been portrayed in art. Its three sections deal with: the landscape, including natural, rural, and urban scenes; life, including social, economic and cultural images; and symbols and nature, which includes flora and fauna, as well as items of popular culture. The paintings reproduced are predominantly from the 20th century, but there are a few examples of earlier work.

750 **Brazilian popular prints.**
Edited by Mark Dineen.   London: Redstone Press, 1995. 106p.

Literatura de cordel (string literature) is a popular literary form in the Northeast, consisting of inexpensive pamphlets containing familiar tales. This book provides examples of their woodcut covers, and explains the genre. It includes an example of the stories and notes on some of the artists.

751 **Iconography and landscape: Cultura Inglesa collection/**
Iconografia e paisagem: coleção Cultura Inglesa.
Carlos Roberto Maciel Levy et al.   Rio de Janeiro, Brazil: Edições
Pinakotheke, 1994. 258p. bibliog.

The art collection of the Cultura Inglesa (Brazilian Society for English Culture) consists of around one hundred paintings of Brazil, dating mainly from the 19th century. The dominant themes of the collection, from which the book takes its title, are the representation of details of topography, wildlife and social customs, and broader landscapes. It is organized by artist, with reference to those born between 1783 and circa 1870, and includes both Brazilian and foreign painters. A major component of the work is more than thirty lithographs by the German artist, J. M. Rugendas, of native peoples and African slaves.

752 **A portrait of Dutch 17th century Brazil. Animals, plants and**
people by the artists of Johan Maurits of Nassau.
P. J. P. Whitehead, M. Boeseman.   Amsterdam; Oxford; New York:
North-Holland Publishing Company, 1989. 360p. map.

The Dutch occupied part of northeast Brazil between 1630 and 1654. Johan Maurits, the Governor-General from 1637-44, commissioned artists, scientists, surveyors and others to record the colony in great detail. Pictures by Albert Eckhout, Frans Post and others provide a very early and superb record of the landscape, wildlife, natives and early economy of Brazil. This book is a meticulous study of the artistic work, and is richly illustrated.

Music

753 **Capoeira. A Brazilian art form: history, philosophy and practice.**
Bira Almeida. Berkeley, California: North Atlantic Books, 1986.
2nd ed. 182p. bibliog.
Capoeira is an Afro-Brazilian tradition which incorporates music, dance and fighting.
This study explores these elements and their history.

754 **The music of Brazil.**
David P. Appleby. Austin, Texas: University of Texas Press, 1989.
210p. bibliog.
This is a comprehensive survey of the history of Brazilian folk, popular, and classical
music, from the colonial period to the present day. It emphasizes the contribution of
major composers, and includes a large number of musical examples.

755 **Heitor Villa-Lobos: the search for Brazil's musical soul.**
Gerard Béhague. Austin, Texas: Institute of Latin American Studies,
University of Texas at Austin, 1994. 202p. bibliog. discography.
Villa-Lobos (1887-1959) is Brazil's best-known classical composer. This study
provides a biography, and an exploration of the nationalist and folkloric elements in
his music. It includes a selective discography of recordings from 1970 to the early
1990s.

756 **Samba: resistance in motion.**
Barbara Browning. Bloomington, Indiana: Indiana University Press,
1995. 190p.
In spite of its title, this book covers not only samba, but *candomblé*, and *capoeira*. It
explores the nature of these dances and their role, and more broadly that of *carnaval*
(Carnival), in racial and sexual identity in Brazil.

757 **Brazil.**
In: *A guide to the music of Latin America.* Gilbert Chase.
Washington, DC: Pan American Union and Library of Congress, 1962,
2nd ed., p. 107-57.
First published in 1945, this is essentially a bibliographical guide to music in Latin
America. Following a brief general introduction, it contains an annotated bibliography
for each country. The Brazilian section includes biographical and critical material, and
sources on Amerindian, African, folk and popular music. Its value is as a source of
historical material, including some from the 19th century.

758 **The prehistory of samba: carnival dancing in Rio de Janeiro, 1840-1917.**
John C. Chasteen. *Journal of Latin American Studies*, vol. 28 (1996), p. 29-48.

A very interesting review of the history and role of samba, tracing its roots back to African dancing in the colonial period, and its emergence as a more social phenomenon in the late-19th century.

759 **Ring of liberation: deceptive discourse in Brazilian capoeira.**
J. Lowell Lewis. Chicago; London: University of Chicago Press, 1992. 264p. maps. bibliog.

Provides a detailed analysis of the practice, music and language of this dance form. The study includes a discography, filmography, and useful glossary.

760 **História da música no Brasil.** (History of music in Brazil.)
Vasco Mariz. Rio de Janeiro, Brazil: Civilização Brasileira, 1985. 332p.

This is an historical survey of the classical tradition in Brazilian music. It concentrates on key figures in the various phases of its evolution, particularly nationalistic forms and the 'independent generations' since the 1940s. Brief chapter bibliographies are included.

761 **Masters of contemporary Brazilian song. MPB 1965-1985.**
Charles A. Perrone. Austin, Texas: University of Texas Press, 1989. 254p. bibliog.

MPB is an acronym for *Musica Popular Brasileira* (Brazilian popular music), which emerged as the urban popular music of the 1960s, and has become an important national and international element of Brazilian culture. MPB is rooted in Brazilian musical traditions and was distinct from international pop music of the period. This book focuses on major composers such as Chico Buarque, Caetano Veloso, Gilberto Gil and Milton Nascimento. Its bibliography contains both English and Portuguese sources, and a short discography lists works of the subject composers.

762 **Os sons dos negros no Brasil. Cantos-danças-folguedos: origens.**
(The sounds of blacks in Brazil: songs, dances, diversions: origins.)
José Ramos Tinhorão. São Paulo, Brazil: Art Editora, 1988. 138p. bibliog.

The African contribution to Brazilian popular music is considerable. This book provides a historical perspective on black music, from its roots in colonial slavery to the samba, and rural and urban work songs.

763 **Música Brasileira: a history of popular music and the people of Brazil.**
Claus Schreiner, translated by Mark Weinstein. New York; London: Marion Boyars, 1993. 312p. bibliog.

An important source on Brazilian popular music, this book traces its evolution from its Amerindian, African and folkloric roots to 19th-century choros and sambas. Its main focus is the modern trends of bossa nova, MPB, and the local and regional diversities of the 1970s and 1980s. The volume also deals with instrumentalists, the organization of show business, and the relations between the State and music, especially in terms of the censorship of the 1970s. It includes a useful glossary of Brazilian musical terms.

764 **Why Suyá sing: a musical anthropology of an Amazon people.**
A. Seeger. Cambridge, United Kingdom; New York: Cambridge University Press Studies in ethnomusicology, 1987. 148p.

An exploration of the place of music in the social organization and cultural tradition of a tribal group of the Xingú region.

765 **A note on the music of colonial Brazil.**
Robert Stevenson. In: *Cambridge history of Latin America. Vol. II.* Edited by Leslie Bethell. Cambridge, United Kingdom; New York: Cambridge University Press, 1984, p. 799-803. bibliog.

A brief commentary on recent discoveries of colonial religious music. It includes a discography.

766 **Heitor Villa-Lobos. The life and works, 1887-1959.**
Eero Tarasti. Jefferson, Missouri; London: McFarland & Co., Inc., 1995. 438p. bibliog.

This substantial volume provides a portrait of Villa-Lobos, and sets his work in the context of the music of Latin America and movements in Brazil. Its particular value lies in its detailed analysis of his music – for soloists, chamber groups, concertos, and orchestral pieces. Numerous musical examples are included.

Theatre and cinema

767 **O teatro Brasileiro na década de Oitenta.** (The Brazilian theatre in the Eighties.)
Severino J. Albuquerque. *Latin American Theatre Review*, vol. 25, no. 2 (1992), p. 23-36.

A useful review of Brazilian theatre in the 1980s, especially of its liberation following the end of the military régime.

768   **A bela época do cinema brasileiro.** (The *belle époque* of Brazilian
cinema.)
Vicente de Paula Araújo.   São Paulo, Brazil: Editora Perspectiva,
1976. 420p.
Presents a detailed study of the early history of Brazilian cinema, covering the period
1898-1912. It is essentially a book for the serious student of the cinematic history of
Brazil. The work concentrates upon Rio de Janeiro, describing the cinemas and their
early programmes.

769   **The art of seduction: representation of women in Brazilian silent
cinema.**
Maria Fernandes Baptista Bicalho.   *Luso-Brazilian Review*, vol. 30,
no. 1 (1993), p. 21-33.
A good summary of Brazilian cinema from 1896, which explores the place of women
in film.

770   **Brasil em tempo de cinema. Ensaios sobre a cinema brasileiro.**
(Brazil in the age of cinema: essays on Brazilian cinema.)
Jean-Claude Bernardet.   Rio de Janeiro, Brazil: Paz e Terra, 1978.
3rd ed. 190p. bibliog.
Bernardet offers a critical review of Cinema Novo films of 1958-66, but sets them into
a broader context, especially the significance of urban films for, and about, the middle
classes. A brief filmography of the period is included.

771   **Twentieth-century Brazilian theatre: essays.**
Fred M. Clark, Ana Lúcia Gazolla de García.   Chapel Hill, North
Carolina: Estudios de Hispanófila, 1978. 122p.
Provides an overview of the evolution of modern theatre in Brazil through an
interpretation of the work of four playwrights. It deals with specific plays by Oswaldo
de Andrade, Nelson Rodrigues, Dias Gomes, and Plinio Marcos.

772   **The modern Brazilian stage.**
David S. George.   Austin, Texas: University of Texas Press, 1992.
176p. bibliog.
A narrowly-focused study of Brazilian theatre since the 1940s, based upon the work of
a few companies and key productions.

773   **Regional depiction in contemporary film.**
Brian J. Godfrey.   *Geographical Review*, vol. 83 (1993), p. 428-40.
A discussion of films relating to environmental and social issues, in this case the
rainforest. It examines *Aguirre, the wrath of God* (1972), *Bye, bye, Brazil* (1980), and
The emerald forest (1985).

774 **The film industry in Brazil: culture and the State.**
Randal Johnson.   Pittsburgh, Pennsylvania: University of Pittsburgh
Press, 1987. 270p. bibliog.

This is an important history of Brazilian cinema from 1896, and deals especially with the role of the State in protecting and supporting the national film industry, particularly in times of economic crisis. The book also explores the role of censorship in times of political crisis, and the difficulties of the industry in the 1980s, due to rising costs, competition from television, and the withdrawal of foreign distributors from Brazil.

775 **Brazilian cinema.**
Randal Johnson, Robert Stam.   New York: Columbia University
Press, 1995. 3rd expanded ed. 492p.

This volume contains an introduction to the Brazilian film industry, but its main value lies in a substantial section of writings by film-makers about their work, each with an editorial introduction, and a set of essays on specific films of the Cinema Novo after 1960. There is also discussion of a number of special topics, such as film music, women film-makers and, as the extension for the third edition, of the trends and difficulties of the 1980s and early 1990s.

776 **Professional theatre education in Brazil.**
Frederic Litto, Antônio Mercado.   *Latin American Theatre Review*,
vol. 27, no. 1 (1993), p. 29-38.

A useful brief history of Brazilian theatre, and an outline of the development of theatrical training since 1908. Commentary is included on current centres of theatre education.

777 **Acting into action: Teatro Arena's *Zumbi*.**
Margo Milleret.   *Latin American Theatre Review*, vol. 21, no. 1
(1987), p. 19-28.

A commentary on the experimental Teatro Arena, established in São Paulo in 1953. It set out to present drama which would best represent national social conditions, and in the 1960s became involved in work against the military régime. *Zumbi*, the last leader of the Palmares camp of escaped slaves, is the title of a play which provides an account of the camp from 1630-94, and thus a symbol of resistance. For a historical account of Palmares, see item no. 286.

778 **Dicionário de cineastas brasileiros.** (Dictionary of Brazilian
film-makers.)
Luiz F. Miranda.   São Paulo, Brazil: Art Editora, 1990. 408p. bibliog.

An essential alphabetical reference work on 700 Brazilian film-makers, which provides brief biographical details, and critical commentaries on their films. It is an invaluable source of reference for anyone interested in cinema.

779 **O negro brasileiro, e o cinema.** (The Brazilian black and the cinema.) João Carlos Rodrigues. Rio de Janeiro, Brazil: Editora Globo, 1988. 110p. bibliog.

An important exploration of the place of Blacks in Brazilian cinema, and particularly its role in sustaining archetypes and caricatures of 'old blacks', 'noble savages', crooks, *favelados*, and sensual *mulatas*. It also explores a range of other themes relating to slavery, music and Afro-Brazilian religion. A listing of relevant national and foreign films is included.

780 **Plano geral do cinema brasileiro: historia, cultura, economia e legislação.** (General review of the Brazilian cinema: history, culture, economy and legislation.) Geraldo Santos Pereira. Rio de Janeiro, Brazil: Editora Borsoi, 1973. 358p.

Though dated, this is a comprehensive review of most aspects of Brazilian cinema: production, distribution and exhibition. It also comments on documentaries, educational films, and links with literature. The volume's particular importance lies in its critical analysis of cinematographic legislation between 1928 and 1966.

Photography

781 **Escravos Brasileiros do século XIX na fotografia de Christiano Jr.** (Brazilian slaves in the 19th century, photographed by Christiano Jnr.) Paulo Cesar de Azevedo, Mauricio Lissovsky. São Paulo, Brazil: Editora Ex Libris, 1988. 80p.

Christiano Junior was a photographer in Rio de Janeiro in the late 19th century. This is a major collection of photographs of slaves, mainly studio poses of street traders, but with some portraits and outdoor scenes. A brief commentary is included.

782 **Pioneer photographers of Brazil, 1840-1920.** Gilberto Ferrez, Weston J. Naef. [s.l.]: Center for Inter-American Relations, 1976. 144p. bibliog.

This is a guide to an exhibition of Brazil's early photography. It includes introductory commentary, portraits of the Imperial family, and examples of the work of fifteen photographers. As they worked in different parts of the country, the photographs provide important records of Brazil at the turn of the century.

783 **Photography in Brazil 1840-1900.**
Gilberto Ferrez, translated by Stella de Sá Rego. Albuquerque, New Mexico: University of New Mexico Press, 1990. 244p. bibliog.
Photography was introduced into Brazil soon after its invention, and this book records and illustrates its application in the 19th century. It is organized by states, with almost half its length devoted to Rio de Janeiro.The volume represents an excellent record of landscapes and cityscapes, and also provides a history of Brazilian photography through commentary on individual photographers and their studios.

784 **Rio de Janeiro.**
Daniel Gluckmann. Madrid: Collección Cuidades Iberoamericanas, 1993. 226p.
Gluckmann presents a photo essay on Rio, of places, people and city life. The work includes a brief historical introduction.

785 **Faces of Brazilian slavery: the *cartes de visite* of Christiano Junior.**
Robert M. Levine. *The Americas*, vol. 47 (1990), p. 127-59.
A detailed analysis and interpretation of these late-19th-century photographs of slaves in Rio de Janeiro (see also item no. 781).

786 **An uncertain grace: photographs by Sebastião Salgado.**
Sebastião Salgado, essays by Eduardo Galeano, Fred Ritchin.
London: Thames and Hudson Ltd., 1990. 156p. bibliog.
The Brazilian photographer Sebastião Salgado (b. 1944) has an international reputation. A member of the Magnum agency since 1979, he has produced startling images of work and poverty in the Third World. This beautifully-produced collection includes some of his graphic photographs of the gold-miners of the Serra Pelada in Amazonia.

787 **In the wake of the Portuguese navigators: a photographic essay.**
Michael Teague. Manchester, United Kingdom: Carcanet Press, 1988. 124p.
A collection of around a hundred contemporary photographs of the Portuguese legacy in Africa, Brazil and the Far East. The dozen Brazilian examples are drawn from Rio, Minas Gerais, the Northeast, and Belém. The book is interesting for comparing the remnants of the Portuguese empire on three continents.

Folklore and popular culture

788　**A mão Afro-Brasileira. Significado da contribuição artística e histórica.**
Edited by Emanoel Araújo.　São Paulo, Brazil: Tenenge, 1988. 398p.
The Afro-Brazilian touch. The meaning of its artistic and historic contribution.
E. Drysdale.　São Paulo, Brazil: Tenenge, 1988. 134p.

This two volume work provides a very wide-ranging history and contemporary review of the African contribution to the arts in Brazil, encompassing art, dance, architecture, music, literature and photography. These are discussed under the headings of: the baroque; the 19th century; the African heritage; and the contemporary scene. The Drysdale volume provides an English translation of the Araújo text.

789　**Dicionário do folclore Brasileiro.** (Dictionary of Brazilian folklore.)
Luís da Câmara Cascudo.　São Paulo, Brazil: Edições Melhoramentos, 1979. 4th ed. 812p.

A wide-ranging dictionary of folk elements in Brazil, covering topics such as food, dress, ceremonies, gods, historical figures, and plants.

790　**Elite intervention in urban popular culture.**
Robert M. Levine.　*Luso-Brazilian Review*, vol. 21, no. 2 (1984), p. 9-22.

This is an interesting exploration of the efforts of the élite to constrain the growing population of urban poor, by repression and cooptation. It suggests that elements of mass popular culture, such as carnival, samba, and Afro-Brazilian cults, are transformed into 'respectable' urban forms by the élite and by state regulation, to make them acceptable.

791　**The impact of African culture on Brazil. FESTAC77, Lagos, Nigeria.**
Clarival do Prado Valadares.　Brasília: Ministério das Relações Exteriores; Ministério da Educação e Cultura, 1977. 296p.

Produced for the Second World Black and African Festival of Arts and Culture, held in Nigeria, this trilingual study provides profiles of Afro-Brazilian contributions to art, sculpture, dance, music and cinema.

792　**Popular culture and regional society in nineteenth century Maranhão, Brazil.**
Matthias Röhrig Assunção.　*Bulletin of Latin American Research*, vol. 14 (1995), p. 265-86.

An interesting historical paper on the emergence and context of popular culture in the Northeast, and the relationship between the élite and the culture of Indians and Africans. It deals with issues such as dress, drugs, and religious beliefs.

793   **Memory and modernity. Popular culture in Latin America.**
William Rowe, Vivian Schelling.   New York: Verso, 1991. 244p.
This is a wide-ranging study of popular culture, but with numerous Brazilian examples. Specific themes of relevance relate to popular theatre, soccer, samba, carnival, and *telenovelas* (soap operas).

794   **Dance of the dolphins.**
Candace Slater.   Chicago; London: University of Chicago Press, 1994. 314p. map. bibliog.
The dolphin has an important role in the folk myth of Amazonia, as an enchanted being which can take human form. A variety of tales are explored here, including the dolphin as lover, as white man, and as supernatural being.

Food and Drink

795 **Brazilian cookery: traditional and modern.**
Margarette de Andrade. Rutland, Vermont; Tokyo: Charles E. Tuttle
Co., 1965. 350p.
This is a comprehensive recipe book, which includes discussion of Afro-Brazilian cookery, staples of beans and rice, and drinks made from *guaraná* and *cachaça*. There is also a useful cross-referencing to the use of egg yolks and whites, which often form extravagant but distinct ingredients in Brazilian desserts.

796 **Wine regions of the southern hemisphere.**
Harm de Blij. Totowa, New Jersey: Rowman and Littleheld, 1985.
256p. maps. bibliog.
A very thorough introduction to the physical and economic geography of viticulture. Although Brazil is much less significant as a wine-producer than Chile or Argentina, its output is increasing and improving. It is discussed on pages 104-20.

797 **The art of Brazilian cooking.**
Dolores Botafogo. New York: Hippocrene Books, 1993. 240p. map.
Presents an introduction to Brazil and Brazilian cuisine, followed by systematic listing – soup, fish, meat etc. – of some 300 recipes. It includes such specialities as *churrasco* (barbecue), *feijoada a brasileira* (black bean stew), and *vatapá* (an Afro-Brazilian shrimp or fish dish).

798 **Viticulture in pre-independence Brazil.**
John Dickenson. *Journal of Wine Research*, vol. 6 (1995),
p. 195-200.
An historical study of the modest beginnings of Brazil's wine industry from the first efforts of Portuguese settlers to the early part of the 19th century.

799 **Cassava and chicha. Bread and beer of the Amazonian Indians.**
Linda Mowat.   Aylesbury, United Kingdom: Shire Ethnography,
1989. 64p. map.

Manioc is widely used in Amazonia to produce cassava bread, *farinha* (flour), and *chicha* (beer). This small book discusses the cultivation and processing of manioc.

Sport

800 **Soccer: opium for the people or drama of social justice?**
Robert DaMatta. In: *Social change in contemporary Brazil.*
Edited by Geert Banck, Kees Koonings. Amsterdam: CEDLA, 1988,
p. 125-33.
Explores the significance of soccer in Brazil, arguing that it is a fundamental element
in the understanding of the country.

801 **Ayrton Senna.**
Christopher Hilton. London: Corgi, 1994. 306p.
A biography of Brazil's most famous motor-racing driver, tracing his career to his
death in the 1994 San Marino Grand Prix.

802 **Brazil and the World Cup: triumph and despair.**
John Humphrey. In: *Hosts and champions. Soccer cultures, national
identities and the USA World Cup.* Edited by John Snyder, Alan
Tomlinson. Aldershot, United Kingdom: Arena, 1994, p. 65-75.
A brief and topical essay, written for the 1994 World Cup in the United States. It is of
interest, despite its brevity, because it summarizes Brazil's record in previous World
Cups, and assesses the wider significance of soccer in Brazilian society and culture.
As other countries are covered by essays in the book, it also has some comparative
merit.

803 **Soccer madness.**
Janet Lever. Chicago; London: University of Chicago Press, 1983.
200p. map.
This is an extensive assessment of Brazil's enthusiasm for soccer. It outlines the
organization of soccer in the country, provides a case-study of the game in Rio de
Janeiro, and discusses its significance for fans.

189

804 Sport and society: the case of Brazilian *futebol*.
Robert Levine.   *Luso-Brazilian Review*, vol. 17, no. 2 (1980),
p. 233-52.

A useful historical introduction to soccer in Brazil, which covers the origin of the clubs and the issue of race. It describes football as a national industry, and as a part of national culture. The paper includes discussion of several famous players, including Pelé of Santos and Tostão of Cruzeiro.

805 Pelé: my life and the beautiful game.
Pelé, R. L. Fish.   London: New English Library, 1977. 256p.

The 'auto'biography of Brazil's most famous soccer player. It details his playing career from 1956-76, during which he scored over 1,000 goals.

806 Ayrton Senna: a tribute.
Ivan Rendall.   London: Pavilion Books, 1996. 174p.

An enthusiast's biography of Brazil's Formula One motor-racing champion. It provides a chronological account of Senna's progress at various levels of motor racing, and includes a record of his results from 1977.

807 The death of Ayrton Senna.
Richard Williams.   London: Penguin Books, 1995. 186p.

A biography of Brazil's leading motor-racing driver. The detailed portrayal of Senna's funeral captures the importance of the man and Formula One racing for Brazilians.

Museums, Books, and Libraries

Museums and heritage

808 **Guia dos museus do Brasil.** (Guide to the museums of Brazil.)
Maria Elisa Carrazzoni. Rio de Janeiro, Brazil: Expressão e Cultura,
1978. 2nd ed. 168p.
This volume provides a basic listing of Brazilian museums by state and city. It gives
addresses, a brief history of each institution, and an indication of the nature of their
collections.

809 **Guia dos bens tombados.** (Guide to preserved buildings.)
Maria Elisa Carrazzoni. Rio de Janeiro, Brazil: Expressão e Cultura,
1987. 2nd ed. 534p.
A detailed and illustrated listing of over 900 buildings protected by Brazil's
conservation agency because of their historic or artistic significance. The classification
is first by state, with a brief general introduction, and then by town. Each property or
site is described, and there are good line-drawings. Similar, more detailed volumes,
exist for some states.

810 **Nostalgia for a gilded past? Museums in Minas Gerais, Brazil.**
John Dickenson. In: *Museums and the making of 'ourselves': the role
of objects in national identity.* Edited by Flora E. S. Kaplan. New
York; London: Leicester University Press, 1994, p. 221-45.
This volume seeks to examine the meaning of museum collections for national
identity, particularly in the Third World. This chapter describes the museums of Minas
Gerais, and the nature of their collections, which are particularly rich in colonial and
religious materials. It seeks to assess their significance for the Mineiro population.

811 **Ad perpetutuam rei memoriam. The Vargas regime and Brazil's National Historical Patrimony, 1930-1945.**
Daryle Williams. *Luso-Brazilian Review*, vol. 31, no. 2 (1994), p. 45-76.
A very useful study of the evolution of the protection of Brazil's historical heritage from the 1840s. It concentrates on the creation of the National Museum in the Vargas period, and of the Service for the Protection of the Historical and Artistic Patrimony (SPHAN).

Books

812 **Directory of publishing and bookselling in Brazil.**
British Council. London: British Council, 1980. 179p.
This is a dated source, but it lists universities and their bookholdings, and the addresses of major libraries. It also lists publishing houses, their fields of interest, date of foundation, and address.

813 **Books in Brazil.**
Laurence Hallewell. Metuchen, New Jersey; London: Scarecrow Press Inc., 1982. 486p. bibliog.
An historical study of the evolution of book production in Brazil since the colonial period. It concentrates on literary publishing, which is discussed with reference to key personalities, and to changing social and economic conditions, and government attitudes. Although it is detailed, the volume provides a sense of the evolution of the book trade, developments in printing, and provincial publishing in the 20th century. It also contains a wealth of data on the industry.

Libraries

814 **Guide des sources de l'histoire de l'Amerique Latine et des Antilles dans les archives françaises.** (Guide to sources on the history of Latin America and the Antilles in French archives.)
Archives Nationales. Paris: Archives Nationales, 1984. 712p.
This is essentially a listing of French sources, in which the source is more important than the subject. Holdings are listed at national, ministerial and departmental levels, with an emphasis on French Caribbean possessions.

815   **The Arquivos das Policiais Politicas of the State of Rio de Janeiro.**
Darién J. Davis.   *Latin American Research Review*, vol. 31, no. 1
(1996), p. 99-104.
The 'opening-up' of Brazil after the military régime has made numerous archives accessible. This collection provides systematic information on the political police from 1900-83, and is of particular importance because it contains federal material for the period 1918-83. The paper includes a list of the holdings of the archive.

816   **Scholar's guide to Washington, D.C. for Latin American and
Caribbean studies.**
Michael Grow, revised by Craig VanGrassteck.   Washington, DC:
Woodrow Wilson Center Publications; Baltimore, Maryland; London:
Johns Hopkins University Press, 1992. 428p.
An extensive listing of Latin American holdings in Washington, DC, in federal and international agencies, universities, libraries and data banks, etc. The emphasis is on the social sciences and humanities, with more than 500 agencies covered, accompanied by addresses and details of their holdings. It is an excellent introduction to the sources held in a single city.

817   **Catalog of Brazilian acquisitions of the Library of Congress,
1964-1974.**
William V. Jackson.   Boston, Massachusetts: G. K. Hall & Co., 1977.
752p.
This volume follows the format of the Library of Congress catalogues, in reproducing entry file cards. Here, however, they are listed by call number, following the Library's classification, and not by author/title, though these items are indexed. The 15,000 entries relate only to a single decade, but one which was important in recent Brazilian history.

818   **Resources for Brazilian studies at the Bibliothèque Nationale.**
William V. Jackson.   Austin, Texas: William V. Jackson, 1980. 58p.
A useful essay and survey of holdings in the national library of France, in the humanities, social sciences, and sciences.

819   **Canning House Library. Luso-Brazilian Catalogue of Canning
House Library.**
Luso-Brazilian Council.   Boston, Massachusetts: G. K. Hall & Co.,
1967. 286p.
1st. Supplement. ibid. 1973. 288p.
Canning House Library is the major UK collection of English and Portuguese material on Brazil. This is a reproduction of the library's file card system, containing basic bibliographical information. It is listed by author and Library of Congress subject class.

820 **Libraries and special collections on Latin America and the**
Caribbean: a directory to European resources.
Roger Macdonald, Carole Travis. London; Dover, New Hampshire:
Athlone Press, 1988. 2nd ed. 340p.

This excellent reference source provides coverage of the Latin American resources of
18 European countries and 467 collections. The collections are listed by country and
city, with address details, information on the history and nature of the holdings, and an
indication of the availability of services such as micro-reading and lending. The
volume includes an index by topic and country.

821 **Library resources for Latin American Studies in the United**
Kingdom 25 years after the Parry Report.
Roger Macdonald. *Bulletin of Latin American Research*, vol. 9, 1990,
p. 265-69.

The Parry Report (1965) established centres of Latin American studies in British
universities. This essay summarizes the consequent provision of library holdings.

822 *Relatorio* **from Portugal: the archives and libraries of Portugal**
and their significance for the study of Brazil.
Ann Pescatello. *Latin American Research Review*, vol. 5, no. 2
(1970), p. 17-52.

A useful survey of the major and minor collections of Brazilian material in Portugal.
As the colonial power, Portugal retains a wide range of archival material on the early
history of Brazil. There are several key repositories in Lisbon.

823 **Publicações da Biblioteca Nacional. Catalogo 1873-1977.**
(Publications of the National Library, 1873-1977.)
Xavier Placer, Nellie Figueira. Rio de Janeiro, Brazil: Biblioteca
Nacional, 1978. 2nd ed. 120p.

This is a useful guide to items published by Brazil's National Library. It contains over
500 titles, on topics including literature, history, geography, and biography.

824 **An annotated guide to medical Americana in the Library of the**
Wellcome Institute for the History of Medicine: books and printed
documents 1557-1821 from Latin America and the Caribbean
Islands, and manuscripts from the Americas 1575-1927.
Robin M. Price. London: Wellcome Institute for the History of
Medicine, 1983. 320p.

A listing of material relating to medicine and surgery. Brazil is covered on pages 7-14,
with thirteen items.

825   **A guide to manuscript sources for the history of Latin America and the Caribbean in the British Isles.**
Peter Walne.   London: Oxford University Press, 1973. 580p.
This provides a listing by county and also of business archives which have Latin American manuscript material. It claims to provide a reasonably comprehensive coverage of such sources. Details of the collections are given.

Mass Media

General

826 **Environmental degradation in Brazilian Amazonia: perspectives in US news media.**
Jacob Bendix, Carol M. Liebler. *Professional Geographer*, vol. 43 (1991), p. 474-85.

Although it has a specific focus, this paper has a broader interest, for it argues that although news media play an important role in shaping public opinion and government policy, coverage of Third World issues and environmental issues is often superficial and crisis-oriented. Using coverage of Amazonian topics in major US newspapers, the authors suggest that though reporting may have some appropriate theoretical base, it is frequently prompted by particular events, such as the murder of the environmental activist, Chico Mendes.

827 **Communication policies in Brazil.**
Nelly de Camargo, Virgilio B. Noya Pinto. Paris: The UNESCO Press, 1975. 80p. bibliog.

This survey was carried out as part of a UNESCO series, and, despite being dated, it is a useful historical source. It contains an interesting review of 'mass communication' from the early colonial period to 1974. Of more value is a comprehensive situation report on mass communication in the mid-1970s. This covers: the policies of the State and the media organizations; training for the media; and public participation in media issues.

828 **Transnational communication and Brazilian culture.**
Carlos Eduardo Lins de Silva. In: *Communications and Latin American society: trends in critical research, 1960-85.* Edited by R. Atwood, E. McCanany. Madison, Wisconsin: University of Wisconsin Press, 1986, p. 89-111.

This essay explores the long history of external influence in Brazil, by Portugal, Britain, France and the United States, and the contemporary strength of foreign influences, particularly in television and recorded music.

Radio and television

829 **'The decision is yours': TV Globo's search for a Brazilian God.**
Francisco J. Pimenta da Rocha. *Journal of Latin American Cultural Studies*, vol. 4 (1995), p. 51-63.

A useful case-study of the nature of Brazilian television, exploring the presentation of regional images on the country's most powerful channel, and the nature and influence of a specific viewer-participation programme.

830 **Expansion of television in eastern Amazonia.**
J. Timmons Roberts. *Geographical Review*, vol. 85 (1995), p. 41-49.

An interesting examination of the diffusion of television across the state of Pará since the 1970s. It notes, however, that though there are one public and four commercial channels, eighty per cent of towns only have access to TV Globo. This is transmitted via satellite, and carries only national programmes and advertising, with no regional input.

831 **Between memory and illusion: independent video in Brazil.**
Ingrid Sarti. In: *Media and politics in Latin America. The struggle for democracy.* Edited by Elizabeth Fox. London; Newbury Park, California: SAGE Publications, 1988, p. 157-63.

A brief but fascinating account of the attempts by independent video-makers to counter the dominance of Brazil's mass commercial television channels.

832 **Television, politics and the transition to democracy in Latin America.**
Edited by Thomas E. Skidmore. Baltimore, Maryland; London: Johns Hopkins University Press, 1993. 188p.

This book explores the role of the media in the return to democracy in Argentina, Brazil and Chile in the 1980s. Three essays on Brazil explore the role of television, especially the major network, TV Globo, in the election of President Collor in 1989.

833 **Television and video in the transition from military to civilian rule in Brazil.**
Joseph Straubhaar. *Latin American Research Review*, vol. 24, no. 1 (1989), p. 140-54.
An exploration of the use by the military régime of corporate organizations and the media. The article suggests that the objectives were to secure social control and to disseminate the ideological values of the government.

Brazilian newspapers and magazines

Newspapers

834 **Estado de Minas.** (The State of Minas.)
Belo Horizonte, Brazil, 1928- . daily.
This is the main serious newspaper of Minas Gerais, with a circulation of circa 65,000.

835 **Jornal do Brasil.** (Brazilian Daily.)
Rio de Janeiro, Brazil, 1891- . daily.
Rio de Janeiro's liberal major newspaper, with a circulation of circa 200,000, has some function as a 'national' newspaper.

836 **O Dia.** (The Day.)
Rio de Janeiro, Brazil, 1951- . daily.
This, Rio's leading popular newspaper, has a circulation of circa 205,000.

837 **O Estado de São Paulo.** (The State of São Paulo.)
São Paulo, Brazil, 1875- . daily.
Brazil's leading 'serious' daily newspaper, with a circulation of circa 240,000.

838 **O Globo.** (The Globe.)
Rio de Janeiro, Brazil, 1925- . daily.
A Rio-based daily, with the largest circulation, circa 350,000, among the serious press.

839 **Zero Hora.** (Zero Hour.)
Porto Alegre, Brazil, 1964- . daily.
Published in Porto Alegre, Rio Grande do Sul, this is the leading daily of the south, with a circulation of circa 115,000.

Magazines

840 **Conjuntura Economica.** (Economic Affairs.)
Rio de Janeiro, Brazil: Fundãção Getulio Vargas, 1947- . monthly.

A monthly economic and financial magazine, produced by the prestigious Fundãção Getulio Vargas economic research institute. As well as articles, it carries a range of economic and financial data. It is a useful source of up-to-date economic data.

841 **Manchete.** (Headline.)
Rio de Janeiro, Brazil, 1952- . weekly.

A weekly photo-magazine, which has a circulation of circa 110,000. It occasionally publishes English-language supplements aimed at the tourist market.

842 **Veja.** (Look.)
São Paulo, Brazil, 1968- . weekly.

A wide-ranging weekly news magazine, akin to *Time*. It has a circulation of circa 800,000.

Other

843 **Antologia do *Correio Braziliense*.**
Alexandre J. Barbosa Lima Sobrinho. Rio de Janeiro, Brazil:
Editora Catedra, 1977. 644p.

Correio Braziliense (Brazilian Post) was Brazil's first newspaper, originally published in London in 1808. It was much involved in the campaigns for independence and for the abolition of the slave trade. This anthology contains material on these issues from the period 1808-22, and is a useful contemporary guide to the debates involved.

English-language newspapers

844 **The Brazilian Gazette.**
London, 1973- .

Several issues a year cover industry, trade, politics and the arts.

845 **Brazil Country Report.**
London: Economist Intelligence Unit. quarterly.

A quarterly publication by the Economist Intelligence Unit, London, and an essential source of up-to-date material for the business person, politician and academic. Coverage includes the political scene, economic policies, the main sectors of the economy, and trade. The same publisher's annual *Country Profile* provides a useful summary of material in these fields.

846   **News and Views from Britain and Brazil.**
São Paulo, Brazil: British Chambers of Commerce. monthly.
A monthly business newsletter published by the British Chambers of Commerce in Brazil.

Professional periodicals

847   **The Americas.**
Washington, DC: Catholic University of America, 1944- . quarterly.
The subtitle of this journal refers to cultural history, but it covers the broad range of Latin American history.

848   **Bulletin of Latin American Research.**
Oxford: Pergamon Press, 1981- . 3 issues per year.
Provides a good coverage of the arts and social sciences. The latter often include topical issues.

849   **Cahiers des Amériques Latines.** (Latin American Studies.)
Paris: Institut des Hautes Etudes de l'Amérique Latine, Université de la Sorbonne Nouvelle, 1985- . (New Series). irregular.
There are normally 2-3 issues per year, dealing mainly with social science topics.

850   **Les Cahiers d'Outre-Mer.** (Overseas Studies.)
Bordeaux: Institut de Géographie Louis Papy, Université Michel de Montaigne, 1948- . 4 issues per year.
Originally concerned with the geography of France's tropical colonies, this journal now covers the Third World more broadly, and includes Brazilian material.

851   **Hispanic American Historical Review.**
Durham, North Carolina: Duke University Press, 1921- . quarterly.
The leading historical journal on Latin America, this publication carries an extensive book review section.

852   **Journal of Interamerican Studies.**
Coral Gables, Florida: North-South Center Press, 1959- . quarterly.
This journal is primarily concerned with foreign affairs issues, as they relate to Latin America and the United States.

853   **Journal of Latin American Studies.**
      Cambridge, United Kingdom: Cambridge University Press, 1969- .
      3 issues per year.
The leading British journal on Latin America, with an emphasis on history, economics and politics.

854   **Latin American Perspectives.**
      Thousand Oaks, California: Sage Periodicals Press, 1974- . 4 issues
      per year.
This journal offers a leftist perspective on Latin America. Its issues are usually thematic – for example, on the city, women, or ethnicity, but sometimes there are 'country' issues.

855   **Luso-Brazilian Review.**
      Madison, Wisconsin: University of Wisconsin Press, 1964- . 2 issues
      per year.
The leading English-language Brazilianist journal. It is interdisciplinary, but primarily covers the humanities and social sciences.

Statistics

856 **Brazil.**
R. W. Howes. In: *A guide to Latin American and Caribbean census material.* Edited by C. Travis. London: British Library; SCONUL; Institute of Latin American Studies, University of London, 1990, p. 128-91.

Provides a very extensive listing of demographic censuses, from Brazil's first, in 1872, to 1970, together with some economic, state and urban material. The location of holdings in the UK is given and there is a select bibliography.

857 **Anuário estatistico do Brasil 1994.** (Statistical Yearbook of Brazil.)
IBGE. Rio de Janeiro, Brazil: Instituto Brasileiro de Geografia e Estatística, 1994. unconventional pagination. maps.

This annual volume is the definitive source of official statistics, and it covers: environmental data, population, the economy, salaries and prices, and macro-economic information. Although it is in Portuguese, it is the most extensive, detailed, and up-to-date source of data on a wide range of topics.

858 **Brazil: a handbook of historical statistics.**
Armin K. Ludwig. Boston, Massachusetts: G. K. Hall & Co., 1985. 288p. maps.

A wide-ranging compendium of historical data, derived from a variety of sources. It is not comprehensive in the topics it covers, but its contents include material on demography, society, politics and economy. The handbook contains useful brief essays on each topic, comments on the reliability of the data, and a glossary of government agencies responsible for material.

859   **International Historical Statistics: The Americas, 1750-1988.**
Edited by B. R. Mitchell.   London: Macmillan, 1993. 2nd ed. 960p.

This is an essential reference source for historical data. Although inevitably not comprehensive, this volume contains much Brazilian information, and is useful for comparative purposes. Its topics include: population, the economy, labour, transport, education, finance, trade, and prices.

860   **Statistical Abstract of Latin America.**
Edited by James W. Wilkie.   Los Angeles, California: University of California Latin American Center Publications, 1995. vol. 31. 2 vols. 1,284p.

This abstract is produced annually and is the best single source on Latin American data. Information in this edition dates to circa 1991.   Material is generally listed in tables for the whole of Latin America, rather than for each individual country. There are, however, some country-specific tables. Coverage is extensive, and includes population, social matters, the economy, politics and religion.

861   **World Development Report.**
The World Bank.   New York: Oxford University Press for the World Bank, 1978- . annual.

The Bank's annual report is a very good source of basic economic and social data at a national level. For Brazil it is therefore useful for the most recent figures on topics such as Gross National Product, population, health, education, trade, commerce, and finance. Each issue usually also deals with a development issue in its substantive text. Thus, the 1992 edition discussed 'Development and the environment', and included a number of Brazilian case-studies, on topics as diverse as sewerage in the Northeast, land zoning in Rondônia, and rainforest protection in Amazonia.

Bibliographies

Latin America

General

862 **Latin America and the Caribbean: a critical guide to research sources.**
Edited by Paula H. Covington.   New York; London: Greenwood Press, 1992. 924p.

An invaluable systematic bibliography, which deals mainly with the humanities and social sciences. For each subject area, there is an introductory essay and an annotated bibliography. There is also a useful guide to special collections. The guide concentrates on post-1960 material, and contains a detailed thematic index by country.

863 **Latin America and the Caribbean: a directory of resources.**
Thomas Fenton, Mary J. Heffron.   Maryknoll, New York: Orbis Books; London: Zed Books, 1986. 144p.

A guide to book, periodical, pamphlet and audio-visual sources. Its specifically Brazilian content is limited, but it is a useful guide to sources, organizations and addresses in the United States.

864 **A bibliography of Latin American bibliographies published in periodicals.**
Arthur E. Gropp.   Metuchen, New Jersey: Scarecrow Press Inc., 1979. 2 vols. 1,031p.

A listing of bibliographies published in periodicals, which are not easily accessible through available indexes. Sources provided are mainly for the period 1929-65. The work draws from over 1,000 periodicals, and lists bibliographies by subject, from

Agriculture to Zoology. The index gives a listing for Brazilian items. There have been
subsequent editions covering later periods (see item no. 874).

865 **Latin America: a basic guide to sources.**
   Edited by Robert A. McNeil, Barbara G. Valk.   Metuchen, New
   Jersey: Scarecrow Press Inc., 1990. 2nd ed. 458p.
This is an essential reference work for any student of Latin America. It is an excellent,
all-round introduction to bibliographical and other work on the continent, which
identifies major libraries in the UK, Europe and the United States; lists their
catalogues; and gives major bibliographies in each field, including those by subject,
country, and personality. The work also lists a wide range of other sources, including
maps, micro-materials, non-print databases, and sound and visual sources. A first-rate
source for tyro bibliographers, it also offers useful advice on travel, careers and
contacts in Latin America.

Systematic

866 **Latin American politics: a historical bibliography.**
   ABC-Clio Information Services Inc.   Santa Barbara, California;
   Oxford: ABC-Clio, 1984. 290p.
Provides an annotated listing by author, with a country and topic index. Specifically
Brazilian references are on pages 155-76, and cover general topics, and the period
1914-45, democracy from 1945-64, and the military since 1964.

867 **An annotated bibliography of Latin American sport.**
   Joseph L. Arbena.   New York; London: Greenwood Press, 1989.
   324p.
Provides a brief general introduction to indigenous and colonial sport, but the bulk of
the book deals with modern sport, by country. Brazil is covered on pages 183-218.
The annotations it provides are good, but many of the Brazilian entries relate to books
on soccer for young people. The volume contains a brief list of Latin American sports
periodicals.

868 **The Latin American short story: an annotated guide to anthologies**
   and criticism.
   Daniel Balderston.   New York; London: Greenwood Press, 1992.
   530p.
Contains a brief listing of short stories published in anthologies. These are categorized
in three sections: general Latin America, regional, and by country. Brazilian material
may be found under the first two headings, as well as in the specifically Brazilian
section (p. 111-55).

869 **Cambridge history of Latin America, vol. XI.**
Leslie Bethell. Cambridge, United Kingdom; New York: Cambridge
University Press, 1995. 1,043p.
This volume brings together the bibliographical essays from the substantive volumes
of this series. Some have been revised, updated and expanded since their original
publication. There are 141 essays, which cite material mainly published since 1965,
and they represent probably the most comprehensive scholarly survey of historical
literature on Latin America. As well as relevant general essays, there are several
which deal specifically with Brazil.

870 **Portuguese language and Luso-Brazilian literature: an annotated
guide to selected reference works.**
Bobby J. Chamberlain. New York: Modern Language Association of
America, 1989. 96p.
A wide-ranging review of reference works which relate to the Portuguese language, or
to Portuguese, Brazilian or other Lusophone literature. The volume covers bibliographies and dictionaries on literature, literary terms, authors, literary movements, and
dissertations. It is a most useful source.

871 **Index to anthologies of Latin American literature in translation.**
Juan R. Freudenthal, Patricia M. Freudenthal. Boston, Massachusetts:
G. K. Hall & Co., 1977. 200p.
This gives access to anthologies of Latin American literature for the period since
1850. Listing is alphabetical by author, and provides dates, nationality, the English
titles of works, and translators. Brazilian items are not listed separately.

872 **Latin America: a guide to the historical literature.**
Charles C. Griffin. Austin, Texas; London: University of Texas
Press, 1971. 700p.
Contains a reference and general listing, followed by a chronological listing of
material, which deals with the colonial period, independence, and post-independence.
Each segment includes country entries. The material dates to 1966, and as the Bethell
volume (see item no. 869) is designed to follow on from this, it provides a valuable
guide to the older historical literature.

873 **Latin American serials: literature with language, art and music.**
Laurence Hallewell. London: Committee on Latin America, 1977.
254p.
Provides a basic listing, by title, of serial publications, and their source, place of
publication, dates, and where they are held in the UK. Brazil is covered on pages
49-65.

874 **A bibliography of Latin American and Caribbean bibliographies, 1985-1989.**
Lionel V. Loroña.   Metuchen, New Jersey: Scarecrow Press, 1993. 224p.
This is a continuation of the work of Gropp (see item no. 864), and covers material from the late 1980s. Coverage here is less extensive, dealing only with humanities and social sciences.

875 **European immigration and ethnicity in Latin America: a bibliography.**
Oliver Marshall.   London: Institute of Latin American Studies, University of London, 1991. 168p.
This is a most useful study on immigration. It lists recent (post-1960) works on immigration since 1800, and includes books, articles and conference proceedings in most European languages. Following a listing of general works, each national and ethnic source is listed, divided up by receiving country. This is an important source on German, Italian, Jewish and Portuguese migration to Brazil.

876 **Latin American literature in English translation: an annotated bibliography.**
Bradley A. Shaw.   New York: New York University Press, 1976. 144p.
A listing of fiction, short stories, poetry, drama and literary essays, with some brief descriptive annotations.

877 **Protestantism in Latin America: a bibliographic guide.**
Edited by John H. Sinclair.   South Pasedena, California: William Carey Library, 1976. 422p.
Provides a useful guide to Protestant activity in Latin America, with an introduction to bibliographical aids and to other churches in Latin America. It contains a systematic listing of topics of special interest to Protestant churches, such as work with Indians and youth, and healing. The volume includes a number of specifically Brazilian sections (pages 134-57 and 313-27), as well as a listing of Brazilian evangelical periodicals.

878 **A bibliography of US-Latin American relations since 1810.**
David F. Trask, Michael C. Meyer, Roger R. Trask.   Lincoln, Nebraska: University of Nebraska Press, 1968. 442p.
Supplement to a bibliography of US-Latin American relations.
Michael C. Meyer.   Lincoln, Nebraska; London: University of Nebraska Press, 1979. 194p.
These two volumes are mainly concerned with general issues of US policy. Books, articles and documents, in a wide range of languages, are listed by author. Brazil is dealt with on pages 372-84 of the original volume, and pages 162-66 in the supplement. The latter includes new categories such as issues relating to multinational corporations and the law of the sea.

879 **Research tools for Latin American historians: a select, annotated bibliography.**
David P. Werlich. New York; London: Garland Publishing Inc., 1980. 270p.
Offers a rich listing of 1,400 items – including reference works, compendia and periodicals, in several languages. The volume covers a wide range of bibliographies, newspapers, official publications, theses, archives and statistical sources. Brazil is dealt with specifically on pages 154-63.

880 **Latin America: a guide to illustrations.**
Curtis A. Wilgus. Metuchen, New Jersey: Scarecrow Press Inc., 1981. 250p.
Visual images are an important source for the historian and social scientist. This study lists pictures in recent English-language books and periodicals. It contains a thematic listing according to the major periods in Latin America's history, and then by country. Brazil is covered on pages 112-23, and material relates to topics including the environment, politics, society, the economy, and culture.

881 **An A to Z of modern Latin American literature in translation.**
Jason Wilson. London: Institute of Latin American Studies, University of London, 1989. 96p.
A short listing by author, which provides titles, accompanied by the name of the translator in each case, and the original and translation publication dates.

882 **Reference materials on Latin America in English: the humanities.**
Richard D. Woods. Metuchen, New Jersey: Scarecrow Press Inc., 1980. 640p.
The coverage of this volume includes bibliographies, dictionaries, guidebooks and essays, etc. Listing is by author, and full bibliographical details are provided in each case, including date of publication, page numbers, and holding libraries in the United States. The index includes a country and subject listing.

883 **Latin American literary authors: an annotated guide to bibliographies.**
David Zubatsky. Metuchen, New Jersey: Scarecrow Press Inc., 1986. 332p.
This is a wide-ranging bibliography covering personal bibliographies about novelists, dramatists, poets, linguists, journalists and literary critics. It is a basic listing, but includes a section of works on individual countries, including Brazil. The book draws upon work in several languages.

Brazil

884 **Bibliografía sul-riograndense. A contribuição portuguesa e estrangeira para o conhecimento e integração do Rio Grande do Sul.** (Bibliography of Rio Grande do Sul. The contribution of the Portuguese and foreigners to the knowledge and integration of Rio Grande do Sul.)
Abeillard Barreto. Rio de Janeiro, Brazil: Conselho Federal de Cultura, 1973-76. 2 vols.
Using sources in a variety of languages, this provides a heavily annotated introduction to the development of the state of Rio Grande do Sul. Its systematic index includes immigrant groups.

885 **A bibliography of Brazilian bibliographies/Uma bibliografia das bibliografias Brasileiras.**
Bruno Basseches. Detroit, Michigan: Blaine Ethridge, 1978. 186p.
This is a wide-ranging listing of some 2,400 items. However, despite the bilingual title, the entries are not given in English. The author/subject is also mainly in Portuguese, and not always cross-referenced.

886 **Bibliografia do Rio de Janeiro. Viajantes e autores estrangeiros 1531-1900.** (Bibliography of Rio de Janeiro. Travellers and foreign writers, 1531-1900.)
Paulo Berger. Rio de Janeiro, Brazil: SEEC-RJ, 1980. 2nd ed. 484p.
A very basic A-Z listing of books by travellers and foreigners on Rio, though it includes much publishing detail. The volume is not indexed.

887 **Periódicos Brasileiros microformas. Catálogo coletivo 1985.** (Brazilian periodicals on microform. Collective catalogue 1985.)
Biblioteca Nacional. Rio de Janeiro, Brazil: Biblioteca Nacional, 1985. 504p.
This is a valuable source of information on the availability on microfilm of Brazilian newspapers and journals. It covers 2,700 titles and 42 institutions, with items listed by state and sometimes by city. The duration of publication of the periodical, along with the location and coverage of the microfilmed holding, is provided. The volume also contains a useful bibliography of material relating to the Brazilian press.

888 **Bibliographia Brasiliana. Rare books about Brazil published from 1504 to 1900 and works by Brazilian authors of the colonial period.**
Ruben Borba de Moraes. Los Angeles, California: University of California Latin American Center Publications; Rio de Janeiro, Brazil: Livraria Kosmos Editora, 1983. 2nd ed. 2 vols.
A rich description of important works on Brazil, which is extensively annotated and indexed in English. Entries are alphabetical, with commentary in some cases, and very

precise publication details. It is an excellent source on Brazilian and foreign literature, and invaluable for the bibliophile and the scholar.

889 **Repertorio critico da literatura Teuto-Brasileira.** (Critical catalogue of Germano-Brazilian literature.)
Oscar Canstatt, translated by Eduardo de Lima Castro. Rio de Janeiro, Brazil: Editora Presença, 1967. 294p.

This volume was originally published in 1902, with a 1906 supplement. It is a study of German writings on Brazil. These include those by early travellers, but the work's main importance lies in its coverage of contemporary material on the important German immigration to southern Brazil in the late-19th century. Its notes provide publication details.

890 **Brazil and its radical Left: an annotated bibliography on the Communist movement and the rise of Marxism in Brazil 1922-1972.**
Ronald H. Chilcote. Millwood, New York: Kraus International, 1980. 456p.

This bibliography covers the Communist Party and other Leftist groups. Material is grouped by author, and includes books and pamphlets, articles, and periodicals, accompanied by very brief annotations. An index is included.

891 **Brazilian slavery: an annotated research bibliography.**
Robert E. Conrad. Boston, Massachusetts: G. K. Hall & Co., 1977. 164p.

The archives of the Brazilian Ministry of Justice were destroyed soon after emancipation, in an effort to erase the record of slavery. The author has collected together a helpful guide to likely sources and to other bibliographies. His material concentrates on African slavery in the 19th century, and the 1,000 items provide guidance on the slave trade and its suppression, the nature of slavery, and its abolition. The volume includes an author index, and useful annotations.

892 **A guide to the history of Brazil, 1500-1822. The literature in English.**
Frances A. Dutra. Santa Barbara, California; Oxford: ABC-Clio, 1980. 626p. map.

This is an essential guide to the colonial period, with a comprehensive annotated listing of modern sources and contemporary narratives. As well as chronological coverage, it presents material on a regional and systematic basis. The latter section includes the economy, religion, women, Amerindians and Africans, culture, and diplomacy.

893 **Human geography in Brazil in the 1970s: debates and research.**
J. H. Galloway. *Luso-Brazilian Review*, vol. 19 (1982), p. 1-22.

Affords a comprehensive review of trends in geographical research on Brazil, outlining the work of both domestic and foreign geographers.

894 **Brazil in the London Times 1850-1905: a guide.**
Richard Graham, Virginia Valiela. Washington, DC: Seminar on the
Acquisition of Latin American Library Materials (SALAM), 1969. 102p.
A terse guide to *Times* entries, mainly those relating to economic and political matters.
It is most useful on topics such as mining, railways, agricultural commodities, and
government. Items are listed by year, month, day, page and column.

895 **Brazil in reference books, 1965-1989. An annotated bibliography.**
Ann Hartness. Metuchen, New Jersey; London: Scarecrow Press,
1991. 350p.
A very useful survey of books, pamphlets, and serials (but not journals), in the
humanities, fine arts, and social sciences. It is an important complement to the present
volume as it includes much Brazilian material in Portuguese. It is also valuable
because it presents such material, where appropriate, on a state-by-state basis. There
are some 1,600 entries.

896 **Bibliografia e índice da geologia do Brasil, 1951-1960.**
(Bibliography and index of the geology of Brazil, 1951-60.)
Dolores Iglesias, Maria de Lourdes Meneghezzi. Rio de Janeiro,
Brazil: Ministerio de Minas e Energia, 1967. 203p.
Though this covers only a decade, it deals with a wide range of European, Brazilian
and North American sources on Brazilian geology.

897 **Brazil since 1930. An annotated bibliography for social historians.**
Robert M. Levine. New York; London: Garland Publishing, Inc.,
1980. 336p.
Provides a listing of some 1,800 items, mainly in English, but with some Portuguese
sources, accompanied by brief notes. Its topics are the State and politics, economics,
society, urban and rural issues, culture, and education.

898 **Brazilian serial documents. A selective and annotated guide.**
Mary Lombardi. Bloomington, Indiana; London: Indiana University
Press, 1974. 446p.
This is a very useful catalogue of serials produced by federal agencies. They are listed
by the Legislature (congress), Executive (president, ministries and their agencies), and
Judiciary. The volume contains an extensive listing of some 1,400 titles, with dates
and place of publication. There are some annotations, but the index is only of the
Portuguese titles.

899 **The Brazilian Amazon: institutions and publications.**
Carmen M. Muricy. Albuquerque, New Mexico: University of New
Mexico Press, 1992. 66p.
A useful source guide for work on Amazonia before 1990. It lists regional and
national agencies, including banks, government offices, churches, and businesses,
which publish items on the region. Almost 300 government and institutional serials,
monographs, and scholarly and cultural journals are included.

900 **Afro-Braziliana: a working bibliography.**
Dorothy B. Porter. Boston, Massachusetts: G. K. Hall & Co., 1978.
294p.

An extensive listing of circa 5,000 books, pamphlets and periodicals written by, and about, Afro-Brazilians, drawn from US repositories. The volume contains a good introduction to the material covered, which includes bibliographies, travel accounts, and publications dealing with history, language, cuisine, the arts, religion, soccer and literature. There is also discussion of selected Afro-Brazilian authors, with critical and bibliographical references.

901 **Brasil. (Brazil.)**
Nicia Villela Luz.   In: *Latin America: a guide to economic history, 1830-1930.*   Edited by Roberto Cortés Conde, Stanley J. Stein.
Berkeley, California; London: University of California Press, 1977, p. 165-272.

This book begins with a general essay in English and bibliography on Latin America. The Brazilian section, however, relates mainly to Portuguese and non-English sources. It covers general economic history, population, economic growth and the various sectors of the economy.

902 **O que se deve ler para conhecer Brasil.** (What one must read to know Brazil.)
Nelson Werneck Sodré.   Rio de Janeiro, Brazil: Editora Bertrand Brasil, 1988. 6th ed. 378p.

This is a very useful introduction to material on Brazil for Portuguese speakers. It provides a listing of principal and subsidiary sources on the history of Brazil for a range of subjects, including: the economy; race; religion; geography; and culture, including literature, the press, science and folk traditions. Each topic is preceded by a brief introductory essay.

903 **Brazil.**
In: *South America, Central America and the Caribbean 1993.*
London: Europa Publications, 1993, 4th ed., p. 132-66.

An invaluable directory of information on Brazilian institutions, covering government, churches, the media, and business. The work lists addresses and other details for many of these, along with the names of incumbents of government and church posts. Brief essays on history and economy, and a wide range of demographic and economic data are included. It is a most useful source of reference.

Accounts of nineteenth-century South America. An annotated checklist of works by British and United States observers.
See item no. 63.

Indexes

There follow three separate indexes: authors (personal and corporate); titles; and subjects. Title entries are italicized and refer either to the main titles, or to many of the other works cited in the annotations. The numbers refer to bibliographical entry rather than page numbers. Individual index entries are arranged in alphabetical sequence.

Index of Authors

215

219

220

Index of Titles

225

Index of Subjects

Tourism 14, 32, 46-53
Trade 140, 216, 531, 617,
  626, 629-30
Trades unions 1, 9, 171,
  211, 247, 404, 507,
  527, 530, 567, 642-55
Trams 634
Transport 230, 595-99,
  631-41
  see also Railways;
  Roads, etc.
Travel literature 46-54, 67,
  701, 704, 886, 889
TV Globo 829-30, 832

U

Umbanda 374, 376-77
United Nations 522
  Food and Agriculture
  Organization (FAO)
  555
United States of America
  165, 194, 203, 322,
  509, 520, 524-25,
  612, 826, 828
  emigration to 333, 335
  relations with 508,
  510-11, 513, 515-16
Universities 443, 658,
  670, 812
Urban poor 5, 97, 251,
  339, 402, 463, 466,
  646, 649, 790
Urban services 213, 224
Urbanization 12-14, 154,
  164-65, 171, 209,
  216, 243, 251,
  394-95, 447-72, 501
  in literature 691, 697

Uruguay 226, 489

V

Vargas, President Getúlio
  125, 127-28, 181,
  190-94, 197-98, 306,
  328, 378, 475-76,
  500, 525, 551, 690,
  811
  and labour
  organizations 643,
  645, 653, 655
Vassouras 231
Vaz de Caminha, Pero de
  (traveller) 158
Veloso, Caetano
  (musician) 761
Venezuela 105
Video 831, 833
Villa Lobos, Heitor
  (composer) 755, 766
Volta Redonda steel town
  465

W

Wagley, Charles
  (anthropologist)
  258-59
Wallace, A. R. (naturalist)
  10, 67
War of 1865-70 128, 165
Water supply 400, 417,
  440, 478
Week of Modern Art, São
  Paulo 1922 735
'Whitening' 321
Whites 248, 257

Wildlife 21, 27, 32, 55,
  61, 65, 83-95, 157,
  280, 752
  see also Fauna; Flora
Wine 53, 796, 798
Women 152, 213, 244,
  257, 277-78, 293,
  316, 336-51, 372,
  425, 494, 654, 769,
  775, 892
  in literature 679, 681,
  695, 697, 699, 701,
  728
Women's organizations 1,
  249, 339, 341, 345,
  349
Workers' Party (PT) 483,
  486-87, 498, 667
World Bank 529, 560,
  595, 661

X

Xingú region 269, 283,
  764
Xingú River 540
Xinguara 456

Y

Yellow fever 415, 430,
  671

Z

Zona da mata 19
Zumbi (slave leader) 286,
  777

Map of Brazil

This map shows the more important towns and other features.

ALSO FROM CLIO PRESS

INTERNATIONAL ORGANIZATIONS SERIES

Each volume in the International Organizations Series is either devoted to one specific organization, or to a number of different organizations operating in a particular region, or engaged in a specific field of activity. The scope of the series is wide-ranging and includes intergovernmental organizations, international non-governmental organizations, and national bodies dealing with international issues. The series is aimed mainly at the English-speaker and each volume provides a selective, annotated, critical bibliography of the organization, or organizations, concerned. The bibliographies cover books, articles, pamphlets, directories, databases and theses and, wherever possible, attention is focused on material about the organizations rather than on the organizations' own publications. Notwithstanding this, the most important official publications, and guides to those publications, will be included. The views expressed in individual volumes, however, are not necessarily those of the publishers.

VOLUMES IN THE SERIES